DOOMSDAY CULTS

DOOMSDAY CULTS

DEATH, DESTRUCTION AND DESPAIR INSIDE THE WORLD'S MOST DANGEROUS CULTS

JONATHAN J. MOORE

NEW HOLLAND

First published in 2019 by New Holland Publishers
London • Sydney • Auckland

131-151 Great Titchfield Street, London WIW 5BB, United Kingdom
1/66 Gibbes Street, Chatswood, NSW 2067, Australia
5/39 Woodside Ave, Northcote, Auckland 0627, New Zealand

newhollandpublishers.com

A record of this book is held at the British Library and the National Library of Australia.

ISBN 9781760790875

Group Managing Director: Fiona Schultz
Publisher: Alan Whiticker
Project Editor: Rebecca Sutherland
Designer: Cyb Elizalde
Cover: Yolanda La Gorcé
Production Director: James Mills-Hicks
Printer: McPhersons, Australia

10 9 8 7 6 5 4 3 2 1

Table of Contents

Introduction 7

The Nature of Doomsday Cults 9

The Children Of God:
David Berg's Sex Cult 19

Branch Davidians: The Lamb of God 41

Aum Supreme Truth: Asian Apocalypse 67

The Family: Horror in Hollywood 96

The Movement for the Restoration of the
Ten Commandments of God: Ugandan Utopia 114

The Church of the Lamb:
Mormon Assassins 136

The Little Ants: Green Apocalypse 166

Heaven's Gate: Alien Intervention 186

Deprogramming 201

Bibliography 206

Index 207

Thanks to my publisher 'straight shooter' Alan Whiticker who has encouraged this book, along with many others, over the years. His wise advice had been invaluable.

Introduction

Adam and Eve may be termed the first doomsayers, the original survivalists. Despite warnings from a merciful but strict God, they were ejected from the heavenly Garden of Eden. Thrust into a world of violence, sickness and moral decrepitude, they had to survive – no matter what. If only Adam and Eve had not succumbed to their base temptations, according to this archetypal tale, humanity would still be living within a Godly Kingdom. The original Biblical couple and all of their descendants have been determined to regain the original blessed state ever since.

The Old Testament Book of Daniel told believers how to regain the Kingdom of the Lord. The Book of Revelation in the New Testament did the same thing. They provide a theological pathway for humanity to follow, and believers hold that by walking that path to righteousness the true followers of the Lord can return to God's graces. All others will perish, spiritually and physically, in the End of Days, the Apocalypse, Armageddon.

These works tell of the impending apocalypse in glorious detail. So rich are the narratives, so gruesome the outcomes and so broad are the warning signs predicting the coming Armageddon that there is no limit to the number of interpretations that can be drawn from the texts.

Each one of the cults within this book is different and reflects its leader's personal preoccupations, but there are some similarities. The Chosen Ones, those that follow the true interpretation of the Bible and carry out God's will, are destined to fight the forces of evil and triumph. They will then establish the Lord's Kingdom on Earth or in heaven.

All other humans follow the Antichrist, the Devil or the Beast, and are doomed to die in flames.

David Berg used Revelation to justify increasingly perverted practices in the Children of God. David Koresh claimed that he was the Lamb who would usher in the apocalypse (once Waco was attacked the prophecy was proved true). Charles Manson and Ervil LeBaron both claimed to be God's emissaries, who would lead the 144,000 listed in Revelation into the new Kingdom of God.

In Uganda the leaders of the Movement for the Restoration of the Ten Commandments used Biblical descriptions of destruction to terrify their followers into blind obedience. Roch Thériault sought to return his flock to an Eden-like simplicity, welding them to him with Bible sanctioned brutality.

While Shoko Asahara of Aum Supreme Truth did not refer directly to the Christian Bible, he used its concept of the coming end to shape his apocalyptic blend of Eastern mystical beliefs.

The doomsday cults in this book took Biblical texts as the foundation of their philosophies. Rather than leading to peace and redemption, their interpretations led to death, destruction and despair.

No doubt this is due to the intrinsically violent nature of the work. In this climactic passage from Revelation, human life is stripped of all worth. Unbelievers are harvested like grapes and blood replaces wine. Such is the slaughter that a tidal wave of blood stretches for 200 miles.

Revelations 14

14 I looked, and there before me was a white cloud, and seated on the cloud was one like a son of man with a crown of gold on his head and a sharp sickle in his hand.

15 Then another angel came out of the temple and called in a loud voice to him who was sitting on the cloud, 'Take your sickle and reap, because the time to reap has come, for the harvest of the earth is ripe.'

16 So he who was seated on the cloud swung his sickle over the earth, and the earth was harvested.

17 Another angel came out of the temple in heaven, and he too had a sharp sickle.

18 Still another angel, who had charge of the fire, came from the altar and called in a loud voice to him who had the sharp sickle, 'Take your sharp sickle and gather the clusters of grapes from the earth's vine, because its grapes are ripe.'

19 The angel swung his sickle on the earth, gathered its grapes and threw them into the great winepress of God's wrath.

20 They were trampled in the winepress outside the city, and blood flowed out of the press, rising as high as the horses' bridles for a distance of 1,600 stadia.

CHAPTER ONE

The Nature of Doomsday Cults

Revelations – Prologue

[3] Blessed is the one who reads aloud the words of this prophecy, and blessed are those who hear it and take to heart what is written in it, because the time is near.

What is a cult? A good definition, that covers all of the organizations in this book, could be: a small religious group that is not part of a larger and more accepted religion and has beliefs regarded by many people as extreme or dangerous.

Another defining characteristic of the groups detailed in this book is the total and absolute power that the cult leader wields over their followers. This power is not used for good, but for evil.

Finally, the cultists feel they are superior to all other members of society – this gives them license to remove themselves from normal behaviors and, in some instances, to seek to destroy society.

History is littered with examples of violent cults. One of the most violent in English history was founded as a reaction to the licentiousness of Charles II's reign. They called themselves the Fifth Monarchists and many of the leading men were Puritans who had signed the death warrant of Charles I. As with many cults, a relatively obscure piece of scripture was the inspiration for their outlandish beliefs. They took as their inspiration passages from the Bible's Book of Daniel, which predicts that the four ancient monarchies (Babylonian, Persian, Macedonian and Roman) were to precede the new Kingdom of Christ - the fifth monarchy. They combined this with the number of the Beast in the Book of Revelation, 666, to predict that in 1666 Christ would descend from heaven, slay all of the unbelievers and place the members of the cult in command as his immortal saints.

The members armed themselves with pistols, muskets and swords and covered themselves with armor. On 6 January 1661, under the leadership of the wine barrel maker Thomas Venner, they sought to overthrow the throne in the name of King Jesus. They regarded Charles II as a traitor to God and a criminal who had to be overthrown.

For four days the center of London became a battlefield. Just as Koresh would do hundreds of years later, the Fifth Monarchists amassed an impressive arsenal of weapons that enabled them to fight off all who came at them, including 700 troops of the elite royal Life Guards.

Finally, the remnants, including Venner, were smoked out of their last stronghold - the aptly named Helmet Tavern - and hauled off for trial. Their end was of course a foregone conclusion and on 19 January 1662 the leader and 12 of his men were executed. They were hung, drawn and quartered at Charing Cross and their body parts were distributed around London's gateways as a warning to others. Needless to say, the world did not end in 1666.

Many of the cults in this book have ended in a similar blaze of violence, madness and bloodletting.

The Millerites are an example of a much kinder cult. They emerged in America in the first half of the 19th century and quickly progressed from fantasy to fanaticism, a typical development model for cults. While the experiences and the teachings of the Millerites are almost comical to our eyes, their history shows how cults begin, flourish and eventually implode, and how the Bible can be used by a cult leader to justify whatever idea takes his fancy.

The Baptist preacher William Miller (1782–1849) used meticulous mathematical precepts to study the Bible and predicted that Christ would arrive in a blaze of holy glory somewhere between March 1833 and March 1844, bringing a whole angelic cavalcade to smite the unworthy and draw all true believers up to heaven.

This is of course the other key component of the cults dealt within this book: an assumption of superiority to all other humans that means they can view their fellow beings as lambs to the slaughter. The Millerites would ascend to heaven, while all others would be condemned to the pits of hell for all eternity.

A critical passage in Miller's theory was Daniel 8:14, which declared that 457 BCE was the start date for a countdown of 2,300 years before the Second Coming. The book actually said 2,300 days, but since that time had obviously passed Miller declared that the Biblical text actually meant years.

Using this innovative interpretation, Miller traversed the width and breadth of the American states converting all who would listen to the righteousness of his cause. His proselytizing mission had a carnival atmosphere; towed behind the good preacher was a massive tent that could hold 4000 people. In the space of several years, Miller delivered in excess of 4000 lectures. The movement he began became known as the Adventists.

Thousands heeded his message of impeding Armageddon, were baptized into his church and sold all of their worldly goods before heading east for the inevitable ascension. The weak minded and gullible readily fell for the ideals of Miller and his Adventist movement. One convert in Port Perry, Ontario gave away a 365-hectare (900 acres) spread of productive farmland complete with stock and equipment. It was all going to be destroyed in the coming apocalypse, so why not?

A follower in Oshawa, Canada decided that ascension was so close that she only had to don a pair of silk wings and leap off a rooftop to be swept up to heaven. Another Adventist convinced himself that he was an angel and announced that he was going to walk across Lake Scugog, near Ontario, to prove it. His neighbors turned out to witness the miracle - and had a good laugh when he sank up to his neck.

Up to 500,000 believers prowled graveyards to welcome the resurrected dead or waited on hilltops for their summoning to heaven. They believed that by standing on elevated positions they would get to heaven that much quicker! The American press had a field day and the antics provided great fodder for cartoonists.

The public held these God botherers in contempt. This increased when March 1844 passed without the predicted cataclysm. Some fancy Biblical footwork was used to extend the date a couple of times, but eventually, as they saw their contemporaries who *hadn't* sold all of their worldly goods going about their daily business, the Millerites experienced what was called the Great Disappointment.

The egotism of this and later cults is revealed through this phenomenon. Disappointment that life on Earth is not expunged, excepting a few true believers who are saved, demonstrates the essentially self-centered nature of these deluded followers.

Most of Miller's followers returned to ordinary life, poorer but hopefully a bit wiser. At least they weren't physically or emotionally scarred by their cult leader. Some continued in the beliefs of Miller, who maintained that he had just got his dates wrong and the Second Coming was just around the corner. The Seventh Day Adventist Church was spawned in the aftermath.

While we can laugh at the crazy doings of Miller and his followers, they do provide a blueprint of how cults begin, thrive and ultimately fail. Miller became fixated on a new interpretation of the Bible and was able to manipulate theology to support his revelation. Carried away with a crusading zeal, the new prophet attracted many needy new followers who suspended disbelief and chose to renounce their everyday life. Under the threat of eternal damnation, they threw away their assets and followed the leader on a perilous journey.

Mainstream society saw the cult for what it was: a deluded sect of believers who arrogantly saw themselves as above their fellow Americans.

Initial disappointment among the cultists at the erroneousness of the doomsday prophesy they had accepted gave way to a rekindling of hope when new ascension dates were revealed. When the world still failed to descend into a maelstrom of divine wrath, the membership of the cult drifted away from Miller and his teachings. Only a small rump remained who, despite all evidence to the contrary, continued to believe in the divine nature of their teacher's beliefs.

Miller made one mistake that most other cult leaders avoid: he gave the date of the coming Armageddon. Much better to say it is on its way in the near future.

The experience of the Millerites pre-empts the modern cults discussed in this work. The big difference is that Miller's cult members did not come to a violent and bloody death, which is a repeated occurrence throughout these pages.

The genesis and the bizarre beliefs of each cult are covered in each chapter. The means by which they attracted, initiated and controlled their members is discussed as is the violent Armageddon experienced by most of the followers.

Genesis

Many cult leaders seem cut from a similar cloth. In fact, it can be argued that many share characteristics of Narcissistic Personality Disorder, as defined by the American Psychiatric Association. Characteristics of this aberrant psychological state include the following:

- An exaggerated sense of self-importance.
- An ability to perceive accomplishments where there are few and a consistent exaggeration of these achievements and talents.
- An expectation that others will recognize their superiority without any real cause for this devotion.
- Intrusive thoughts of success, power, beauty and brilliance dominate waking hours and conversation.
- A disdain for most others as mere mortals.
- Requiring constant admiration and a pervasive sense of entitlement.
- An expectation that all other individuals must meet their wishes with unquestioning compliance.
- An inability to see another's point of view and a willingness to use or manipulate others in pursuit of their own goals.
- An arrogant or haughty manner of behavior, except when the charm needs to be turned on to achieve some goal.
- An inability to understand other people's feelings, a lack of empathy for their suffering and a lack of true emotional connection with other people.
- The proverbial 'glass jaw.' Underneath their confident, domineering exterior, there is a lingering paranoia and feeling of inferiority. Questioning or refuting their ideas can lead to a catastrophic breakdown, such as that shown by Jim Jones of the Peoples Temple when he ordered the mass Kool-Aid suicide in Guyana.

(Lightning Guides, *Cults: In Too Deep From Jonestown to Scientology,* Sonoma Press, 2016)

While psychological profiles are fairly loose devices that can be seen as something of a catch all, there is no doubt that most of the leaders featured in this book could be readily diagnosed with Narcissistic Personality Disorder.

The leaders of the cults described in this book took their flocks down destructive paths. Why did these figures so badly mistreat the people who put their wellbeing in their hands? Some, such as Charles Manson, suffered abysmal childhood neglect that instilled a fierce hatred of society. Others, such as Shoko Asahara and Ervil Le Baron, appear to have been born bad, with manipulative and narcissistic tendencies emerging early in life even though they were raised in loving and supportive environments.

Many, such as Dominic Kataribabo and David Koresh, displayed an early fascination with the Bible and, under the influence of drugs or sex, gradually began to develop a perverted theology that led to death and destruction. Roch Thériault began life as a cheerful individual, but seemed to lose his grip on reality after several intensive surgeries. And of course there are those who realize that with every sucker there is a piggy bank full of cash and set out to take them for every last penny. The Church of the Lamb and the Children of God are perfect examples of the cash cults.

Despite the many and varied backgrounds of the leaders, they all had this in common: an overweening ego combined with a good deal of charisma that allowed them to attract followers and get them to accept as the absolute truth a load of theological rubbish.

Bizarre Beliefs

During childhood, adolescence and early adulthood, these cults' leaders developed a set of beliefs that set them apart from more mainstream churches. Many utilized a grab bag of ideas and manipulated them to suit their own ends. David Koresh studied the Book of Revelation and decided that he was the Lamb of God. Shoko Asahara combined several Buddhist theologies with modern technological advances to create a doomsday scenario, which his cult attempted to bring about with their Sarin attacks in the Tokyo subway. Ervil LeBaron perverted Mormon teaching to allow him to become judge, jury and executioner in a bizarre series of assassinations in Texas.

Attraction, Initiation and Control

Different organizations have different methods of attracting and controlling members, but there are several principals they all follow.

Cult recruiters are experts at finding vulnerable prospects. Lonely, confused and disenfranchised individuals are perfect. Some recruits have substance abuse problems; all are malleable or open to suggestion.

Specialist recruiters can target particular demographics. Aum Supreme Truth set 'honey traps' where attractive females lured lonely professional males. Manson's Family used sex-on-tap to attract male followers and LSD induced orgies to sway any reluctant members. The Rajneesh movement, which originated in India, targeted wealthy white Anglo Saxons who were going through midlife crises.

A group's leadership will present itself as a benevolent authority concerned with the wellbeing of the individual, offering tips or benefits to lure them into return visits. The recruits are often given personal attention through sharing exercises or confessions, which are designed to assess the individual's strengths and weaknesses and to find out their desires. In small cults it might be the leader who does this. In larger organizations a mentor, or mentors, will be assigned.

This process can be formal or informal in nature, although the outcomes are the same. The personal attention boosts the recruit's self-esteem and gives them an emotional hook to plunge deeper into the cult.

Advertising material and 'gospels' can be introduced at this stage. The recruits are introduced to other members and a group-think mentality is developed. Other organizations and social mores are denigrated and the superiority of the cult's own ideals is reinforced through testimonies and sharing activities with large groups.

With all of this softening up, successful cults entice their new members to cross a vital threshold; the new recruit must acknowledge that their happiness and wellbeing in the future depends on adopting the cult's change program. This can involve lifestyle changes, such as moving in with the cult, or financial, such as signing up to an increasingly expensive set of courses to attain enlightenment. In one remarkable example, Shoko Asahara sold his used bathwater to gullible acolytes, who would swill it down in the pursuit of divine inspiration.

Once a new member has been lured into the cult's orbit, it is imperative that they stay there. Any psychological or physical means will be exploited to ensure that they remain as functional assets.

Techniques controlling the members' daily lives are intensified. Leaders will use the sins extracted during the early confession stage as weapons to be pulled out and deployed at will. Critical thinking is reduced through exhausting but largely pointless sessions of chanting, meditating, speeches and the continuous playing of movies and recordings. A negative tone comes in. The new member is shown many disastrous scenarios that may occur if the change program is not adhered to.

Eventually the new member will realize three crucial points:

1. Enlightenment can be attained with continual striving on a well-defined route.
2. The cult is never wrong.
3. The past life must be abandoned.

All those who are not on the correct path to righteousness are deemed unworthy and the pre-cult self is discarded as worthless. Any doubts or anxieties about the new lifestyle must be ruthlessly squashed – either by the individual or through a process of confession/absolution.

It is often at this phase of indoctrination that a recruit must make a choice. They can reject the cult and move on, or they can give themselves over to a complete trust of the cult leadership. Those who choose the latter course abandon any reservations and commit to the new theology, mentally erasing any flaws they may have detected in the cult's logic.

The member is often required to surrender all of their worldly assets to the cult. This can include property, inheritances or a 90 percent tithe on wages. At the same time, the last links with family and friends are severed. Cult members cut off all contact and refuse to answer letters, emails or phone calls. The family structure is often abnegated, with husbands and wives being separated and children ending up in a foster care or dormitory situation. These steps solidify the cult leader's hold over the member.

The member is given a function within the cult to validate their new existence. This can be as simple as handing out brochures or as complex as attending to the cult's property portfolio.

With the destruction of the old support network, the new 'family' can exploit the member's dependence on the cult by threatening them with force if they do not toe the party line. This can involve violent punishment, or psychological techniques such as threatening to shun them for their 'unworthy' thoughts or condemn them to hell.

If a member leaves, they feel the wrath of the jilted organization. Persecution can range from hate mail to goon squads beating up members and trashing their houses. Mail may be tampered with. Manson's Family may have been involved in up to 20 unsolved killings. Aum Supreme compounds dotted through Japan had shipping containers converted into cells; members were starved to death before being vaporized in giant microwaves.

The most heinous crime a cult member can commit is to question the authoritarian leadership of the cult, or the closed system of belief to which it adheres. Beliefs can only be modified by the top-down leadership and to doubt their wisdom could be a capital offence.

Armageddon

Commitment to a cult can reverse an individual's moral compass. Heinous acts such as suicide or mass murder become virtuous. Rather than believing that it is important to get along with everybody, the ideas of 'us versus them' or 'right versus wrong' become dominant. The world is framed in terms of good versus evil; the cult, of course, is good. A successfully indoctrinated cult member is able to carry out acts considered immoral in the mainstream; their moral compass is so warped that they feel guilt if they don't carry out the act.

Cults thrive by infecting their recruits with what could be called a mind virus. Just as an actual living virus can thrive within a host with a weakened immune system, cults seek out individuals with psychological issues so that they can 'infect' them. Through remorseless conditioning and propaganda, the individual will lose touch with any reality but the reality sought by the cult leadership.

Once a recruit has been thoroughly brainwashed, the mind virus is absolutely dominant. They are able to perform horrific or bizarre acts that they would not have contemplated before induction into the organization. Whether it is pouring arsenic down the throats of their children, beating dissidents to death or blowing themselves up in a suicide pact, indoctrinated cult members are bound to follow their leader's instructions.

Although individuals could come to see the error of their ways, in the cults examined in this book the realization came too late. Roch Thériault's Little Ants descended into a mad world where body parts were hacked off, testicles were removed and children were beaten to death. The members of the Branch Davidians and the Movement for the Restoration of the Ten Commandments died in a maelstrom of fire, murder and suicide. Youths who suffered years of emotional and sexual abuse within the Children of God still grapple with suicide and substance abuse. Members of the Church of the Lamb and Aum Supreme Truth are still rotting in jail, decades after their crimes.

The Millerites could be considered fortunate in that they escaped a cult situation with little more than a loss of some assets and a bit of public embarrassment.

CHAPTER TWO

The Children Of God: David Berg's Sex Cult

Revelation – Book 7

15 Therefore, 'They are before the throne of God and serve him day and night in
his temple; and he who sits on the throne will shelter them with his presence.'
16 Never again will they hunger; never again will they thirst. The sun will not
beat down on them, 'nor any scorching heat.

The Children of God sect is a particularly secretive and difficult to access organization. This is for a reason. Its founder, David Berg, was determined to use the word of God and the threat of nuclear annihilation to satisfy his pedophiliac urges.

A mysterious inner circle known as 'The Unit', consisting of Berg and his most trusted followers, roamed the world, staying one step ahead of governments and worried parents. Even though they were rarely glimpsed, this inner sanctum exercised an iron control over the cult members. Day to day activities were rigidly monitored and behind a glossy exterior of evangelical joy, members endured a grim reality of unrewarded, unremitting labor and rampant child abuse.

The Children of God were given other names, such as The Family, Family of Love and The Family International. For simplicity's sake we will refer here to the cult as The Children of God.

Berg was no newcomer to the evangelical scene. He came from a long line of snake oil salesman and knew how to manipulate those who came in search of religious and sexual freedom.

The emotional and psychological scarring experienced by the young cult members continues to leave a trail of murder, suicide and mental illness in its wake. Despite the best efforts of the modern day Children of God - The Family International - to disassociate themselves from the cult's dark past, many questions remain.

Genesis

David Berg founded his church on the counterculture movement that swept through America in the 60s and 70s. He learnt his proselytizing techniques from his mother, Virginia Brandt, who had done exactly the same thing four decades earlier. She learnt the techniques from her father, Reverend John Lincoln Brandt.

Reverend John Lincoln Brandt was a wealthy Methodist preacher who joined the Campbellites, a group that followed the teachings of Alexander Campbell (1788-1866). They had a mistrust of church hierarchy and sought a purer church, less concerned with the trappings of wealth and privilege and more concerned with personal salvation as espoused in the New Testament. Brandt was born in Somerset, Ohio; a descendant of migrants from Stuttgart, Germany, who were members of the sect known as the Dunkers thanks to their predilection for full body immersions during baptism ceremonies. This willingness to immerse the whole body and soul in religious fanaticism dominated the family for generations.

It seemed Brandt's mission in life was to question orthodoxy, whether it was Catholic, Mormon or Protestant. His desire to make his spiritual mark was inherited by his daughter, who was born on 27 May 1886 in West Virginia. Virginia Brandt married Hjalmer Berg, who shared her view of established churches and became ordained as a minister in the Disciples of Christ. Founded by Campbell when he was ejected from the Presbyterian Church, this sect still exists today.

Fundamental to these practitioners is a belief that each individual can take their own path to spiritual fulfillment as long as they follow the teachings of Christ. The other key factor that holds these congregations together is a fundamental mistrust of organized churches or creeds that seek to impose their will on their congregations.

David Brandt Berg was born into this spiritual cauldron on 18 February 1919. His mother's background instilled in her the belief that it was right to have a flexible interpretation of the scriptures. She also had a flexible understanding of the truth.

In 1911 Virginia was thrown from a vehicle and broke her back in two places. For the next five years she suffered unimaginable pain as a bedridden paraplegic. Fortunately, after much prayer she awoke and found herself perfectly healed, returning to Hjalmer's church with newly restored mobility. Doubts about the legitimacy of her injury aside, this miraculous intervention formed the basis of Virginia's new ministry.

The couple's strident claims of divine intervention and faith healing alienated the normally tolerant Disciples of Christ, and Hjalmer lost his ministry. The couple were forced onto the road. The 'Berg Evangelistic Dramatic Company' adopted the techniques of the Pentecostal Movement that was sweeping America. With much fanfare the troupe would sweep into town and begin their evangelical mission. Adopting all of the tricks of the holy rollers, the meetings were tumultuous affairs and involved faith healing and speaking in tongues.

Virginia was one of the first well-known female evangelists and she used the press and radio to advertise her mission. No claim was too big. Newspaper ads called her 'the Miracle Woman' and a 'Modern Prophetess'. Soon she had a flock of thousands. People came from all over the country to listen to her tale of redemption and healing.

It all came crashing down in 1926. A hurricane destroyed the Miami church that she had built using donations from wealthy benefactors. At this time Virginia had all but separated from her husband. With this financial setback, just before the Great Depression, she became just another itinerant preacher.

David Berg's mother was not entirely happy with her son. At an early age Berg had issues with his sexuality; at six years old he became a compulsive masturbator. One of his earliest memories was Virginia threatening to cut off the offending member if she found him playing with it. Not helping things, according to Berg, was a nanny who used to lull him to sleep by administering oral sex and giving him, even at this young age, orgasms.

Virginia, curious as to why her son was still having naps even though he was no longer a toddler, secretly observed the goings on and fired the nanny. Nevertheless, the damage may have already been done. This early child abuse may have been the key factor that led to the rampant pedophilia that arose in Berg's own church.

Berg's siblings left the family's ministry and, once he got his driving license, it was left to David to drive his mother around the country. This continued until 1947, when he was ordained into the Alliance Churches as a pastor.

The young preacher was given his first ministry in a struggling town in Arizona in 1948. He arrived at the Valley Farms Church with his wife Jane, young children Linda and Paul, and a desire to step out from his mother's shadow. Within two years the young family was run out of town due to shady accusations of sexual misconduct.

Being sacked due to sexual misconduct did not seem to trouble Berg. Soon after this event he convinced himself that his calling was too large for the strictures of an establishment church.

He would no longer be bound by others but would instead forge his own relationship with God. Berg began to believe that he alone was the Christian God's one true prophet. In the meantime, he fell in with evangelist Fred Jordan, with whom he stayed as his media advisor for 15 years before the pair fell out.

Berg and his family then set out on the road as an evangelistic touring band. Paul and Jonathan Emanuel, Berg's sons, proved to be talented and creative musicians. They would soon use their talents to attract many adherents to the faith.

Virginia was by now living on the coast of Southern California in Huntington Beach, which was developing a hippie milieu. As Virginia gazed out of her cottage window at the drugged out, rootless community, her old proselytizing instincts kicked in. Here was a fertile field where a canny evangelist could reap quite a harvest. She called Berg to her side.

In 1967 Berg dropped straight into the Summer of Love. This counterculture movement was centered on the Haight-Ashbury neighborhood in San Francisco, but was echoed up and down the Californian coast and even across the Atlantic. Hundreds of thousands of youths were seeking alternative meanings for their lives than the ones offered by their conservative parents. Drug taking and spiritualism were central to the experience of many.

Cults proliferated by offering radical new perspectives. Charles Manson founded the Family and groomed them with LSD, racism and sex. Another broad movement were the 'Jesus-freaks'. These individuals combined counterculture lifestyles with a message of peace and love. Berg saw his opportunity and founded the Teens for Christ. This would eventually become the Children of God.

An active campaign of recruiting 'babes' began (from the term 'babes in the wood' or 'babies for Christ'). These were the innocent, the lost and the lonely; perfect fodder for Berg and his cult.

Bizarre Beliefs

Berg's experiences with established churches and the counterculture movement of the late 60s formed a nexus for the crystallization of his belief system.

He founded a radical sect based on anti-establishment ideas. Government, churches, business and parents were all to blame for a dysfunctional world that was heading for Armageddon. The Vietnam War was at its height in the late 60s and Berg pointed out the hypocrisy of a Christian world performing mass slaughter and war crimes on a regular basis. Only by returning to the origins of Christianity and by breaking down the barriers that separated individuals could peace on Earth be regained. He regularly referred to the Bible's Book of Acts, which features all Christians living together without personal possessions.

Berg proclaimed himself to be the end time prophet. He was instituting a 'Revolution for Jesus' and God's prophesy poured through him. It was necessary for all true believers to follow his every world.

Berg painted a vivid picture of what was coming. California was to be destroyed by earthquakes. The rest of North America and all of Europe would be destroyed by nuclear war. That was why it was crucial to have Children of God compounds throughout the world. An Antichrist was soon to rise and he would rule the entire world as a dictator. His acolytes would be recognized by a microchip implanted under their skin inscribed with 666, the number of the Beast. He would form a One World Government until the Great Tribulation, which was bound to occur in 1993 and persist for seven years. Finally, in 2000, Jesus would return in the Second Coming and the Children of God would be raptured to heaven.

The war was inevitable in Berg's eyes. The signs were there and in fact the conflict had already begun.

Personal possessions were no longer necessary. Children did not need to be prepared for life outside of the church. Secular education was a waste of time. In fact, all teachers, university professors, and even pastors and priests were the emissaries of Satan, who permeated and corrupted these institutions. The CIA and the American Federal and State governments were all representing the interests of the Antichrist.

Berg had a deep mistrust of Big Pharma. Faith alone, declared Berg, could cure any illness. Children within the cult were not inoculated, and medical professionals were deemed to be devils. Systemites (i.e. non-Children of God members) were given pills. These pills were addictive and allowed the Antichrist to control the minds of the population. Medicine was considered evil. If a child scraped their knee or had a minor injury, they were not treated. They were told they were warriors of Christ and had to toughen up and 'get the victory.' Home remedies were employed by the cult; for example, cloves of garlic were inserted up each member's rectum to kill infestations of worms.

In Berg's eyes it was vitally important to breed as many children as possible within the cult. These youths would become 'Warriors for God' and when Christ descended from heaven in 1993 the children would all develop super powers with which to smite the ungodly foe. Berg offered all kinds of powers to the children: laser missile eyes, X-ray vision, super strength, fantastic speed. As well as magical powers, the children would be issued with laser pistols and flying suits, all illustrated in detail within various forms of cult literature.

Fortunately for the young warriors Berg had a stepson, the child of his wife, Karen Zerby. Ricky Rodriguez (known as Davidito within the Children of God) was to be a mighty fighter who would lead the children against the Antichrist. He would have extraordinary powers and leadership abilities beyond the understanding of all mortals. It was his role to be slain by the Antichrist and be raised up to heaven to sit at the right-hand side of the Lord. The greatest martyr of all.

Once the end time battles had finished, all of the members of the sect would be called to Heaven, a Heaven with three pearly gates and a giant pyramid twice the height of the Empire State Building. Each family would have their own apartment in the pyramid. The more bravely they had fought or the more painful their martyrdom, the more elevated and fancy their apartment would be. The chosen did not have to walk or drive: they would be given the power of flight.

Any attempts by governments or families to interfere with the Children of God proved that they were acting upon the orders of Satan. It was crucial that all contact with the evil world outside the church be severed. Systemites were to be avoided, unless they were handing over cash or being ensnared into the faith.

Even shopping in the supermarket was dangerous. One song was titled 'Cathy Don't Go' and told the story of a member of the church who wanted to go to the supermarket and buy bulk rice that was on special. The lyrics warned Cathy that a mind-controlling chip would be inserted into her hand at the register.

How could such tripe be swallowed by so many rational beings? Like all good cult leaders, Berg maintained a steady stream of propaganda aimed at suppressing rational thought and allowing 'group-think' to take over. His increasingly deranged theology was communicated through his Mo Letters.

Berg adopted several nicknames, Moses, King David, Father David, God, Father and Grandfather being among his favorites. The Mo Letters were written by his chief alter ego, Moses David. They sought through striking visuals to inculcate his thoughts into the flock. Titles included 'God's Law is Love' and 'It Is Later than You Think' and they featured images that placed Christ and Moses figures within the context of Berg's worldview. They often espoused a perfect world where all was good with a loving community. Others portrayed the end of times with Berg as the end time Prophet. While the bulk of society was going to be shredded by a nuclear holocaust, the Children of God would be shielded by Moses David's loving vision. A range of artists contributed to the literature.

Even the earlier publications featured voluptuous women dominated by strong biblical male characters. Scanty tunics and robes barely concealed the women's curves. 'The Law of Love,' which proclaimed that monogamy was sinful, was a frequent topic. Sexual liberation was espoused, along with the idea of a loving world community accepting of all regardless of race, age or sex. The Mo Letters frequently condemned abortion and contraception. The taking of drugs and alcohol was frowned upon.

Over time the Mo Letters turned from a steady flow to a deluge. At least 2800 were sent from cult headquarters. They provided guidance on all aspects of life, including hygiene, automobile maintenance and how to brush your teeth. There may have been many more than 2800, but many had the instruction BAR on the cover: Burn After Reading. Concurrent with the Mo Letters were taped sermons from Berg that also dispensed his wisdom. As in the letters, these recording gave 'suggestions' on how to live according to Berg's teachings. Of course any who strayed from these 'suggestions' would be called out by other cultists.

Chief among Berg's targets was the American government and the American people. They were the chief Antichrist – The 'Beast' of Revelation. Mo Letters dealt in glorious gory detail with the terrible fate God had in store. Nuclear weapons weren't the only coming calamity; a comet named Kohoutek would appear in the sky before plunging to earth and wiping Washington, DC off the map.

As time went on, the number of Mo Letters and taped recordings of Berg became overwhelming. There was no time to study the Christian Bible, as there had been in the early years of the organization, and it was beyond even the most ardent devotee to keep up with the stream-of-consciousness material emanating from Berg. He was unapologetic about usurping the New Testament. He was, he explained, God's true living prophet. What were more important, pronouncements that the Lord had made 2000 years ago, or those he made today? Those who doubted Berg's revelations were spreading poison. They were inhabited by demons.

Berg's attitudes to sexuality shifted from the late sixties to the eighties. While he remained a staunch critic of alcohol and drugs, he moved from a position that demanded celibacy to one that endorsed sexual experimentation. An avowed anti-homosexual, Berg finally consented to allow threesomes where two women had sex with one man. A long as the females were not lesbians and were primarily attracted to men it was OK by Berg if they wanted to engage in bisexual love.

Attraction, Initiation and Control

When Berg and his family turned up at Huntington Beach in the late 1960s, they stood out like sore thumbs. The Berg Family Singers were dressed in their Bible-belt best. The suits, ties, polished shoes and clean-cut looks were soon discarded. The family set up in a coffee house on the beach and founded their new church, Teens for Christ.

Every good charismatic evangelist movement needs a honey pot to attract the bees. Berg was blessed with his four children, who could turn on a show to wow the most cynical drugged out hippie. Anyone who came into the coffee shop would be approached by members of the church, who would tell of the blissful existence they lived.

Paul was the oldest son and it appears that he had a genuine talent. His songwriting abilities were outstanding and with a guitar on his lap and a willing audience he could bring anybody to ecstatic enjoyment. Handsome, tall and blonde Aaron was responsible for bringing countless young women into the cult. His brother Jonathan Emanuel was also talented and the two sisters Faith and Linda could turn on the charm like holy laser beams to entrap impressionable young men.

The cult began growing exponentially on the back of the Berg children's evangelical skills. But how was Berg to take his place as the leader? At 50 the gaunt and bald figure seemed to have little to offer the children of the Summer of Love.

He imposed himself with his counterculture, anti-establishment views. Berg railed against 'the man,' 'the system' and the straightjacket of parental expectations. The middle-aged man became the mouthpiece of youth. Abandoning his straight-laced look, Berg adopted a goatee beard, long hair gathered with a leather tie, sandals, loose cotton trousers and, of course, a turtleneck shirt.

His message had a tremendous appeal to those who fell into the cult's orbit. The Teens for Christ had a great old time at first. They roamed American highways, spreading their revolutionary gospel. Individuals would be surrounded by singing, hugging youths whose one goal was to attract new members to the faith. Many members tell how they would be drawn into conversations with the Jesus-freaks and be so smitten with their ideas and joyful demeanor that they would drop everything and join up immediately.

The band Fleetwood Mac's guitarist Jeremy Spencer disappeared after a gig one night. A couple of Berg's followers had been in the audience and, after a brief chat, they managed to lure him away from playing in one of the most popular bands of the time.

Berg had so many recruits that he began to send them on international missions. They were renamed as Children of God. It was important, claimed Berg, to spread their message around the world and help people avoid the nuclear holocaust.

Life in these communes would have been enjoyable for the enthusiastic young Christians. Once the strictures against sex had been dropped, a sexual free-for-all developed. The mission in Paris, France was typical. Between 100 and 200 dedicated young people lived in the heart of the city. Young women wandered around in diaphanous and revealing outfits. Five or six individuals would share a room and few were monogamous. There was a feeling of having a divine mission and a joy in being among the chosen who would bring in a new age of peace and love. Three hours of Bible study was intermixed with ecstatic prayer, dancing and singing. These sessions were called inspiration classes and they included lots of loving hugs, kisses and affection. This was termed 'love bombing' and reinforced the message that their new family was within the commune. All connection with the cultists' past life was severed.

Acts 2:44 describes how the disciples lived together and held everything in common. They referred to each other as brother and sister. This was the ideal, according to Berg. Rather than living in family units and attending church on Sunday, the communes shared all their possessions and lived with God's word 24/7. Their only roles were worship and evangelism. Getting 'high on Jesus' was the aim.

Only a successful evangelist could eat. Recruits to the commune had to sell the cult's literature or raise money by busking or begging. They could keep 10 percent of what they earned for food and necessities. All of the rest had to be given to their overseer – 40 percent of the funds were spent on rent, rates and services to the commune premises, the remaining funds were sent to the cult leadership.

Behind the seemingly anarchic, freewheeling lifestyle, there was very clear hierarchy in place. Each commune had several overseers who were responsible for a group of individuals. The overseer could demand written reports from their subordinates that accounted for every minute of their day. They were also asked to confess to any impure or doubting thoughts.

These reports were called Open Heart Reports. In some communes they had to be completed daily, in others once a week. Adults were required to write down who they had 'shared' with, the frequency of their sexual encounters and even what positions they had adopted while engaged in sexual intercourse. Along with writing their own impure thoughts, adults were required to inform on any commune members who had broken guidelines.

Children's Open Heart Reports detailed 'spiritual battles' they had engaged in, the number of times they had been to the toilet and whether the stools were hard or soft. They were also required to 'snitch' on other children. A culture of informing and spying grew up in the communes. It was wise to make up a story about an individual even if it had no basis in fact. Children or adults who did not report misdemeanors could be punished on the suspicion that they were holding something back.

Above the overseers were the Home Shepherds, who were in charge of individual communes. Coordinating a country's outposts were the Regional Shepherds. It was these individuals who made sure that everyone followed the word of Moses David. Even though the Shepherds were often the hardest working in the Church's flock, there was no stability in the role. Berg was jealous of anyone who gained a favorable reputation and would routinely sack his officials and return them to the ranks.

Many who turned up to coffee shops or missions run by the organization later reflected upon the remorseless proselytizing used by members to inveigle them to join. Once they had committed to the organization, there was no letup in the pressure. Complete obedience was required. Everyone had to attend regular meetings, and if there were any questions thrown at the local leadership or the precepts issuing from Berg the dissenters would be cruelly shouted down and rebuked. These meetings could go for hours.

Every part of the day was strictly controlled. Members were told what to wear, how their hair should be cut, how many coffees could be consumed a day (a maximum of two), bed time, how many sheets of toilet paper could be used – nothing was off limits. Three sheets of toilet paper was seen as wasteful, and if a cultist used more there could be dire repercussions.

The list of activities the cult members were not permitted to perform was lengthy. None were allowed out into the community on their own. No books, comics or television shows were permitted unless they came from cult headquarters. Reading was seen as a waste of time and unholy. Medicine was forbidden. Much better to die and ascend to heaven than to take the potions of the Antichrist.

Even the leaders of the various cult compounds were subject to unremitting pressure. Using the medium of the video recorder, they were forced to be accountable to the cult's shadowy leadership with regular updates on their subordinates' activities. These regular camcorder productions depicted every aspect of the members' lives. Their meetings, the food that was provided, happy people dancing, singing and proselytizing for new converts – everything had to be regularly produced and sent to 'Mo' to avoid demotion and disgrace.

Members of the community were engaged in remorseless evangelical activities. Children would dress up in their best clothes and visit restaurants, where they would serenade customers with catchy Christian numbers. Groups within a mission were given territories where they were required to go 'witnessing'. Quotas of recruits and presentations were rigorously enforced and any individual who fell short would be punished with emotional and physical deprivation. Tips were accepted, but it was a real achievement to get as many souls as possible. At other times adults were forbidden to wear contraceptives – there was more than one way of adding to the flock.

These efforts were spectacularly successful. By 1979 there were Children of God missions in 76 countries worldwide.

Women were ordered to stay at home. Housekeeping and procreation were their duties. A culture of fear permeated the cult. There were warnings of what would happen should they leave. A vengeful God would strike the unfaithful down. Maybe the traitor would be hit by a car, or else a lethal disease would take hold.

Once within the cult, there was no escape and no support system should someone wish to leave.

Where did this extraordinary level of control emanate? Most cults within this book were dominated by the charismatic presence of their leader. In contrast, the huge majority of the members of the Children of God never saw David Berg in the flesh and only heard taped recordings of his sermons.

He and his chief lieutenants were firmly ensconced in what was called 'the Unit'. This was Berg's inner circle of enforcers. The Unit was a shadowy organization, not only to the members of the cult but also to law enforcement worldwide. As tales of abuse, extortion and tax evasion began to spread, Berg and his coterie continued to move around the world, one step ahead of the authorities. Tenerife, Paris, Germany, Madeira, Portugal, Switzerland, Lisbon, Malta and myriad other countries and cities played host to the cult leadership.

Sometimes they stayed for a year or so, sometimes for less than a week. Like many criminal enterprises, the Unit was in a perpetual quest for a safe haven or tolerant judiciary.

A very different rationale was reported to the cult members. Moses David had to keep his location secret. Only through this routine was he able to remain clear-headed and focused; able to receive revelations from his spiritual helpers. Additionally, cult members were informed, their prophet's location was kept secret so that the Antichrist could not launch an assassination attempt.

Berg's relatives and selected fanatical supporters were members of the Unit. Berg used the members as his sexual playthings. The women of Berg's circle followed an informal roster deciding who would satisfy his sexual urges on a daily basis. He regularly abused his grandchildren. No one was off limits to Berg's depredations.

There were regular gatherings where Berg and his 'wives' would strip, consume copious amounts of alcohol and engage in group sex. Several Unit members became disenchanted with what they witnessed and left.

Rather than being a wise and benign figure, Berg was in fact a charlatan and a chronic alcoholic. One of the holy messengers who visited and passed on God's word to Berg was Abraham. This spiritual being loved a drop. He promised he would tell all, but demanded more and more alcohol to loosen his tongue. Members who left the inner sanctum described how a drunken Berg would carry on for hour after hour, becoming increasingly incoherent as the night wore on. Any pronouncement was treated as gospel by his followers and a bewildering stream of contradictory commands was issued to Berg's confused flock.

The funds pouring into the Children of God headquarters allowed them to live a lavish lifestyle. Palatial homes were occupied for longer stays, while whole floors of luxury hotels could be booked for shorter stays. The supply of food and drink was unlimited.

Meanwhile, the people working the streets for Moses David were living in squalid poverty. The days of interminable labor, proselytizing and malnutrition were broken up by one major festival: the celebration of Berg's birthday. For three days before the great date, the entire community fasted. All normal activities ceased and the time was spent in daylong prayer vigils and lengthy sessions of reading or listening to the latest missives from the prophet. They were then primed for a day of ecstatic feasting, singing and celebrating the day of Moses David's birth.

After several years Berg's prohibition of contraception had begun to bear fruit. Hundreds of children were born into the church every year. Fresh fodder for Berg's warped worldview.

While adults chose to join the cult, their children did not, and children fared particularly badly. They had no freedom – they were helpless pawns in the creation of a cult dedicated to satisfying its leader's every whim. Thrust into large communes, they had to call every adult aunty or uncle, and obey them no matter how dire the consequences.

The daughter of a young woman who joined the cult remembers a childhood stripped of joy. Her earliest memory is of being a four-year-old child gazing out of a window in the Jamaica cell. She looked on enviously as other children ran about, playing games in the midday heat. She was only allowed out once a week, to hand out food to impoverished families. Every waking moment was dedicated to working for God. The small family – brother, sister and mother – moved into different compounds around the world. Each was identical in the strict regime they forced the children to follow.

Families were broken up and most children slept together in a dormitory-like 'children's room'. This sterile space contained the barest necessities and lacked humanizing decorations. They all woke at 7 am on the dot. Woe betide any child who had wet the bed – this was construed as a sign of possession and a severe beating was the only way of expelling the demon. Berg also proclaimed that any child should be able to sleep the entire night without needing to use the toilet. It was a case of damned if you do and damned if you don't.

As soon as they climbed out of bed the children were forced to kneel and say their prayers. A meager breakfast followed, and then another session of prayer. The well-behaved children were then allowed out of the compound, chaperoned by an adult, to beg for funds from passers-by. Most of the money went straight into Berg's coffers as 'donations'.

The poor diet and gut-wrenching anxiety experienced day after day led to many children becoming malnourished. They were then put on the 'Minnies' program. These were established within each commune to ensure that the authorities would not be alarmed by conditions within the compound. The Minnies were forced to eat large portions of stodgy rice pudding packed with powdered milk and butter.

The intellectual fare that was dished out to the children was no better. School days consisted of Word Time, which involved reading and discussing Berg's teachings, followed by Memorizing Time – memorizing the teachings – and Jesus Job Time, which included scrubbing toilets, cleaning linen and cooking. Then the children had School Work, which not surprisingly involved answering questions about Berg's theology. The morning would be wrapped up with Quiet Time, when children had to take a nap.

After an inadequate lunch, the young members of the Children of God spent the afternoon doing PE. Competitive games were forbidden. Instead it was hour after hour of grueling exercise designed to toughen the young ones up for their role in the Army for God. Armageddon was just around the corner and it was their responsibility to bear the standard of Christ for Berg. It was their task to overthrow the evil Antichrist dictator.

After an exhausting day that avoided any reference to a basic school curriculum, the impressionable youngsters were force fed a diet of horror stories. Wicked outsiders were just waiting for the opportunity to invade the compound and even the youngest would be burnt at the stake or placed in front of a firing squad if they broke in. The only hope was to do exactly as they had been instructed and toughen up for the coming confrontation.

Severe physical punishment went hand in hand with affectionate displays. A misplaced frown could earn a beating. This was followed by lavish affection, confusing the poor children and leading to lifelong emotional scarring. Children, even babies, were thrown up against walls or tossed out of windows.

The children were fed a steady diet of cartoons and films produced by the Children of God. Some of these showed happy family members doing chores and singing the praises of Moses David. Others were horrific, Crumb-like cartoons showing the horrors of Armageddon and mass murder.

Two hours a week would be Family Time, when members of a family could spend time with each other. Once a week there was a movie night. Few movies were approved by Berg; children recall watching *The Sound of Music* more than a hundred times. To be allowed to see the movie, children had to prove their spirituality by talking in tongues.

These were the experiences of children who, knowing no better, accepted the strict regime enforced by the leadership.

However, as the second generation of children grew larger and larger there were more and more who acted out against their draconian, Spartan and abusive existence. Berg called these 'Terror Teens' and he moved ruthlessly to demonize any rebellious behavior. Those who questioned the state of affairs were sent to one of several 'Victor' camps.

Even among the most faithful adherents there were whispers about the horrific state of affairs at the Macao Victor Camp. While it was meant to run a voluntary program for children who needed special attention, it was actually a location where child abuse under Berg's rule reached its worst. Cult literature described a caring and personalized counseling service, where wayward individuals were cocooned in a loving environment. It was in fact a place of unremitting psychological and physical torment. Children, already traumatized by their experiences in the Children of God, were beaten, deprived of food, slapped repeatedly, placed into isolation, forbidden from communicating and even put to hard labor.

This exacerbated pre-existing psychological conditions. Many children were sent over the edge into madness. One teenage girl was slapped around so badly that she lost all powers of communication and could only stutter incoherently.

The response of the 'counselors' at Macao Victor Camp? These children were obviously possessed by evil spirits. Faux exorcisms were held, complete with lit candles and leaders talking in tongues over the distressed children.

Sometimes the exorcisms were violent. Children would be beaten and their heads bashed against a brick wall. If they blacked out, the children would be revived and the violence began anew. Many vomited, which was a good sign according to those conducting the exorcism – the children were vomiting out demons.

There were also Victor Camps in Japan and Brazil. While not as violent as Macao, the camps still tried to mold the thinking of individuals through fear and intimidation. One victim recalled being forced to pull down his pants and receive a spanking in front of 50 other teenagers. His crime? Taking a banana out of a fridge.

The first task for reprogramming was to remove the child from their family. One 12-year-old child was sent to a camp in the Philippines. For 18 months, she and her brother were confined within the camp. Armed guards stood at every entrance, preventing escape. The two were subjected to brutal abuse. They were forced to fast. Talking was forbidden, and if any child dared to laugh their mouths would be taped up. Without their passports or parental guidance there was no hope of escape.

Armageddon

The Teens for Christ and Children of God movement began life as a celibate cult where the members were encouraged to 'get the victory' for Christ. When Berg realized that there was a bevy of beautiful young woman around him willing to satisfy his every urge, he decided that his spiritual teachings should be altered to justify his lecherous longings.

This started off harmlessly enough. In the early 70s he began promoting the Law of Love. He took a few lines in the Bible and interpreted them less as a platonic love of mankind than as an encouragement to 'share'. It was not right, the Mo Letters said, for single members of the cult to feel lonely. It was important that married members share their partners and allow them to sleep with other cult members (as long as they were of the opposite sex). Lovemaking was, in Berg's view, a symbol of God's love.

Many members embraced this ideal and it was during this time that the Children of God gained a new name – they were dubbed the 'Love Cult' by the press.

The communes became rife with extramarital, free-for-all sex. 'Aunties', 'uncles', 'brothers' and 'sisters' would engage in intercourse at any hour of the day and in any location. Children would be exposed to this lovemaking and there was no attempt to hide the activities from them. Children came upon adults groping in the hallways, or having loud orgies in the lounge rooms and dormitory bedrooms.

Mo Letters began to espouse the new ideology and it was common for children as young as four to spend 'Word Time' poring over images of men and women having sex in fields while a benign and bearded 'grandpa' looked down upon the copulating couple.

Not all were enamored with the new directives and several left the cult. Even some who stayed behind were uncomfortable. A man could express his willingness to bed a cultist's wife. No matter how physically repulsive they found the proposal, neither partner could refuse. To do so would see them labeled as selfish and a note would be made in the Open Heart Reports. Partners could be shamed publicly or even separated and sent to different compounds to learn humility.

In 1975 Berg had a revelation. The Unit had fled the USA when authorities took too much interest in their activities, and he had taken his close circle with him to London. These included several of his wives and some of the most attractive women in the cult. He began 'witnessing' in London nightclubs (always a good excuse to combine drinking with proselytizing), and he noticed that young men were keen to talk to his wives and the fashionably dressed acolytes. Strangers seemed more receptive to his heavenly message while gazing into the mascaraed eyes of the young women. Berg realized that he could use the women within the sect to go 'flirty fishing': they could solicit donations by exchanging sex for cash, or use sex to recruit new members into the cult.

It took a while to hone the techniques and approaches that constituted 'FF', but by 1976 Mo Letters explaining what was required were being sent to his communes throughout the world.

Children and adults had a good set of clothes for when they went 'witnessing' in the outside world. This was stepped up a level for women engaged in flirty fishing. Whole posses would dress up in the latest low cut fashions and the nicest makeup and head into town to enrapture and ensnare unsuspecting men.

Many of the young women took to it with a will. They were already following Berg's 'law of love' in the cult compounds, so it wasn't much of a step to take it into the real world. The attractive young women could still pick and choose who they wanted to bed and it was good to bring in cash for the Children of God's coffers.

In line with all of his other operations, Berg ran it as a business. He leased large houses and effectively turned them into brothels. The girls had to write reports detailing who they had talked too, what sexual acts they had performed and how much they had earned. They were told to keep their eyes out for particularly well-heeled marks or men who seemed to be spiritually vulnerable. Berg would identify the best targets and a succession of FFs would 'love bomb' the mark to either bring him into Berg's fold or extract as much cash as possible.

Powerful government officials were also targeted; they could hardly move against cult communes if they had been beneficiaries of targeted 'loving'.

Berg gave himself a new name: The Fisherman.

The women called themselves God's Whores. The Mo Letters issued telling them exactly how to behave included titles such as 'God's Love Slave' and 'The FF Explosion'. Posters were stuck up in communes showing a scantily clad woman writhing on a fishing hook with the caption 'Hookers for Jesus'.

Eventually Berg was so enamored with his new project that he had his disciples sign up with local escort agencies. The advantage of this technique was guaranteed income, although it meant that the FFs couldn't pick their marks and had no right of refusal. Some questioned this arrangement, because it placed women in a vulnerable position and subject to violent attacks. Berg was not concerned. He compared the women to the Christian martyrs. They should take any injuries or trauma on the chin, for Jesus.

There were several other consequences. Berg's ban on contraception meant thousands of children were born into the cult, most without fathers. There was also an outbreak of STDs.

But the program was bearing fruit. Berg could claim thousands of compounds throughout the world. Some had as many as 400 people while others were living in houses as family units, carrying out Berg's 'good works.'

In 1982 a new and disturbing trend arose: institutionalized child abuse.

Berg had great plans for his stepson. In 1982 the cult published a work entitled 'The Book of Davidito.' This set the young man up as the future leader of the cult, destined to fight on God's side in his chariot at the end of the world. It placed the young man in many different scenarios and became a seminal teaching aid for the youth growing up in the cult.

There were several disturbing chapters where his 'Aunt' Sara describes masturbating the boy even as he was an infant. This sex play extends through his youth and he is invited to watch and even partake in adult activities. Sara gave birth to a daughter and encouraged her and the Prophet Prince to carry on as adults and develop a sexual relationship even though they were not yet teenagers.

This 'revolutionary sexuality,' as Berg liked to describe it, was soon being promulgated throughout the cult. Mo Letters with DAR written on the cover were distributed, urging adults to have sexual interaction with children. Glossy covers showed adults lying in bed with children, or children standing in fields witnessing adults copulating. Graphic illustrations of women 'spooning' with or masturbating young boys were some of the milder images. Second generation cultists were encouraged to experiment with their friends and stimulate sex acts even if they were not capable of intercourse. Videos, showing girls as young as four performing provocative striptease acts, were sent to the compounds with the request that they produce similar pieces and send them back to the Unit.

Children were ordered not to demonstrate any of these behaviors in front of systemites. The ongoing corruption of the young was to be a closely held secret.

Predatory men and women used the new license given them by Berg to move on young children and perform unspeakable acts. Children who are sexually abused are often reluctant to discuss the horrific acts perpetrated upon them with their parents or guardians due to shame and fear. Within the Children of God there was a whole new level of control, urging children to fight against their instincts and accept what was happening. Children that were removed from their families were particularly vulnerable as 'aunties' and 'uncles' gained sexual satisfaction by exploiting their young charges. Even within smaller units, children were routinely abused when cult members visited or boarded with the permanent residents.

Many adult members left the cult when they realized what was going on. Sadly, many did not, preferring to turn a blind eye to the abuse in order to maintain their standing within the organization.

Many survivors tell how innocent functions would turn seedy when 11- and 12-year-old children were asked to perform stripteases in front of adult audiences. Literature targeted children. Titles such as the 'Basic Training Handbook' sought to educate prepubescent teens in the arts of love, and 'My Little Fish' showed photos of a grown woman and a young boy embracing.

There is a clear correlation with the 'Terror Teens' and the rise of sexual abuse impacting the children of the cult. Seeking to escape the horrific conditions, children would act up, try to flee or descend into madness. As usual with the Children of God, Berg was at the center of the exploitation. His granddaughter began, like Davidito, as an example to the cult's children, but after years of abuse at her grandfather's hands she became difficult and rebellious. Repeated beatings could not expel the 'demon' that took up residence in the 13-year-old girl's body. A lengthy spell at several Victor camps led to her total breakdown.

Many second generation cultists fled as soon as they were legally old enough to do so. But this has not ended the torment. Many experienced, and still suffer from, what can only be termed Post Traumatic Stress Disorder. They have difficulty forming relationships, are not equipped to operate in the outside world and often descend into lives of petty theft, substance abuse and prostitution.

They are the lucky ones. At least 25 children from the cult have committed suicide. Some have leapt off buildings, others have taken overdoses and some have gassed themselves in cars.

'Davidito' Ricky Rodriguez left the cult. Years of abuse had turned the one time Prophet Prince into an extremely angry young man. Ricky was determined to take revenge and execute his mother, Karen Zerby, who by that time had taken over the cult following Berg's death.

Ricky lured 'Aunt' Sara to his flat in Tucson, Arizona, on 5 January 2005. The Prophet Prince was hoping that she would reveal the whereabouts of his mother. She did not do so and was stabbed multiple times. Sara bled out on the floor of the cheap rental apartment. Ricky drove for 24 hours, stopped at an industrial lot near Blythe, California, and committed suicide with a gunshot to his head. He would no longer be able to fight the Antichrist at the side of God.

Berg's cult lives on, despite his death in 1994. They still expound the 'Law of Love' and pamphlets describing the apocalypse are still distributed by the members. How they rationalize the late arrival of Armageddon is not known. After all, it is at least 25 years overdue!

CHAPTER THREE

Branch Davidians: The Lamb of God

Revelation – Book 5

[13] Then I heard every creature in heaven and on earth and under the earth and on the sea, and all that is in them, saying: 'To him who sits on the throne and to the Lamb be praise and honor and glory and power, for ever and ever!'

The horrific suicide of 900 Americans in 1978, deep in the forests of Guyana, forever changed the government's perception of cults. Once seen as harmless dwellers on the lunatic fringe, they were now perceived as unpredictable and dangerous.

When word came of a millennial cult taking root and attracting adherents in the center of Texas, alarm bells went off in several agencies. Alerts went to code red when it was heard that the Branch Davidians were stockpiling weapons. Their self-proclaimed messiah, David Koresh, was becoming increasingly certain that Armageddon was imminent.

A move was made against the compound at Mount Carmel, outside Waco, Texas. Due to many errors, the raid degenerated into a 51-day armed standoff. However, the biggest mistake made by the authorities was their inability to understand that the man at the heart of the conflict had one goal and one goal only: to go down in fire and flames in a final shoot out with the unbelievers.

Genesis

Vernon Wayne Howell, the Lamb of God, the divine personage who would prize open God's right hand to open the Seventh Seal on the Scroll of Armageddon and usher in the end of the world, was born on 17 August 1959. His mother, 14-year-old Bonnie Clark, was an unmarried high-school dropout. Vernon's father, Bobby Wayne Howell, didn't see much of his son and soon got hitched to another woman.

Bonnie then moved in with a man who had just finished a stint in prison. This fellow was a nasty piece of work and soon Bonnie and Vernon were the subject of repeated violent assaults. After 18 months of this the young boy was sent to his grandmother, Earline Clark, for protection. Earline had several children still at home and raised them along with their nephew.

Vernon called his maternal grandmother 'Momma', but there was no such intimacy with his grandfather. He was a distant figure, a hard-handed, hard drinking Texan. While he wasn't too keen on demonstrating affection, grandpa was always willing to give his charges a good hiding for poor behavior.

Vernon was taken back by his mother, who had married Roy Haldeman. He too believed in corporal punishment and the young fellow often had his 'tail whomped' for a bad report card. By all accounts this was pretty common for the time and most reports paint the Haldeman household as stable and cheery. However, Vernon was still attached to 'Momma' and would pedal after her on his trike, tears trickling down his face, whenever she left after a visit.

The earlier beatings may have had a permanent effect on Vernon's progress. At a Dallas public school, he soon fell behind his peers and was diagnosed with a learning disability. He completed first grade twice and in third and fourth grade he was put into special education. Bullying became a feature of life for the young boy. There is a possibility that he was sexually abused by some older boys, although this is probably apocryphal.

Vernon moved back in with his grandparents when he was 14. This was a happy time in his life. A shed in the back yard became his private domain and with a bit of hammering and a bit of fixing it was transformed into a cool 'pad.' It was a classic 70s teenage hangout, with pictures of guitar legends covering the walls, a couch and an amplifier which Vernon used to practice his licks. He also developed a liking for tinkering with cars, something that would last his lifetime. Girls were attracted to the long-haired, laid-back and increasingly handsome young man.

But while Vernon was living the good life, being cool and riding around the neighborhood on his dragster, the problems at school continued. He dropped out of junior high.

He continued some study on his own. Often he was found in the back shed poring over a well-thumbed copy of the Bible. It seems that although some things came hard for the young man, he had a near photographic memory for scripture. He could repeat verbatim most of the New Testament by the time he was 13.

Vernon's mother and grandmother were practicing Seventh Day Adventists. They followed strict moral codes that taught a rigid adherence to the Ten Commandments. Vernon got caught up in their fervor and his behavior began to become somewhat obsessive. He spent many a long hour listening to fiery radio preachers banging on about the promised land.

Vernon's late adolescence became troubled. He was shuttled back and forth between his two families and lacked a positive male role model who could teach him appropriate boundaries in a consistent manner. He was exposed to one aspect of life in Texas that would have an effect on later decisions: a 14-year-old female relative married a sailor. What would now be termed pedophilia was accepted as commonplace.

Outwardly the 18-year-old teenager seemed happy. He worked at a construction job and bought a hotted-up Silverado pickup truck complete with red velour interior and a cranked up sound system. He continued to hone his guitar skills and worked out at the gym, becoming quite a catch for the young ladies. Howell had the gift of the gab and often had a group of admirers trailing behind him.

But something was missing. Despite a joyful reunion with his biological father, Vernon lacked purpose. He couldn't hold down a steady job, he had no college degree and his band could not get any gigs.

What could give him direction?

After a messy breakup with one of his many girlfriends, Vernon began to attend the Seventh Day Adventist Church in Tyler, Texas. He realized that he had not been following 'the Way' and went through a crisis of guilt. Seeking atonement, Vernon attended services and Bible classes as often as he could and spent many hours in fervent prayer.

At first the troubled teenager was welcomed in the church. He appeared to wear his heart on his sleeve and seemed genuinely interested in accepting advice and healing his troubled conscience. He did tend to bang on a bit about obscure sections of the Old Testament but overall he was welcomed as a new acolyte who had a real and genuine interest in the teachings of the Bible. He perceived himself as a newborn lamb seeking to have his intercourse with the devil (premarital sex and rock and roll) washed from his soul.

Soon the young disciple tried to become the master. His exhaustive knowledge of the Bible and his newfound zeal for leading a pure life saw Vernon emerging as an ideologue who was increasingly unable to deal with dissenting views. When disputing a point of faith, he could pull out a lengthy quote to support his point. Vernon became less and less hesitant about trying to impose his will on the other members of the church. This would stand him in good stead as leader of the Branch Davidians later on.

From being one willing to accept 'counsel,' Howell decided he was better placed to dish it out. All of sudden, women whose skirts were above the knee became immodest and young girls in particular were admonished for any 'loose' behavior. Vernon would break into conversations and seek to dominate proceedings.

Vernon may have remained something of a minor oddball within his group, a difficult character with an inflated sense of his own importance and lacking direction. He was, however, given a shot at glory and he seized it with both hands.

The Seventh Day Adventists sponsored a fiery evangelist called Jim Gilley to run what were called Revelation Seminars. These were, and still are, used by the church to describe what the coming apocalypse will look like. The multimedia display from Gilley was particularly dramatic. Graphic pictures of unbelievers being dragged down to hell were interspersed with images of all of their worldly goods and chattels being consumed by earthquakes and fiery volcanoes.

Gilley would dwell on the nature of that final conflict, and how all believers would be tested. Even those who followed the teachings of the Seventh Day Adventists would have their faith stretched to the limit. Just as they were about to surrender to temptation and fall in with the unbelievers, Armageddon would occur, leading to the Ascension and the establishment of God's Kingdom on Earth.

Vernon lapped it up, especially the graphic videos that revealed how contemporary world events seemed to be fulfilling Biblical prophecies for the end of days. All that was lacking, explained Gilley, was the true prophet who would unlock the Seventh Seal. The Book of Revelation describes seven seals that bind a scroll in God's right hand. Only the Lamb of God would be able to open the last seal and bring on the impending apocalypse.

Vernon began to believe that he was the new prophet who would lead the Seventh Day Adventists in the coming crisis.

As the young man's fantasy life began to grow on the spiritual plane, this was reflected in his sex life. The pastor of the Tyler congregation had a daughter, and the 20-year-old Vernon decided that they were destined to marry. Fortunately for the aspiring groom, God was there to lend a helping hand. Vernon was immersed in prayer when he had a divine experience. He floated upwards towards heaven and entered a wonderland of celestial clouds. Pillowed within the bosom of one cloud was the pastor's daughter, entreating him to join her. Vernon heard the voice of God declaring that it was His will that the two be joined in matrimony.

A breathless Vernon rushed to his pastor to tell of the glorious vision. Supporting his point, he quoted exhaustively from the Bible, finding tracts that supported the idea that all people should have a mate. By this time the pastor was well aware of the manipulative shenanigans that Vernon got up to and promptly banned him from even looking at his daughter.

Vernon had another vision at this time: he was summoned to heaven to find God extending his right hand with a scroll.

One other aspect of Vernon's behavior troubled the Tyler leadership. His learning difficulties made it hard for him to put pen to paper. But as a foil to this disability was an awakening idea that he was able to speak with such passion and authority that he could mesmerize any audience and bend them to his will. Self-belief and perhaps a touch of charisma allowed Vernon to attract a large portion of the congregation, particularly the young, to his world view.

His increasingly delusional and strident behavior led to his formal expulsion from the congregation in April 1981.

He soon found a new cause. Word had been circulating among members of the Seventh Day Adventists that Lois Roden, the leader of the Branch Davidian compound at Mount Carmel, had also been in direct communication with God. Vernon made his way there in late 1981.

The Seventh Day Adventists were a relic of the Millerites. While they did not put a date on the 'Advent of Christ' they were nevertheless convinced that it would come sooner rather than later. Most people would find the Adventists' lifestyle fairly restrictive, but in the 1930s one group thought the lifestyle too permissive and split off into a sect known as the Davidian Seventh Day Adventists (Davidians). In 1955 an even more strict branch was founded: the Branch Davidians (the Branch). The Branch Davidians were convinced that Armageddon was just around the corner and that their leader had a direct line to the heavenly host – this individual was known as the 'living prophet', a title held in the early 80s by Lois Roden.

Branch Davidian founders had bought a large sprawling estate of many acres outside of the town of Waco. Using pooled resources, they built a dormitory and a meeting hall. Primitive cooking and sanitary arrangements were provided, although there was little running water. Over the years, large parcels of the original estate were sold off and the compound began to take on a ramshackle air, with abandoned vehicles and castoff building materials littering the area.

Vernon made his first visit into this environment in 1981. After a short stay, he left with some theological reading material. Over the following years his visits became longer and longer. Proving a dab hand at working on the sect's cars and doing handy work, he was soon accepted into the community. Vernon attended Bible study classes and slowly raised his profile within the community. His knowledge of the scriptures, his passionate belief in the need for redemption and his growing confidence as a public speaker led to an acceptance among many that he was possibly the new 'living prophet'. Indeed, Roden and some of the top people of the Branch Davidians saw him in this light.

In 1983 Vernon, by now well ensconced in the Waco community, was invited by Lois to present a series of eight sermons that were intended to spell out the increasingly detailed revelations he was receiving. The presentations became known as the 'Serpent's Root' meetings and established him as a worthy successor to the elderly woman.

How powerful the young man must have felt. Barely into his twenties, he had an enraptured audience of all ages who would hang on his every word, who were becoming convinced that he was the one man on Earth who could bring salvation during the apocalypse. For an ambitious individual it must have been an addictive experience. And Vernon was ambitious.

In 1984 Vernon married 14-year-old Rachel Jones, who was the daughter of Roden's chief lieutenant. It has been speculated that soon after his marriage he began a sexual relationship with Roden herself, a woman over 40 years his senior. One version has it that Vernon complained to the older woman that he was suffering from an inability to stop masturbating, and only her heavenly loins could stop this foul practice! The unlikely pair hoped that a child from their union would be the new Christ – something of a miracle indeed considering her advanced age.

Whatever the rationale for this behavior, there was one individual who was determined to stop Vernon being anointed the prophet when Lois passed on. Her son, George Roden, was convinced that he should have become leader of the group when his father died. He resented his mother, who had taken what he saw as rightfully his, but considering her advanced years he decided to bide his time. When young Vernon came along and seemed about to hijack his succession plans, George, who was known to have a short temper, was understandably upset. He chased Vernon out of the compound, threatening him with a pair of six shooters.

Vernon beat a hasty retreat, but not before he gathered 40 or so of his acolytes. While he may have lost a battle, he was determined to win the war and return as the new leader. The new splinter group from the Branch Davidians (who had splintered from the Davidian Seventh Day Adventists who had splintered from the Adventists) moved to Waco before relocating to an encampment on a 40-acre site near Palestine, Texas. This was a rough existence; the group seem to have lived in tents, buses and rough-hewn log cabins. There were few amenities but, when salvation is at hand, who cares?

Despite the exile from Waco, Vernon and his wife continued to work on his message. Part of this involved a visit to Israel in 1985. While in Israel, Vernon was visited by seven angels who, rather than flying with the aid of wings, traveled from Orion in spaceships to deliver their divine message. Vernon had recently watched *Chariots of the Gods*, a documentary based on the book of the same name by Erich von Däniken, and some of this message may have rubbed off on him. It was while in Israel that Vernon decided his real name was David Koresh. Henceforth he will be referred to by this name.

During this time in exile, Koresh visited Australia and several other countries. He and his chief lieutenants were frequent attendees at Adventist prayer meets and Howell was able to gather more and more adherents.

Soon the brash young man felt he had enough earthly assistance to oust George Roden from the Davidian HQ.

George Roden was aware that the pretender was continually undermining him. Both men traveled around the country drumming up support, but the problem for poor old George was that he lacked charisma or a novel divine message. The alternative – the young, passionate and messianic figure of Koresh – began to attract more and more support. While few would actually challenge George to his face, he began to see that his hold was slipping. Once his mother died, on 10 November 1986 at the age of 70, there was even less likelihood that he could stay in charge.

Koresh had been ramping up the pressure and was claiming that once he was the head of the Davidians he would gather the 144,000 chosen folk who would live through the time of troubles and lead them into the new age of Christ.

Being from a long Texan heritage, George sought to head his challenger off at the pass by challenging him to a shootout – not with guns but with prayers. George fired the opening salvo of their stand off by claiming that, as the true living prophet, he would use the power of prayer to resurrect a long dead member of the cult: Anna Hughes, who had died in the 60s at the age of 84. Hughes had died a spinster before being buried in the compound's graveyard, where she had all but rotted away, leaving only the proverbial bag of bones left to be resurrected.

George had obviously not done his history study, because he promised the faithful that within one week he and his 'mighty men' would complete their task. As the Millerites had discovered, it is never good to put a date on a miraculous event, just in case it doesn't eventuate.

Nevertheless, George and his followers dug up the creaky old coffin, draped it in a flag with the Star of David and carried it triumphantly into the main meeting hall. The Davidians then threw themselves into some serious prayer. Acting in relays, the worshipers ensured that God was being properly beseeched around the clock. Despite their best efforts, poor old dead Anna Hughes stayed just that - old and dead.

While Koresh obviously had delusions of grandeur, he still had some link with reality and decided that such a task was not for him. Instead he hatched a cunning plan for the Texas authorities to sort out George Roden. With an unusual respect for secular law, Koresh surmised that if he was able to seize the coffin and bring it to the sheriff, they could nail George for interfering with a corpse.

In the early morning of 3 November 1987, Howell and seven of his followers crept stealthily into the Waco compound, past the recently erected sign reading 'Rodenville'. All eight men were dressed in military fatigues and camouflage and were armed with a variety of semi-automatics and rifles. A sharp-eyed Davidian saw the party snaking across the grounds and a firefight soon erupted, with the two factions emptying magazines at each other.

George Roden was wounded in the chest and the right arm. The tree he was sheltering behind was so full of lead it was a miracle it didn't topple over. George was pulled out of the compound and Koresh made a triumphant return.

The Waco sheriff and a few of his deputies drove out to Mt Carmel and asked for the cult members to hand over their weapons. This was done without incident (in contrast to what was to happen five years later) and Koresh and his followers were arrested for attempted murder.

In 1988 the eight men stood trial. Koresh tried to convince the judge that he was a God-fearing man who had all the provocation he could stand. Every day a bevy of his followers, including many women carrying babies, turned up to support the accused in a respectful and polite manner. This seemed to do the job and Koresh and his men were released without conviction.

It was all too much for George Roden. His bizarre behavior escalated until he found himself committed to a psych ward in 1989.

David Koresh was now the undisputed master of the 77-acre Davidian compound at Waco. He would soon turn all who lived there into tools to help fulfill his messianic vision.

Attraction, Initiation and Control

The extent of Koresh's control over the cult is made clear by studying psychological reports on the 21 children who were released during the siege. For weeks after their release the children, many as young as four years old, remained afraid of Koresh. Although some were quite aware that Koresh was dead, they still feared his wrath if they did anything that went against the strictures placed on their behavior. They were in no doubt that he would be able to return from the dead to mete out a range of punishments.

Part of any cult conditioning is to produce a fear of the outside within the members. The Davidian children had had it pounded into them that those outside of the compound were evil.

Within the compound, rigorous discipline was maintained. Many of the surviving children still had raised wheals on their buttocks. For the slightest sin, such as spilling milk or talking out of turn, they would be struck with 'the helper', a crude paddle device. Other punishments included being separated from their peers or deprived of the paltry meals given to the rest of the community. These meals reflected Koresh's obsessions regarding frugal living; fruit and vegetable were often mashed up and served in a cold collation.

They were also conditioned to survive the coming apocalypse. Male children woke at 5 am to train for the final battle. This included drill, weapons training and hand-to-hand fighting. If they did not fight hard enough they were paddled for that too. The children had to refer to their parents as 'dogs'; only Koresh was their 'father'.

Young girls had an altogether different upbringing. They were allowed to sleep in as long as possible. Girls as young as 11 were given a plastic star of David, which indicated to the cult members that these girls had 'the light' and would soon be taken as a wife by the leader. In what would now be termed classic grooming behavior, Koresh discussed sex openly with the young girls, even working the topic into the sermons he delivered.

Children in mainstream society can usually expect the unconditional love of their parents, regardless of minor misdemeanors or disagreements. Within the Davidians, confused messages of hope, fear, love and religious intolerance were intermingled to produce confused children who knew that if they were to escape punishment they had to attend to the every whim of their leader. This ensured that they were continuously on tenterhooks, caught between being condemned to a hellish inferno or praised as one of Koresh's angels.

Rather than being brought up in a loving environment, the children were manipulated by a range of destructive emotional techniques including coercion, fear, shame, humiliation, guilt and aggression. Children who dared to question Koresh would be placed in solitary confinement in small underground chambers, as well as being beaten on the buttocks until they bled. The last message delivered by their parents as the children left the compound was that they would all soon be dead and they would meet up in heaven – something the children did not see as odd at all.

How was it that Koresh managed to prepare more than 100 people for certain death?

In Israel, Vernon Howell had decided that his 'Biblical' name was David Koresh. This name is laden with meaning. David relates to the House of David, a royal line that ruled ancient Israel during some of its most glorious achievements. It is a tenet of Christian faith that Jesus was an heir to the House of David. Koresh has multiple meanings. It can refer to the Persian Emperor Cyrus, who overthrew the Babylonians, but it has another meaning: the destroyer.

Vernon Howell had re-titled himself as Christ the Destroyer. He became the font of all knowledge within the sect; as Christ he had to be looked upon as perfect. Bible study was not a free flow of ideas, it was Koresh laying down the law.

Initially the new leader seemed to bring improvements to the Waco acreage. Old dilapidated buildings were torn down or rebuilt. Junk that had been allowed to accumulate under the Rodens was cleared off the property, including many old cars that had been cannibalized for spare parts. A proud new tower rose over the compound, which was turned into a large monolithic collection of buildings rather than a hodgepodge of unconnected structures. The tower and compound now had a clear field of fire stretching for hundreds of meters in either direction.

Other techniques were utilized to strengthen Koresh's bastion. 'Rodenville' was knocked down and the property was renamed 'Ranch Apocalypse'. On the top floor of one of the buildings a large secure armory was built. The leader was one of the few who had a key. Some of the larger buildings were reinforced with concrete sheeting. Water wells were dug, as were a network of tunnels linking the buildings. An old bus was sunk into the ground to act as a bunker.

Along with these defensive preparations, never-ending training sessions were held within the compound. As mentioned before, the males were expected to be ready for armed combat. Taking a leaf out of the Bible, Koresh anointed some of his most trusted followers as 'mighty men'. These hardcore fighters helped enforce his will.

Many cults maintain control by keeping the members tired and disorientated. Ranch Apocalypse was no different. Most individuals woke before the crack of dawn and spent long hours in exhausting pursuits. Some worked in the fields, others went into town to spend long days working in the cult businesses. Food was issued sparingly and was often used to discipline the members. It could be withheld for perceived infractions or doled out in larger portions for those who earned favor in Koresh's eyes. A light breakfast and a light lunch were sometimes all that was served up – they did not always get dinner.

Koresh was under no such constraints. He often rose after noon and had access to any foods he desired. If he needed a bit of variety, he would take a quick trip into Waco to his favorite bar with a couple of the mighty men.

There was no respite for the exhausted members as darkness fell. They would all be summoned to the meeting hall. There they would sit on a tier of hard wooden benches and be exposed to Koresh's crack theology. It would be hard for anybody to sit perched on a shallow bench without back support for any amount of time, and these sermons would go for hours. Sometimes they were harangued as Koresh found passages from the Bible to reinforce his message. At other times he would amp up his guitar and sing his greatest hits – no doubt he took the opportunity to show his talent by cranking out an ear-splitting solo.

Koresh would show violent movies to young and old in these meetings; *Apocalypse Now, The Godfather* and *Platoon* were often played. These helped Koresh reinforce his ideas regarding the evil and threatening nature of the outside world. If anyone fell asleep during the exhausting sermons, they would be hauled out and paddled in front of the rest of the flock by one of the mighty men. On the paddle were inscribed the words 'it is written'.

While we may wonder how people could sit through this, in fact many of his disciples still recall these times fondly. There was a perception that Koresh's knowledge was special; that they were working together for a bright future. These sermons, tiring as they were, did serve to reinforce the values of the cult and pull them together into a tight-knit group, prepared to resist the blandishments of the outside world.

Unbelievers in Waco and the surrounding towns had no cause to complain about the cult. In everyday dealings the members appeared neatly dressed and polite, if a little reserved.

Most of the group were keen to stay within the cult. An ex-member described how Lois Roden would deliver a complex message that had to be 'wrestled' with to gain understanding. In comparison, Koresh was able to speak with the clarity of a clarion bell. He made scripture come alive; dry and dusty passages of the Old Testament would be related to the present as if they had been written in the modern day. Many of the Davidians were familiar with spending hours poring over the Bible, so to them it was no chore. It was a delight to have Koresh throwing out new, exciting interpretations. To many his presence was intoxicating. Despite the fact that they were sleeping in spartan dormitories and were forced to excrete into primitive buckets, it did not matter. Spending 8, 9 or even 16 hours a day on Bible study in Koresh's presence was manna from heaven.

Even though the cult members were often out and about, Koresh kept a tight financial stranglehold over them. Most had sold off all of their assets and handed them into the cult coffers. Social service payments and 90 percent of wages were all tithed into Koresh's accounts.

Financial independence was not allowed; neither was emotional independence. Families were broken up, with separate dorms for men, women and children. Koresh became the font of all love, intimacy and wellbeing.

What was Koresh planning with this cohort of robotic followers? The money provided was going towards the creation of a huge arsenal of heavy weapons, grenades and ammunition. The cult began selling arms at fairs around the country, always using this cover to stockpile more and more weapons at Ranch Apocalypse. Neighbors often heard automatic weapons crashing out on firing ranges within the estate. Armed guards began to patrol the perimeter and took station at the main entrance.

Bizarre Beliefs

In the aftermath of the destruction of the Waco compound there was shock that reverberated throughout America and the world. Many assumed that the members who had been incinerated were crazed fanatics, perhaps deserving of their fate. Others closer to the cult had a much more nuanced perception of the deceased. Despite a certain aloofness, they had seemed to be able to operate in society in an appropriate manner. Some of the Davidians had even left the compound on a periodical basis to earn money as far away as California, before returning to the bosom of their faith.

What were the ideals that turned such people into automatons that would gladly die at Koresh's command?

As with many millennialists, Koresh focused on the Book of Revelation to fuel the fears and hopes of his flock. The beauty of Revelation is that it has such a range of images, cataclysms and obscure symbolism that it can be interpreted in any way a prophet wants it to be.

Koresh's preoccupation was with the passage describing the seven seals. God holds a scroll locked with seven seals. On these seals are written prophecies about the end of time. By unlocking the seals, 'the lamb' will usher in the end of time. But who was the lamb? Through close reading of the scriptures, Koresh was able to prove that he was the one destined to open the seventh seal. He was not, Koresh explained, Christ; he could not perform miracles such as raising Lazarus from the tomb or walking on water. However, there was one thing God had instructed him to do: open the seventh seal.

Once Koresh had decided that he was the lamb, he had an excuse to engage in all kinds of reprehensible behavior. Using typical cult leader doublethink, Koresh believed that in order to gain a greater understanding of sin, he was permitted to engage in as much drinking, swearing and womanizing as he liked. While the Davidians sweated from dawn to midnight in almost medieval conditions, their leader was able to indulge any whim.

Koresh's interpretation of Revelation saw that after the end of time a new Kingdom of David would be created. Koresh's role was to select 144,000 worthy disciples to inhabit the new land, where he would rule alongside God. Koresh would father 24 'judges' to aid him in this task.

Since all possessions in the new age were to belong to Koresh, so it was at Ranch Apocalypse. Women, men and children were his chattels. Wives of cult members were summoned to his bed. Most came willingly, although some left the compound with their husbands.

Children as young as twelve were soon in his sights. Koresh taught Bible classes to prepubescent girls that justified his ability to take them sexually and dealt in graphic detail with the practical workings of sexual intercourse. Once these girls were suitably conditioned, they were told to wear a plastic Star of David, an insignia designed to indicate to all of the cultists, even their parents, that these girls were destined to receive the seed of the prophet. Texas law at the time prohibited marriage or intercourse under the age of 14. In the eyes of the law, if the judiciary chose to pursue the matter, Koresh was an avowed pedophile and rapist.

Koresh was not averse to engaging in a pornographic interpretation of the Testaments. A phrase from the 45th Psalm discusses the practice of using 'the oil of gladness' to anoint the 'head' of the king. Koresh decided that the oil was in fact vaginal lubricant and that his penis was the king's head.

Koresh was successful in his project: by the time of the siege he had his 24 heavenly offspring and a bevy of compliant wives.

There was one more crucial aspect of Koresh's belief system. Even during his trial for the shoot out he had warned his flock that eventually the authorities would come for them. He believed that the final showdown with the Philistines was coming. Any of his flock who wavered in this belief were taken aside and given the full force of Koresh's evangelical fervor. It was righteous to die at the hands of unbelievers; resurrection was guaranteed.

The theological interpretation took on an even darker hue. Adults and children began to be told of the merits of suicide. Koresh himself explained to the children that it was best to place the barrel of a gun in their mouth before firing.

Whispers of these preoccupations came through to various government agencies. One of the reasons that the decision to break up the cult was made was because they felt a mass suicide like that of Jonestown was becoming increasingly likely.

However, there was one part of Koresh's teachings that they missed.

Within the Bible are references to times of trouble, conflict and battle - a period that must be endured before the new age is ushered in. Koresh was supposedly chosen by God to break the seventh seal. Before that time, the fifth seal had to be broken, heralded by a time of battle. Between the breaking of the fifth seal would be a time of waiting, a false calm before bloodshed, which would open the sixth seal. Once this was broken, Koresh would be ushered into the presence of God to break the seventh seal, read the prophecies and usher in the new Kingdom of David.

By attacking Waco, in the rhetoric of the cult, the American government broke the fifth seal. For Koresh to be able to open the seventh seal, he and his followers had to perish in fire and violence. Every moment the siege dragged on reinforced this idea and strengthened the Davidians resolve not to surrender.

Armageddon

Koresh's idea of building a heavenly kingdom on Earth, where he would be surrounded by angels and his 24 Judges, came to naught. All that remained of the cult after the siege were the incinerated and charred corpses of his 100 followers. Some were unrecognizable; a foot, complete with charred ankle and shoe, were all that remained of one person. Other adults had been burnt until they were the size of small children. Individuals could only be identified by recourse to dental charts. Some corpses had been exposed to such heat that not even their teeth survived the inferno.

On the morning of 28 February 1993, the Davidians were inside the compound, loading weapons, preparing fire positions and building barricades out of furniture. On most mornings cult members worked in the fields and workshops from dawn until their meager breakfast was served. Why was this day so different?

As the sun rose over Waco, a TV crew had driven up in their van and set up their cameras looking down the road towards the entrance to the compound. An associate of one of the cult members had pulled up and asked what happening. He was told that they had been tipped off that an ATF raid was imminent. This information was conveyed to Koresh, who sounded a general alarm. Armageddon was upon him.

The ATF (the Federal Bureau of Alcohol, Tobacco and Firearms) had been keeping an eye on the increasingly deranged cult leader's activities. Almost by accident, a delivery driver had realized that he was delivering hand grenade cases to the compound. The driver had alerted his superiors, who alerted Federal authorities. They began to take a keen interest in the masses of material delivered into the compound. Agents were inserted into the delivery runs and it was noted that armed guards seemed to be controlling traffic in and out of the main entrance.

Local sheriffs were also taking an active interest in the goings on at Camp Koresh. Neighbors had complained of the noise created by intensive weapon training going on in the adjoining fields. Even in Texas, constant fire from semiautomatic and automatic weapons was a bit disconcerting. Agents hired out a vacant house with a clear view of the road in and out of the compound, keeping a 24-hour watch. It seems that federal agents had implanted fiber optic cables into some walls of the compound, allowing them to see and hear everything that went on in selected rooms. Innocent-looking phones were in fact radio transmitters that allowed them to listen in to the heart of Koresh's empire.

Well before February 1993, Koresh was well aware that the authorities were perhaps planning to move on him. He called members from overseas to return to Waco just in case they should be needed. He cleared out the other homes, making sure that all of his 24 children were in his presence – ready for the coming Armageddon. At least a year's supply of food and water was laid in, ready for any eventuality.

Koresh's Davidians were so well conditioned that the apocalypse was coming that all Koresh had to do was arm them and tell them where to point the weapons. They had a huge arsenal, thousands and thousands of rounds in magazines and ammo boxes, distributed in all the defensive sites within the compound. Men were armed with AK-47 sub machine guns, Beretta semiautomatic pistols and Glock 9 mm pistols. There were stores of hand grenades and incendiaries placed at selected sites chosen by Koresh.

The ATF made a fatal miscalculation in tipping off the press. In fact, the whole raid was a colossal, unnecessary stuff up. Despite his increasing paranoia, Koresh still made regular trips into town. While the cultists lived a hard-scrabble life in the compound, their guru would go into town and spend hundreds of dollars at his favorite music shop or chow down on a hearty steak at a local saloon, the Chelsea Street Pub. The Davidians owned a car repair shop in town and David often spent an afternoon there, tinkering with engines.

It would have been easy to nab him away from his armed coterie. Why wasn't this done? It appears that the ATF was planning a media triumph. The raid was 'coincidentally' timed to occur just before Congress decided the next tranche of funding.

It is quite bizarre that such an obvious slip was made in the security measures employed by the raiders. Many of the ATF planners had seen action in Vietnam and were well versed in the methods of launching a surprise attack. Two specially built pickup trucks towed what appeared to be cattle trailers. Concealed inside the trailers were more than 50 ATF personnel ready to launch the raid. They had all been exhaustively drilled and were given specific objectives. They had practiced their assault on a full-scale mock-up of the compound's buildings during several weeks of intensive training. Nothing was allowed to go awry.

At 9.55 am the vehicles burst into the compound and squads covered in flak jackets and bristling with weaponry piled out of the cattle trucks. They proceeded to storm their objectives at the front of the compound. In what was another classic snafu, a Ford Bronco packed with local media types was allowed to follow along behind the agents. The ATF agents placed their ladders up against the wall of the main compound and climbed up towards the roof to gain access through the upper floor windows. It was suspected that one of the main weapon caches was situated on the top floor.

Other teams were intended to seize Koresh and his mighty men, or to protect the women and children. One of these teams rushed the front double doors, waving a warrant and shouting 'Federal agents - we have a search warrant.' As the assault crews swarmed over the front of the building, two ATF apache attack helicopters and one military Sikorsky Black Hawk helicopter buzzed the compound from the rear.

Everything was going to plan. The raid seemed perfectly timed.

One survivor claimed that as the agents closed in Koresh was initially calm and thought the situation could be resolved peacefully. The cult leader apparently told all of the members to go to their rooms while he sorted out the situation. Koresh then went down the main corridor to the front door, but when he opened it and saw the charging ATF he yelled out that they had to back off, as there were women and children there.

Then the Davidians opened fire. Machine gun and rifle fire poured into the agents. Much of it came from the central tower. Others fired through walls on the top stories to take down the agents on the roofs. A 50 caliber machine gun opened up, shattering vehicles and blowing tires. Snipers, who had been well trained in the use of tunnel warfare, seemed to pop up from all angles, shooting at the ATF and pinning them to the ground or making them take shelter behind vehicles and buildings. The three helicopters, intended to overawe the inhabitants, were almost immediately chased off by the intense gunfire.

Four ATF members were not so lucky and were not able to make an escape. They died or were mortally wounded in the initial hail of gunfire. A further 16 were wounded. Most of the others, including the local media in the Ford Bronco, were pinned down and could not extricate themselves.

Many ex-military ATF members recognized the heavy discharge of 12 mm bullets fired from a 50-caliber machine gun, a lethal weapon that could destroy soft skin vehicles from a mile away.

At 10.15, Department of Public Safety officials evacuated any members of the press who were not pinned down. By 11.20 a fragile truce was organized, allowing the wounded to be evacuated by helicopters that had set down in a field north of the compound. By 1 pm most had been airlifted to Providence Medical Center, Waco, where doctors strenuously worked to save their lives.

The next hours saw a peaceful standoff until, at approximately 6 pm, a cultist began shooting. He met with swift retaliation and died in a hail of gunfire.

The FBI were called in to manage the situation. Unknowingly, the ATF had played into Koresh's rich fantasy life and brought about the final confrontation he had been prophesizing for so many years. When negotiators managed to get in touch with the prophet, they encountered a man not concerned with helping the wounded Davidians, not concerned with ensuring the safety of up to 40 children and not concerned with arriving at a peaceful outcome. Koresh seemed to be in a religious ferment and sought only to discuss the unlocking of the seventh seal.

Koresh had been wounded in the side during the initial exchange of fire. Playing the martyr for all he was worth, he posed with members of his family, claiming he only wanted a peaceful outcome. Other members of the cult were taped discussing the situation, exonerating themselves of any responsibility for the dire situation they found themselves in. Koresh was determined to go down in a blaze of glory; not only in God's eyes, but in the eyes of the American media too.

The administration of Bill Clinton was embarrassed by one of the longest sieges in American history. It was no doubt made clear to the FBI head that the situation had to be resolved as quickly and efficiently as possible. From 28 February to 19 April 1993, no expense was spared to bring the Davidians to their knees.

The 50-caliber machine gun was a real threat to the surrounding forces, as was the arc of fire provided by the central tower. M113 APCs had thin aluminum sides that made them vulnerable in an intense firefight, so a squadron of modern M2 Bradleys was brought in to surround the compound.

Soon a small army surrounded the besieged Davidians. Some reports estimate that the total included 10 Bradley APCs, 2 Abrams tanks, 4 tracked combat engineering vehicles, 668 FBI agents, 15 soldiers, 13 members of the Texas militia, 6 US customs officials, 131 Texas firemen and medics, 17 sheriffs and deputies and 18 Waco police officers. In all, almost 900 representatives from federal, state and county organizations were trying to control the situation. Not only did they have to deal with the Davidians, there was a hungry press pack that needed to be kept in line.

High-tech surveillance equipment was deployed. Infrared devices deployed in circling aircraft and from the ground penetrated the building to determine exactly where Davidians were located within the complex. Thermal imagers scanned outside walls to track body heat and isolate individual locations. Sensitive equipment, which included fiber optic cables and listening devices planted by agents, was even able to pick up conversations. Special lasers picked up vibrations in glass windows and used the signals to reconstruct speech. It appears that the Davidians were equipped with night-vision goggles that relied on thermal sights to pick out any sneak attack that may be made during the evening. As a counter to this, the FBI deployed powerful arc lights that could temporarily blind anyone using night-vision goggles. Specialists from the SAS in Britain and Delta Force members from the American military were brought in to offer advice.

Huge stereo speakers were set up in the siege lines. Earplugs were issued to members of the FBI, but the Davidians were not so lucky. An eclectic soundtrack was blasted at the besieged compound. Tibetan chants, Nancy Sinatra's 'These Boots Were Made for Walking,' police sirens, chopper blades, Christmas carols and discordant trumpet or synthesizer-like noises were played around the clock. What was no doubt particularly distressing for the children in the compound were the sounds of sheep and cows being slaughtered. There was no rhyme nor reason for the playlist – it was meant to disorientate and harass the cultists, preventing sleep wherever possible. This strategy may have been a bit of payback aimed at the guru. Before the power was cut, he enjoyed blasting out some of his own numbers, complete with discordant guitar, at the besiegers. Floodlights and laser beams swept the walls or were reflected off clouds; no doubt it seemed as if night was turned to day.

Koresh was aware of the trauma that he was putting his flock through. There seemed to be some hope that he would act rationally and at one stage he made an offer to the FBI: if they allowed him to broadcast a one hour sermon throughout the nation, he would saddle up his flock and bus them out of their dire situation into the hands of the authorities. The FBI stuck to its part of the bargain, and for one hour Koresh's deluded ramblings could be picked up from Hawaii to New York.

Three bright yellow school buses drove up to the main entrance. Surviving cult members recall that everyone still in the compound was looking forward to the evacuation. Everybody packed their bags, ready for a final blessed journey to freedom. Some elderly members and offspring from other cultists had been allowed to leave, 29 children in all. Hopefully the entire compound would be evacuated without further loss once Koresh's demands had been met.

However, it seems that Koresh was off his game. The sermon was flat and uninspiring – maybe he realized that the deal would not be honored. While the buses were idling outside the compound, God had words with Koresh. God told him to stay put. One frustrated fed explained, 'You can't argue with God.'

There was something deeper to Koresh's change of mind. The Davidians saw the initial attack by the federals as the opening of the fifth seal. They were prepared to wait the 'little season' before the sixth seal – the time of bloodshed before the ultimate unraveling of the seventh seal.

There was one more matter. Koresh released a film where his offspring came and sat on his knee. He declared that this was his family and he intended to defend them from all who attacked him. As all fathers do, he loved his children and would protect them against any aggressors. In his mind, his children were the 24 Judges who were destined, in the words of Revelation, to help him bring on the Kingdom of David. They were necessary for Koresh to fulfill his mission. If Koresh was to surrender his children, he would just be another crank who had gone a bit overboard.

Koresh could never surrender. He could not give up his delusional sense of superiority over the rest of mankind. This condemned his 24 children to death.

On the other side of the continent, another figure was losing face. The Clinton administration decided to move on Ranch Apocalypse after 51 days of stalemate. Once more the brightest minds in the American federal government played into Koresh's hands.

For months the FBI had been considering smoking the besieged cultists out of the compound by using tear gas canisters and specially evolved heavily armored Combat Engineer Vehicles (CEV). By the morning of 19 April, their patience had run out.

Four specially equipped CEVs, with jury-rigged gantries placed above where turrets may have been located, approached the cordon surrounding Mt Carmel. Each gantry was equipped with a point that allowed it to punch a hole through walls and a hose that could pump hundreds of thousands of canisters worth of CS tear gas into the space beyond. In the pre-dawn gloom the Davidians on sentry duty would have heard the heavy diesel engines revving and their tracks creaking as the vehicles approached. A phone call followed. At 5.55 am an FBI negotiator rang to say that the government's patience was exhausted. The FBI had been instructed to smoke out the Davidians and clear the compound. Koresh could hear Armageddon approaching in the form of the CEVs. The Biblical endgame was here. The phone, the last contact with the outside world, was tossed out of the top floor window – there would be no further communications.

Keen-eyed FBI agents noticed something else – some members could be seen frantically placing some kind of objects around the interior. Mines, grenades, ammo caches? The authorities couldn't be sure. They turned out to be incendiary devices; the sixth seal was about to be broken.

At 6.05 am the first engineer vehicle nosed its way up to the building where the men's quarters were located. It breached a window and started to pour tear gas into the building. At the same time, loudspeakers blared out a warning instructing all of the Davidians to evacuate the building. Their response was clear. After the action it was found that almost one hundred rounds had been fired at the vehicle. They had not penetrated its armored carapace, but had ricocheted harmlessly off. For the next six hours the CEVs roamed around the compound's buildings, bursting through or pushing down thin ply walls or reinforced concrete structures with ease.

One survivor recounted how, while he sought to shelter with some others in the chapel, huge chunks of concrete crashed down around the terrified people. They were huddled between the pews, low to the ground in an attempt to escape the gas.

Just before midday, a bizarre event occurred: a large sheet was unfurled from the topmost observation tower. Written in large letters were the words 'We want our phones fixed.' Was this a last desperate effort by some of the Davidians to re-establish contact with the FBI and negotiate a peaceful exit for the cultists? It is unlikely that Koresh took this initiative. He finally gave the order to usher in Armageddon.

By 12 pm large portions of the compound's buildings had collapsed. Whole portions of wall had tumbled down and a section of the roof had also collapsed. At 12.05 a small flame was seen near the southern end of the building. Within minutes, other points within the building were burning. Some of Koresh's mighty men had been ordered to set the incendiary devices alight until all the fire points coalesced into a towering inferno.

In another staggering federal stuff up, no fire trucks were on hand to meet such a contingency – it would be half an hour before the first arrived.

For the men, women and children sheltering inside the compound, the fire created an almost paralyzing fear. While sheltering between the pews they were hit by a massive wall of heat. One survivor prayed for a miracle – he saw a hole in the wall and crawled towards it. As he emerged into the smoky daylight, the FBI loudspeakers continued to blast out the message 'David, you have had your 15 minutes of fame. You are no longer the Messiah.' As the fugitive staggered out of the hole in the wall, it suddenly filled with a wall of flame. He knew he would not be joined by any other survivors.

Nine adults escaped the inferno, many with third degree burns to their face, hands, feet and neck, but they earned no sympathy from their FBI captors. The Davidians were told that if they made any false moves they would have their heads blown off. The wounded Davidians were sent by helicopter to the burns unit at Waco Hospital, tied down into stretchers and with FBI guards accompanying them as security.

They were the fortunate ones. As the flames took hold, many were eaten alive by the raging fire or crushed by falling concrete and steel rafters. It appears that many tried to escape the evil pull of Koresh's cataclysmic vision. Koresh made sure they didn't. Of the 25 children who perished that day, five had lethal stab wounds to their bodies and one had been bludgeoned to death with vicious blows to the head. Other adults had bullet wounds in their backs – a clear indication that Koresh's mighty men had executed any who tried to flee.

And what of Koresh himself? Was he resurrected to become the agent who would open the seventh seal? Was he joined by 144,000 individuals who were the chosen people intended to live in the new Kingdom of David while all unbelievers perished?

Not on this earth. All that remained of Koresh was a fragment of his skull, with a bullet wound that showed he had died by one shot to the head, as well as some charred remains. Whether he had inflicted the fatal shot himself or asked his closest confidant to perform the act is unknown.

What is not in doubt is that his mortal remains have not been resurrected, and they will not be.

Postscript

The controversy regarding the federal authorities' handling of the attacks on Mt Carmel dogged the Clinton administration for years. These controversies continue, with all kinds of conspiracy theories seeking to blame larger forces for the deaths rather than seeing it as caused by human error and incompetence.

There was however one much more serious consequence. Timothy McVeigh was already wary of the federal government and saw its handling of the siege of survivalist Randy Weaver and his family in the shootout at Ruby Ridge Idaho in 1992 as an affront to liberty. With the demolition of the Mt Carmel, he and some associates decided to give the federal authorities some payback.

At 9 am on 19 April 1995, the Alfred P. Murrah Federal Building in the center of Oklahoma City was shattered when a pickup truck packed full of homemade explosives was detonated.

McVeigh had entered Oklahoma City at 8.50 am and at 8.57 he lit a long fuse to begin the ignition process of his 2-ton bomb. Two minutes later, as he saw the target building's precinct, he lit the shorter fuse. Pulling up in the drop-off zone directly under the building's day care center, he then got out and locked the truck before hastening to his getaway vehicle. Two blocks away from the Alfred P. Murrah Building, he dropped the truck keys.

This building housed many federal agencies and included a day care center called America's Kids; it was full of babies and toddlers just dropped off by their mothers at the start of the working day.

The bomb, which was the equivalent of 5000 pounds of TNT, was detonated in front of the building. It shattered one third of the structure, killed 168 people - including 19 children - and wounded more than 680 others. Buildings within a 16-block radius were also damaged and the center of town was reduced to a glass-strewn wreck, with 86 cars burnt out and more than half a billion dollars in damage. Of those who died, 5 percent were killed in the maelstrom of flying glass. There were 361 occupants of the building: 47 percent (168) were injured, 45 percent (165) were killed and only 8 percent (30) survived uninjured. The blast was heard up to 88 kilometres (55 miles) away and was recorded as a level 3 earthquake on the Richter scale. The crater under the rented Ryder truck was 2.5-metres (8 feet) deep and 9 metres (30 feet) in diameter.

When the bomb detonated, all nine floors of the building were devastated. The front of the building was completely destroyed and, with half of the structural supports gone, floors began to concertina into each other. More than 500 rescue workers from emergency services were deployed and they were faced with a truly horrible spectacle. Trapped survivors were screaming from the rubble and bodies and body parts were scattered in all directions. Covering the entire site was a thin film of unexploded fertilizer. Many of the corpses were naked; the force of the blast had blown off their clothing.

An unrepentant McVeigh was executed by lethal injection on 11 June 2001, but Waco continues to echo in American society.

CHAPTER FOUR

Aum Supreme Truth: Asian Apocalypse

Revelations – Book 9

[11]They had as king over them – the angel of the Abyss, whose name in Hebrew is Abaddon and in Greek is Apollyon (that is, Destroyer).

In this age of super-sensitive security, it is difficult to grasp that for many years one of the deadliest cults of the 20th century was able to experiment with means of mass destruction for years before they embarked upon an attack on the very fabric of Japanese society.

Trucks patrolled remote townships, spewing out deadly Sarin; the top floor of an office tower in the heart of Tokyo became a factory dedicated to spreading anthrax spores into the air of one of the biggest cities in the world; large assembly lines produced Kalashnikov sub machine guns, along with tons of ammunition; hit teams took out whole families whose members sought to interfere with the cult; and members who died from malnutrition or violence were dissolved into their constituent atoms in huge room-sized microwave ovens. Tons of some of the most lethal nerve agents known to man were stockpiled in large underground reservoirs, while dissident members were kept in shipping containers converted into jails deep within the bowels of large cult compounds that mushroomed throughout Japan. The cult operated internationally. In Australia, Sarin was tested on merino sheep tethered to the rocky soil of the outback. In Russia, members bought attack helicopters and tried to purchase armored vehicles and nuclear bombs.

All of these activities were carried out under the nose of the Japanese government. The post-war Japanese constitution forbade the government from interfering with religious groups.

On 20 March 1995, thousands of innocent civilians were wounded and 12 were killed in Sarin gas attacks designed to bring down the government. The Japanese government could no longer ignore the fanatical doomsday cult in its midst.

Genesis

Some cult leaders have frightful childhoods. Many suffer abuse or are brought up in an emotionally barren home. This might be, in a small way, an explanation for their actions as manipulative and destructive martinets as adults.

Shoko Asahara has no such rationale to fall back on. It seems that from a young age he was bent on manipulating and exploiting his fellow man for his own benefit.

The future doomsday cult leader was born as Chizuo Matsumoto in 1955, the sixth of seven children in a large family. His parents were poor and the main family income came from weaving mats from local grasses, rice straw and reeds. The residents of the family's village of Yatushiro noticed nothing strange about the family, although their poor diet led to several of the children developing eye problems. An older brother went totally blind, while Chizuo developed infantile glaucoma. He lost all of the sight in his left eye and most of his vision in the right. This proved to be something of a blessing, as he was pulled out of the local school and sent to a school for the blind in the nearby town of Kumamoto.

Maybe his parents were sad to see their strong willed six-year-old depart for the city, maybe not. At least he would receive free board and accommodation and help relieve the family's desperate finances. While the family produced mats that were used as the basic floor coverings in most houses, they could not afford their own and lived in a basic shack with a dirt floor.

There is an old saying: in the land of the blind, the one-eyed man is king. This proved to be the case with the young Chizuo. But rather than using his partial vision for good, he used it to manipulate, scam and bully his fellow students. This was a trait that stuck with him throughout his life. The solidly built young man was happy to use violence on his blind peers and would extort funds from them. He regularly challenged his teachers and would throw massive tantrums where he would threaten to burn down the school. Sometimes he behaved in a seemingly altruistic manner and would guide his blind peers into town for a meal at a restaurant; not so – he demanded that they pay his bill. More usually he was known for demanding that other students do his chores and collect noodles and cakes from town without paying them for their trouble. One dorm mate described living with him as 'hell'.

Chizuo became proficient at judo. He seemed to possess extraordinary strength and could launch himself into the air while sitting cross-legged. The grades he achieved at school were generally higher than those of his peers.

But after many years the dominant memory that his fellow students and teachers have of Chizuo is of a rather unpleasant and domineering character. He often picked fights and at one stage ruptured a classmate's eardrum. He was quick to anger, but just as quickly would turn around and act in a fawning, wheedling manner in an effort to escape punishment. He frequently abused his dorm-mothers. He rebelled against rules such as strict bath times and 'lights out', and if the dorm-mothers tried to enforce the regulations he would turn on them in an aggressively hostile manner. He screamed at one teacher 'I'll shoot you to death!'

The young tyrant confused fear with respect and ran for President of the Student Association. On at least three occasions he was rejected by his peers and received almost no votes. Nevertheless, when Chizuo left school he had a healthy bank account – the years of extorting funds from his blind peers had paid off.

He graduated from high school in 1975 and developed grandiose ambitions. Friends and relatives from the time remember that he wanted to be, among other things, the Prime Minister of Japan, the ruler of a robot kingdom or a high paid lawyer trained in the prestigious law faculty of Tokyo University. To enter college required rigorous entrance examinations, but he was unable to pass the required tests and never entered college. He instead paid his way working as an acupuncturist.

In 1977 he set up a business in Tokyo as an acupuncturist and seller of herbal remedies. This latter revenue stream became more and more important. Early clients found the earnest young man to be quite convincing in his claims and Chizuo soon found out that people were willing to shell out large amounts of money for foul tasting placebos. Eastern philosophies and spiritual practices were another path Chizuo pursued and in 1984 he set up a small mediation workshop with the modest title Aum Inc. He sold remedies and literature and was also able to attract a large flock of almost 3000 people who were willing to spend a bit of time dabbling in New Age mysticism.

Chizuo was a fun leader at this time and any ideas of leading a messianic doomsday cult were still in the future. He did enjoy showing off his physique and 'levitated' by sitting cross-legged and thrusting himself into the air with violent thrusts of his thighs. What began as a party trick in 1985 would later be used to prove his divinity.

Chizuo always had an eye out for good publicity. On one of his overseas trips he encountered the Dalai Lama and posed next to him as if they were long lost brothers and spiritual equals. The Dalai Lama had no idea who the Japanese acupuncturist was, but these photos were exploited for all they were worth in later years.

Hubris soon took over. Chizuo began to realize the potential that his fledgling cult could achieve. Yes-men and hangers on surrounded him and eagerly listened to the tall tales he began to weave. In 1985 Chizuo was meditating on a beach when he was visited by the Hindu god Shiva, who declared that the young Japanese man was now the 'god of light who leads the armies of God' (Brackett 66). In 1986 Chizuo, the son of a mat weaver, attained Nirvana. In 1987 the organization was renamed Aum Shinrikyo (Aum Supreme Truth) and Chizuo Matsumoto became Shoko Asahara.

Thousands of followers flocked to the new religion and its coffers began to swell exponentially. A large tract of land in the shadow of Mt Fuji was purchased and a vast compound began to sprout in the land located in Fujinomiya.

Bizarre Beliefs

Asahara drew on a wide range of spiritual traditions. Like all great 'gurus' he was able to pick and choose the beliefs and practices that best suited the needs of his growing cult. He began by studying traditional Chinese medicine and astrology. Soon he was studying many Buddhist tracts. One in particular stood out: the writings of Shinji Takahashi, who founded a new religion called the God Light Association. In these writings Takahashi claimed to be an incarnation of the Buddha – something which Asahara himself would claim.

Two schools of thought clarified Asahara's ideals. The first was the idea of 'Primitive Buddhism.' This belief system taught that the outward trappings of the religion were an impediment to true spirituality. Only by clearing away distractions and fripperies could divine understandings be reached. Long, involved, step-by-step meditations were required to strip away bad karma and attain enlightenment.

Asahara then found the *Yoga Sutras of Patanjali*. This ancient text breaks down a sequence of yoga practices to be completed on the path to enlightenment.

By combining these ideas Asahara was able to create an elaborate sequence of meditations and skills that aspiring followers had to achieve on their spiritual path.

Being the wise and compassionate leader that he was, Asahara decided to fast-track the progress of his devoted flock. The first initiation ritual, *Shaktipat*, was made available. For a modest fee, equivalent to about a thousand dollars, the young guru would place his thumb on to the forehead of the disciple, the location of the third eye. Asahara would absorb through this spiritual conduit all of the subject's bad karma while injecting his positive spiritual power in return. Of course, there was only so much bad karma that Asahara could absorb. Just as an advertisement might claim that the special is available only until all stock is sold out, so Asahara claimed he had a limited number of *Shaktipat*. By 1988 he no longer performed this ritual, but his leading disciples filled the breach for half the price.

With this came a new innovation. Training credits were required to ascend to new levels of consciousness – these too had to be purchased. At this time Asahara became an author. In his early tracts he discussed in fantastic detail the different levels that an acolyte had to pass through to attain Kundalini (awakening). These included the six desire realms, the lower astral realms and the higher astral realm, followed by the lower, middle and higher causal realms. To reach each of these streams, intensive meditation had to be followed and hefty sums of cash had to be paid out.

Asahara did encounter one problem: some of his followers were so devout that they moved too quickly up the spiritual ladder. It was necessary for him to continually add levels of spiritual attainment so that he could be at least one step ahead. Each new step led to extra revenue.

In 1988 a new and dangerous thread appeared in cult literature. Asahara appointed himself as a messiah acting on behalf of the god Shiva. Soon Armageddon would come and only he could lead his disciples to *gedatsu* (emancipation) so that they could join Shambala, the kingdom of Shiva. Fujinomiya would be the 'lotus village' and its example would lead all of Japan to the path of enlightenment. After Japan, his movement would direct the entire world to the correct path, bringing salvation to all who believed.

These initial ramblings could be seen as harmless. However, by 1990 Asahara's growing obsession with Armageddon began to filter down to the lower echelons of the cult. Dire warnings of the upheaval of the Pacific Plate and a war that would begin in Japan and spread around the globe were frequently referenced in cult literature or in Asahara's speeches. Only those who had progressed along the cult's ascetic path would become 'superhuman' and survive the coming apocalypse, which Asahara confidently predicted would occur in 1996.

By the early 1990s his cult had amassed an estimated 200 million US dollars in assets. He used much of this wealth to amass a huge array of conventional and chemical weapons. Hundreds of cult members were engaged in cranking out Kalashnikov sub machine guns. Combat suits that utilized the latest Kevlar armor were produced. Massive laser arrays were built. It was hoped that if such a weapon was unleashed in central Tokyo, whole office towers could be bought crashing to the ground. Aum agents in Russia were openly seeking to purchase nuclear weapons from ex-Soviet arsenals. Attempts to buy T-72 tanks were made. While these were fruitless, the cult did manage to bring a disassembled heavy military attack helicopter to the compound. Thousands of cultists were trained by ex-military specialists in the latest combat techniques. And of course there were stockpiles of nerve agents and high explosives that could be employed by Asahara.

Aum Supreme Truth transitioned from being a religious spiritual organization to a government in waiting. Rather than writing spiritual tracts, Asahara planned a coup to bring about Armageddon. X-Day would begin with the seizure of the Japanese parliament by elite combat squads of Aum shock troops. It was planned for the first day of parliament so that the Emperor would be in attendance and he could go into the bag along with the rest of the government. Aum loyalists would have insinuated themselves into command positions within the Japanese military, ensuring that they would declare their support for the new regime. At the same time, cult helicopters would spray tons of Sarin over administrative buildings and the media, effectively paralyzing the state.

Waiting in the wings was a new hierarchy of Aum devotees, ready to take up the reins of government. Asahara would of course be the new Emperor, untrammeled by constitutional niceties. Below him would be a secretariat and reporting to all of the ministries of a modern state: commerce, defense, education, home affairs, labor, justice etc. There would also be a Household Agency tasked with ensuring that every need of the new Emperor was met.

By 1994 Aum Shinrikyo barely resembled a religion at all; it was turning into a paramilitary industrial chemical complex that had at its base 10,000 members bent on following even the craziest whims of its delusional leader.

Attraction, Initiation and Control

With the move to Fujinoyama, there was a desperate need for revenue. Previous to this expansion, Asahara could rely on the existing membership to meet the cult's needs. Now a recruiting drive was launched that would see numbers grow to tens of thousands in Japan alone, as well as large numbers of cultists in Russia and several other countries.

Post-war Japan proved a fertile ground for the recruiters. Urbanization in the large cities saw hundreds of thousands of young people living in soulless apartment buildings, existing in the cold shadows of their parents' work ethic. Lacking direction or spirituality, cults such as Aum Supreme Truth offered these youths an escape from their dreary existence.

Attractive cult members around the country acted as honey traps for these 'seekers,' using propaganda, music, drugs and meditation courses to ensnare them. Wealthy individuals were targeted, along with professionals and members of the military. As in all cults, prospective members often did not realize that a meditation class or a small donation were actually the first steps to initiation and indoctrination.

Small sums soon became significant amounts of cash as ever-greater spiritual goals were dangled in front of members.

Asahara had form selling dodgy remedies from an early age. When acting as an acupuncturist he was arrested and jailed for a short stint for selling orange peel soaked in alcohol as a cure-all medicine.

He offered the chance for his followers to connect with him up for cash in various ways. His old bath water, samples of his semen or blood could be purchased by his acolytes to earn 'credits' on their way to salvation. Cultists wore badges like medals – these had bits of the master's energy that transferred straight to the wearer's heart. The most spectacular piece of kit was the 'Perfect Salvation Headset'. A nylon framework dripping with electrodes and wires allowed followers to plug straight into Asahara's mind. The honor of wearing this outlandish item could cost as much as a thousand dollars a month.

There was no respite for those who dipped their toes in the muddy waters of Aum Supreme Truth. An initial payment would be followed by demands to spend more. Fellow cultists would hound the individuals with letters, phone calls and visits, urging the initiate to pay for more courses or more advanced meditation practices. Many individuals had mind-altering experiences; they were given a formidable mix of hallucinogens, which included LSD and morphine.

The ultimate aim of the recruiters was to move part time cultists, the 'lay' practitioners, into the compounds that were sprouting up all over Japan, converting them into 'monastics'. Once the believers took this fatal step, all of their worldly wealth was signed over to the cult's lawyers. Land titles, bank accounts and shares were swallowed up by cult coffers while all property was sold off to second hand stores. This practice extended beyond Aum members. Many reported that their elders were ill and, under cult pressure, agreed to shift their ailing parents and grandparents into cult hospices, where their health would deteriorate until a premature death occurred – after power of attorney was signed over to the cult.

Apart from contacts like these, all communications with families and work colleagues was ruthlessly cut off. Phone calls were prohibited and mail was intercepted. Should a concerned relative have the temerity to turn up to a compound in search of a loved one, they would be met by an armed guard and told in no uncertain terms to vacate the premises. Should the relative or friend persist in such intrusive behavior, the cult member concerned would be quickly whisked off to another compound as far away as possible.

In common with most cults covered in this book, families were broken up. Men and women slept in separate dormitories and any sexual contact was prohibited.

Most monastics toiled night and day on repetitive, mindless tasks. Whether it was producing weapons parts or attending to cult publications, their constant companions were mantras or sermons blaring over loudspeakers, combined with pervasive fatigue and hunger.

Few managed to escape. At the heart of 'lotus village' were containers packed with non-cooperative cultists. Special rooms were built where errant members were force fed drugs, subjected to a barrage of cult propaganda and repeatedly submerged in water heated to just below boiling point. If a member did manage to escape, that was not the end of the matter. Specialist recovery teams would stalk the escapee, tracking them down throughout the length and breadth of the land and harassing family members for information. There were several instances of individuals being snatched off the street and tortured in an attempt to ascertain the whereabouts of their absconding relatives.

Those who were retrieved would be locked in tiny cells where it was impossible to either stand or lie down. They were subjected to constant barrages of sermons until they saw the error of their ways, or died. At least 80 individuals died within the cult. Aggressive Aum lawyers ensured that relatives were forced to keep their distance from these tragedies.

At the heart of this state network was the compound that had been originally intended to bring enlightenment to Japan and then the world. Fujinomiya grew into the nerve center of the worldwide Aum empire. Large buildings began to sprout on the once bare land. Aum structures were called 'satian,' which was derived from the Sanskrit for 'truth.' The entire compound came to represent a nightmare scenario that blended the terrors of a Hieronymus Bosch painting with the regimentation of the society in George Orwell's *1984*.

Satian 1 was the administrative center of the empire and the first floors were given over to office buildings. The top floor was used to confine and re-educate errant cult members. Here were the hot baths and intrusive multimedia platforms that would be combined with drugs to break their psychological resistance. Satian 2 was a printing factory that spewed the increasingly paranoid fantasies of the guru out of state-of-the-art publishing facilities.

Satian 4 was the guru's home. Space was provided for his concubines and spacious meeting rooms hosted gatherings of the top leaders, who would gather to discuss the ongoing arms production and evolve strategies to bring about Armageddon. Weapons caches were built into the walls in myriad hidden compartments, as were a series of boltholes containing food supplies, cash and false passports in case Asahara was ever pursued by the authorities.

Satian 10 was designated the hospital. Rather than curing cult members, it was increasingly used to keep dissidents sedated and let them waste away through malnutrition.

Satian 7 was known as the Supreme Truth Research Institute of Science. Coming out of the walls were a series of protuberances made up of pipes, valves and barrels, seeming to sprout out of the wall with no ordered structure. Noxious fumes that evaded the most modern air purifiers emanated from the building. Transport containers littered the grounds. Within these containers, members who had sought to escape from the cult were confined in cages built within the cold metallic structures. All light was blocked from these miserable cells and individuals were prohibited from talking or washing. Starvation diets combined with minimal sanitation or bedding led to these prisoners wasting away in filth and despair.

Half-starved and sleep-deprived cultists scurried around the compound. The members were always on the alert for any dissenting voices, though these were few and far between. Anyone who questioned the leadership or complained about the conditions would be likely to be re-educated – or worse, end up in the giant industrial microwaves that reduced human beings to their composite ashes. After exhausting days laboring in the kitchens, the arms factory or the admin wing, the dazed members crashed onto their uncomfortable cots in draughty dormitory buildings, where they fell asleep to the never-ending pronouncements of the guru echoing out of the cult's PA system.

Asahara had created a true hell on Earth.

Even the family of Asahara were not spared. One of his daughters was born six years before the cult was broken up. She told a horrific tale of a loveless upbringing. From the time that she was two his fourth daughter lived alone in a barren store chamber without windows. She was kicked out of her mother's bed as soon as her younger brother was born. The unloved young girl never had normal relations with her father and always had to call him guru. She was forced to eat thin rice gruel or omelets with broken crockery mixed in. The girl was so undernourished that her growth was stunted and she could place her fingers between her emaciated ribs. TV was banned and Asahara's daughter was forced to listen to tape recordings of her father, which played, along with his videos, 24 hours a day. Like other members of Aum she was forced to get into scalding baths; she often lost consciousness while pinned down in the 46 degrees Celsius (115 degrees Fahrenheit) water.

Armageddon

Aum Supreme Truth was similar to many cults in that its descent into violence was a response to a perceived threat from government authorities. Just as Jim Jones instituted Revolutionary Suicide as a response to an American Senator's visit and Koresh responded violently to an actual raid, Aum Supreme Truth began their violent attacks to pre-empt and outmaneuver the authorities, who were taking an increasing interest in their shady goings on.

The bloodletting began with an attack on a small family.

Up-and-coming lawyer Tsutsumi Sakamoto was keen on carving out a political career for himself. He had raised his profile by defending the rights of certain families, who felt that their children or siblings had been dragooned into Aum Supreme Truth and were being held against their will or exploited in other ways. The families were of course correct with their concerns and Tsutsumi Sakamoto became the high-profile advocate for this group of citizens. He was not afraid to use the media when pursuing the cult and he was rapidly becoming, in Asahara's view, a real problem.

It was decided that the lawyer had to die. In November of 1989, four members of Aum Supreme Truth, led by Kiyohide Hayakawa, were summoned to meet with their guru. Over the course of a couple of days a diabolical plan was hatched to get rid of the offending lawyer, his wife and their 14-month-old baby, Tatsuhiko Sakamoto.

Doctor Tomomasa Nakagawa was to carry out the killings. He equipped himself with several hypodermic needles filled with potassium chloride, which he would use to wipe out the young family.

With three other members of the cult, all wearing black clothes and rubber shoes, the doctor broke into Sakamoto's apartment in the dead of night. They stealthily entered the couple's bedroom and found the 14-month-old baby sleeping between his parents. One of the 'Special Action Squad,' as they named themselves, hauled the baby out of the bed and clamped a hand over his mouth. The man pulled up the child's nightgown and presented his buttocks to the doctor. Nakagawa had a needle poised and soon the potassium chloride was coursing through the baby's circulatory system. With barely a whimper, Tatsuhiko Sakamoto was dead.

The child's parents may have been woken by the noise of their son being murdered, or perhaps it was just a sixth sense that danger was present. Whatever it was, Tsutsumi and his wife Satoko launched themselves at the Special Action Squad. A furious melee followed, where the outnumbered and dazed couple fought desperately for their existence while the cultists sought to pin them down and kill them. Satoko was the first to succumb; one of the squad pinned her down and a lethal dose of potassium chloride was injected into her torso.

With the death of his wife and child the whole Special Action Squad turned their attention to the lawyer. Tsutsumi's death must have been unimaginably painful, physically and mentally. No doubt the relatives of the cult members who had appealed for his help had warned the lawyer how dangerous the cult was and urged him to take precautions to guarantee his safety. Tsutsumi had underestimated the danger may have felt personally responsible for his family's deaths. This perhaps leant him a superhuman strength born of despair and anger. While putting up a desperate fight, he managed to bite a chunk out of one of his attacker's arms. He was then wrestled to the floor and a hypodermic needle slid into his buttock to deliver its lethal payload.

It was not enough. Tsutsumi continued to writhe around and almost broke out of the clutches of his attacker. Kiyohide Hayakawa straddled the distraught man and strangled him to death.

Once the dust had settled and the team had regained their breath, Hayakawa initiated the rest of the plan. The family were wrapped in their bedding and hauled out to a waiting station wagon. They were taken to the cult compound in the remaining hours of darkness. It was decided that the bodies were to be buried in widely dispersed locations, so that if they were found there would be little the police could do to link the killings. The attack was successful from the point of view of Asahara; several investigations into his activities were stopped in their tracks and Aum Supreme Truth was not linked to the disappearances.

Asahara played a direct role in these killings. On 2 November he had summoned the team of five men to the sect's headquarters at Fujinomiya. He personally selected the men due to their unswerving loyalty. He told them of their task and within 30 minutes the 5 men and their leader planned the hit. Originally they were only going to take the lawyer off the streets, on the evening of 3 November, murder him and incinerate the corpse in the compound. When that did not work, the team made a call to Asahara. It was in that call that he ordered the murder of the entire family in the early hours of the fourth. When the team returned with the corpses, Asahara ordered that they be buried in the three different prefectures.

The guru noticed that Nakagawa was distressed by his role in the killings and he was at pains to praise the doctor for his actions.

Emboldened by this successful hit, Shoko Asahara decided to remove another legal nuisance. This time he would deploy a weapon of mass destruction: Sarin.

Aum Supreme Truth had been experimenting with biological and chemical weapons of mass destruction for several years. The first attempt at mass murder was made by the cult scientists when they cultivated large amounts of the lethal bacterium – *Clostridium botulinum* – that causes botulism. The bacterium comes in various lethal strains and at its worst is 16 million times more lethal than strychnine. A human can be killed by one millionth of a gram. It can infect a person through inhalation, food or into a wound. Initial symptoms involve twitching facial muscles, double vision, drooping eyelids and problems swallowing. Nausea, vomiting and constipation can be followed by a dry mouth, difficulty talking and decreased blood pressure. As the toxin attacks the nervous system, the subject experiences difficulty breathing, which can lead to respiratory failure and death. Botulism achieves these horrific outcomes by inhibiting neurotransmitters that communicate between motor neurons and muscle cells, leading to paralysis.

This was a perfect weapon for the cult, as symptoms appear many hours after the bacteria enter the body. It was hoped that millions of Japanese could be infected before the authorities were alerted to the attack. In April 1990 a specially equipped truck made its way through the center of Tokyo, spraying several kilos of emulsified bacteria and its toxin through the government and financial district. Asahara hoped to knock off the administrative head of the Japanese federal government. Fortunately, nothing came of this. The toxic compounds were destroyed in the oxygen rich atmosphere.

Another attempt at mass murder was made by cult scientists. This time Tokyo was subjected to a sustained biological attack with lethal anthrax spores.

Everything about anthrax is dark. The circular sores that they cause on your flesh, the color your lungs turn if you catch it and the color that your blood turns when it gets into your bloodstream – even the nasty little rod-shaped bacilli are dark. They can hang around in black soil for hundreds of years. When animals fall prey to this dreadful disease there are few outward signs until the animal drops dead. Once dead it starts decomposing incredibly quickly, all thanks to these voracious little spores.

Once anthrax gets into animal or human blood streams it begins to breed. The bacteria itself is not the cause of death, but the waste matter known as exotoxin it produces, which are lethal poisons. This exotoxin swamps the blood, causing it to break down. The blood can't carry oxygen and the entire cardiovascular system turns black. It causes a particularly bleak end for humans. After inhaling the spores an individual will develop a flu-like illness that includes vomiting and a high fever. As the spoors attack the circulatory system, the person's skin begins to blister and turn black. Eventually they choke to death as the lungs fill with toxic phlegm.

The animal or human dies and the black blood oozes out of every orifice. In the blood are millions and billions of anthrax spores that escape into the atmosphere ready to infect other unsuspecting animals.

That is how anthrax survives. It infests one animal, reproduces in huge numbers and then enters the atmosphere. Once they are in the atmosphere these little baby anthrax spores are almost impossible to eradicate. These bacteria have double shells, which make them incredibly tough, and they live for years and years in soil waiting for a plant to grow and carry them into the path of an unsuspecting herbivore.

In fact, the spores are so successful they are found on every continent, including Antarctica. If animal graves containing victims of the deadly bacteria are disturbed, it can lead to new infections 70 years after the animals were buried. Such a lethal agent has a long history of use in biological warfare, and can be deadly when released into the environment.

Aum Supreme Truth built an anthrax factory in the middle of Tokyo. They hired an eight-story building and developed an anthrax delivery sprayer. For several weeks this machine blew out anthrax spores right in the heart of one of the biggest cities in the world. Like something out of a science fiction movie, cultists clad in biohazard suits fed the diabolical machine with a steady stream of *Bacillus anthracis*. Fortunately, the conditions for the spores were not right and nearby residents only noted a couple of dead sparrows and a funny black cloud that smelled bad.

The next scheme was equally ambitious. In 1992, hearing tales of the rabid hemorrhagic fever, Ebola, 40 members of the cult were soon winging their way to the Republic of Zaire. Ebola is a highly contagious virus that can be transmitted in any bodily fluid. Once it enters a person's bloodstream it breaks down their internal organs and streams out of their stricken body through unstoppable diarrhea, vomiting and even bleeding through any or all orifices. The mortality rate from this disease can hit 90 percent and death usually occurs after six or seven days.

Fortunately for the good citizens of Japan, this exploratory team did not manage to obtain samples of this virus or harness the lethal microbe to satisfy their diabolical purposes.

Despite these failures, the cult's scientists ensconced in the main cult headquarters at Fujinomiya managed to distil one killer chemical weapon: Sarin.

The scientists were aware of their importance. They understood that Asahara relied on them to establish the key component of the coming Armageddon. In the center of the Mount Fuji compound was a three-story building named Satian 7. As the building's personnel filed in each morning they passed a large statue of Shiva, the Hindu god of destruction. A budget of 10 million dollars was allocated to this labyrinth of laboratories and industrial chemical processing plants. Money was not an object. Asahara had thousands of cultists living on starvation rations and any surplus or profits from his multimillion-dollar empire went into biochemical warfare research.

The security measures were extreme. Armed guards patrolled the exterior and guarded the entrance and loading bay. Meticulous records were kept, detailing who entered and the time spent within. Approximately 100 trusted cult members were allowed within the building.

Rigorous contamination protocols were followed. Pressurized biohazard suits were worn by the staff. Controls were not perfect, however; neighboring communities began to complain of noxious fumes emanating from the facility. Livestock became ill and crops were stunted.

The cult's chief scientist, Masami Tsuchiya, who held a PhD in organic chemistry, was able to purchase the most modern equipment possible.

On the ground floor were temperature-controlled storage facilities maintaining tons of chemicals in their optimum state. The cult had bought so much hazardous material that several other warehouses were required to store the chemicals. The amounts were mindboggling. Tons of sodium fluoride, steel drums filled with phosphorus trichloride and gallon upon gallon of isopropyl alcohol. These were the base ingredients to make hundreds of tons of Sarin. Three tons of nitric acid and 10,000 gallons of glycerine were purchased. These are, of course, the basic ingredients required for nitroglycerine, a very powerful explosive. The labs also bought the materials for psychoactive drugs such as LSD, which was produced for use by the cult members. Aum was able to amass such huge quantities of chemicals by purchasing through a range of front companies.

The second floor contained five large, self-contained reactor labs. Large steel drums were equipped with heating elements, piping and ventilation ducts, as well as closed circuit TV monitoring every stage of chemical production. The entire system was automated, allowing precise amounts of precursor chemicals to be added to produce noxious chemicals such as Sarin. The finished product was piped into an industrial packaging machine that injected the nerve agent into vacuum-sealed polyethylene bags. The production facilities were matched by state-of-the-art research labs with the best chemical analysis devices available from Switzerland.

On the third floor of Satian 7 were the offices of the scientific staff. A central computer controlled the entire operation and no expense was spared purchasing the latest scientific literature or IT equipment.

After years of experimentation, in November 1992 the chief scientist was able to proudly report to Asahara that the facility had managed to produce a deadly chemical: Sarin. Soon the staff at Satian 7 were cranking out larger and larger amounts. In fact, at the height of production almost 10 litres (almost 3 gallons) of liquid Sarin was being produced within Satian 7 every day. Almost 70 tons were produced. A tiny droplet of 6 milligrams could kill an individual. Asahara had his doomsday weapon.

Today Sarin is seen as one of the less dangerous nerve agents, but when it was first developed in 1938 by a group of German scientists it was a state-of-the-art killer. Ten tons were manufactured by the German war machine. Thousands of rounds of ammunition and bombs were filled with the agent, but Hitler – a soldier during World War I – refused to countenance a return to gas warfare. In 1945 the stockpile was captured by the Soviets, who also set up manufacturing plants, as did the Americans.

Mustard gas, like Sarin, is odorless. In World War I, soldiers fighting in the trenches were often unaware that they had been exposed to mustard gas. Several hours later their eyes would begin to water and their skin, particularly in the groin or armpits where there was moisture due to sweat, would begin to blister. Severe cases would experience blistering in the mouth, eyes, throat and even lungs. Mucus would build up and the scalded lungs would collapse, leading to a slow and horrific death through suffocation.

Pure Sarin was also odorless, but its effects set in much more quickly. A tiny droplet inhaled into the lungs or deposited on the skin rapidly sets off a catastrophic chain of events. The nerve agent halts production and distribution of an enzyme that regulates the actions of glands and muscles. Once these enzymes are stopped, the body's system goes into overdrive – muscles begin contracting or expanding at a furious rate, while mucus and wastes are produced in large quantities. Initial symptoms are stinging eyes, nasal passages and throat. Vision is impaired and a tightness in the chest is experienced. Disorientation soon follows, as well as muscle weakness and drowsiness. As the Sarin penetrates deeper into an individual's nervous system, the symptoms become lethal. The victim vomits, urinates or defecates uncontrollably as the body goes into violent spasms. The heart goes into overdrive, leading to coronary arrest and the collapse of the respiratory system.

Even if an individual survives exposure to Sarin, permanent damage is often the result. Many survivors of the Aum Supreme Truth attacks were permanently blinded or experienced significant brain damage.

Asahara had the first target for a large-scale biological terror attack in his sights: the idyllic mountain town of Matsumoto.

The first assassination planned by Asahara had been aimed at removing the legal problem of the troublesome lawyer Tsutsumi Sakamoto. In June 1994, Asahara decided to take out the entire judiciary of Matsumoto prefecture.

Nowadays Matsumoto is known as a beautiful mountain town with one of the best-preserved samurai castles in Japan. The town of 200,000 people has a proud heritage and during winter thousands of tourists pour out of Tokyo, three hours away by train, to enjoy the area's skiing and snowfields.

In 1991, Asahara turned his gaze on the idyllic town and decided to set up a new branch there. By this time the cult was getting quite a reputation for underhanded business practices and, to get around local issues, front companies were set up to allay suspicion. A large block was purchased in town by what purported to be a food manufacturing plant, but as soon as construction began on a two-story cult outpost the locals were up in arms at this intrusion into their peaceful environment. The original owner was particularly incensed and launched an action in the local court to invalidate the sale. He argued he had been convinced to sell the land under false pretenses.

As the case ground through the courts, Aum began a campaign of harassment, following a pattern of intimidation they had developed over several years. Locals were bombarded with nuisance calls that threatened dire consequences if they did not accept the new cult headquarters. Some found themselves being tailed by sinister sedans. Children were photographed leaving school and walking home.

In May 1994 the trial ended with all witnesses making their submissions.

An inside source leaked to Asahara that he would lose the case and the new outpost of his empire would have to be abandoned. He was having none of it. In April 1994 he summoned his top men, including the scientist Hideo Murai, and ordered that an attack on the Matsumoto law courts had to be launched before the decision was handed down. Satian 7 became a hive of activity as a suitable delivery mechanism was created.

Several months earlier a Sarin attack on a rival religious leader had ended in farcical circumstances when the truck that was carrying the deadly payload burst into flames. Hideo Murai was determined that the same thing would not happen again.

The problem with delivering Sarin in a terrorist attack is that it has to be heated from a liquid into a gaseous form. Even as a gas Sarin has a tendency to settle, so it is necessary to project it into the environment from an elevated position. A 2-ton refrigerated truck was purchased and in the following weeks it was converted into an efficient Sarin dispersal unit. A large tank was bolted to the bed of the truck and this was filled with liquid Sarin. Thirty batteries fed power into a large heater. Small amounts of the toxin were fed into the heater and turned to vapor before powerful fans blew the gas through pipes and out into the atmosphere.

The five-man Sarin delivery team must have felt similar to the early tank crewmen driving to battle in World War I. As the overladen truck lurched up the mountainous roads to Matsumoto on 27 June 1994, it swayed around on its overloaded suspension. Within the rear bay the vast array of batteries took up more than a third of the space, while the crew were crammed around the lethal gas and a maze of swaying pipes and wires. Although each man was to be injected with an antidote, they were also issued crude gas masks. Plastic bags connected to an oxygen pump were placed over their heads as the truck ascended the windy mountain road.

Despite the hours of preparation that had gone into the attack, Hideo Murai had overslept on the day and they arrived in the square before the law courts several hours late. Court had been adjourned. Fearful of returning after a failed attack, Murai decided on a different course of action. The judges were known to sleep in a dormitory within a densely populated residential area. That was where the attack would take place.

The truck settled in a parking lot to the east of the judge's dorm, at about 10 pm. A light easterly breeze was blowing – perfect for conveying the gaseous Sarin to the target building. That it would pass over or through several other apartment blocks was neither here nor there – casualties were to be expected.

At 10.40 the complex array within the truck was fired up. Things began to go awry almost immediately. Rather than a clear gas, a problem with the heat exchange produced a dense cloud that spewed from the truck. That was not all. The easterly wind changed, sending the gas in another direction – away from the targets. After 10 minutes the van took off.

The gas remained and moved into several apartment buildings. Residents at first felt a trace of nausea. One man heard a strange scratching noise, looked out his door and saw his dog writhing in absolute agony and foaming at the mouth. Soon people were dropping. One woman suffered so much that in her death struggles she had shredded her straw tatami mat.

Dead trees, grasses and shrubs showed the course of the gas. Some, who were sleeping in sealed bedrooms with their doors and windows tightly shut against the winter chill, had almost no symptoms. Others began coughing, lost their vision and went into uncontrolled muscle spasms before choking to death. This Sarin was almost 100 percent pure and 13 innocent civilians died, three of them while being conveyed to hospital. Many more were badly injured and required months and even years of care.

Only one of the judges and his wife were affected, but both survived without long term damage.

Fortunately for the cult, one of the first victims to raise the alarm was an industrial chemist. The police did not even suspect Aum and for many months they had this innocent man firmly in the frame. His wife had been desperately wounded in the attack, but this did not allay police suspicions. In a nasty taunt, Aum sent the poor man an offer to treat his wife in one of their hospital wards – an act of cruel hubris.

Similar hubris would lead to the Sarin attacks in the Tokyo subway, and bring the cult undone.

Ever since Asahara bought the compound in the lee of Mount Fuji, the cult had run roughshod over the concerns of the locals. While loudspeakers banged out cult sermons or prayers and mantras around the clock, members drove over crops or left industrial waste in the form of discarded chemical drums around the local environment. Construction work was carried out at all hours and local requests to keep the noise down were ignored. Cult members paraded in a threatening manner through local towns and locals who kicked up too much of a fuss were subjected to a barrage of hostile phone calls or threatened by cult lawyers.

Noxious odors emanated from the compound and it was noted that many cultists wore gas masks. Farmers who had inherited their land from previous generations noticed disturbing changes in the environment. The leaves of trees began to turn brown and soon there was a barren wasteland in the immediate environs of the complex. Not even weeds would grow there. Cattle stopped producing milk and some sickened and died. Chickens stopped laying eggs and small birds disappeared from the area.

Despite many complaints from the cult's neighbors, the local authorities were loathe to take any action – tangling with Asahara was not something one did lightly.

In the middle of July 1994, all this changed. Production pressures had led to the Aum scientists in Satian 7 taking short cuts. The result was a potentially fatal leak of chlorine gas. Frantic emergency klaxons led to a mass evacuation of the building. Soon a large cloud of gas had left the compound, where it settled onto adjoining properties. Another leak soon after led to soil samples being taken form the surrounding area.

Chemicals related to the production of Sarin were found. More and more of the nation's law enforcement agencies were taking an active interest in the activities of the increasingly arrogant cult.

By February 1994 more than 300 formal complaints had been launched against the Aum Supreme Truth. Late in that month a member fled to her brother in Tokyo. He was a public notary and Asahara ordered him snatched while walking home from work. After prolonged torture he was disposed of in the microwaves in the basement of Satian 2.

Local law enforcement decided to act; a series of raids were planned that would shut down the cult's nationwide facilities. It would take place in late March. Aware that such an act would expose their members to dangerous chemicals, the organizers requested hazmat suits (Hazardous Material Suits) and gasmasks from the military. Two sergeants, members of Aum, heard the unusual request, put two and two together and immediately tipped of Asahara about the coming raid.

He decided to strike first.

Shoko Asahara may have been blind, but his plot to bring down the Japanese government was visionary. The first Sarin attack had been aimed at some provincial judges in an out of the way jurisdiction in regional Japan. In the Tokyo attacks,

Asahara aimed to bring down the entire law enforcement infrastructure of one of the largest cities in the world. The attacks were planned for 8.30 am on a busy weekday. He well knew that the night shift of Tokyo police would be pouring onto the underground railway network to go home at the same time as the daytime shift was in transit to their stations and workplaces. If the Sarin attacks went to plan, he would be able to knock out the law enforcement officers of Tokyo. This would cause chaos in the government and of course delay and disrupt any looming investigations into his nefarious activities. Some 2.5 million other commuters would also feel the effects of the poison and create another blind to his true intentions. Asahara surely thought he could usher in global conflict and fulfill his prophecies.

Nevertheless, he was not leaving anything to chance. In the days leading up to the attacks, his assassins practiced piercing plastic bags with their sharpened umbrellas and worked out how best to spread the lethal nerve agent. The drivers rehearsed their routes into the heart of Tokyo and visited the drop off and pick up points that would be used on that fateful day. The plotters were helped by the efficient and punctual Japanese rail network. They knew exactly what station to get on their train and when to exit down to an accuracy of seconds.

The plan was diabolical in its simplicity. Each of the 'ultra terrorists' would carry the Sarin onto some of the busiest subway routes: Hibiya, Marunouchi and Chiyoda, which all converged on central Tokyo. As the trains moved through stations 5 to 10 kilometres (3 to 6 miles) from the CBD, each of the operatives would spread the Sarin throughout their carriage before disembarking. The trains would be turned into carriers of lethal cargo, transporting death and destruction into the heart of Tokyo. Spreading through the subterranean stations or being carried into office blocks on the shoes of unwitting commuters, the nerve agent would be able to infect hundreds of thousands, or even millions of people. The lines all converged on the Imperial Palace; it is likely that Asahara hoped that the Emperor too might be infected.

There was one miscalculation made by the guru. Previously, a huge cache of 100 percent pure Sarin was destroyed upon his orders. Nervous that the authorities were about to raid the installations where the lethal liquid was stored, and concerned that it was too pure, Asahara had ordered its disposal. The substance to be used was a diluted form of the gas. This saved countless lives.

The other factor that saved thousands of innocent Japanese civilians and emergency-services workers was the powerful smell given off by the impure amalgam. Normally Sarin is entirely odorless. A person can be exposed to a lethal dose and be none the wiser until terrible symptoms take hold.

This would be a small consolation to the thousands who were hospitalized after the attack, many of whom experienced lifelong disabilities, or to the families of those who died.

The gates of Satian 7 swung open in the pre-dawn light of 20 March 1995 and at 6 am five modern cars emerged from the compound. Each one held a driver and a terrorist. Most of the five men embarking on the first large-scale biochemical terrorist attack of the 20th century possessed science degrees. Each carried a small duffel bag containing two or three reinforced plastic bags, filled with a solution that was 30 percent Sarin. Each man also carried a sharpened umbrella.

So thorough was the planning that each vehicle arrived at the designated station at least an hour before the appointed time. On the way, each car stopped to allow the assassins to buy a newspaper. They wrapped the deadly packages in the newspapers to make them appear inconspicuous. Millions of Japanese were making their way to work with similar parcels, wrapping snacks and lunch treats.

At least two of the assassins displayed a perverse sense of humor. One wrapped his Sarin in the Japanese equivalent of the *Wall Street Journal*, while another chose the Japanese Communist Party's rag.

After dropping off their passengers, the vehicles drove to the designated pick up spots. The assassins made their way to the escalators and traversed the underground stations with their Sarin bags wrapped in newspaper, trying to ignore their fellow commuters. It was important to distance themselves from any potential victims. Sarin would leach into the newspaper once the bags had been punctured, allowing the noxious cocktail to evaporate into the air rather than running over the carriage floors and perhaps out of the doors. Each man had taken his antidote and the attack was ready to proceed as planned.

Looking entirely indistinguishable from the other passengers, each cultist squeezed into the designated carriage - those most likely to be filled with police workers - and found a seat near a door. The five duffel bags were placed on the floor, unzipped and the umbrellas poised above the vacuum-sealed Sarin bags. It seemed that Armageddon, so often prophesized by Asahara, was about to strike into the heart of Tokyo.

Maybe not. One of the attackers began to have second thoughts. Ikuo Hayashi was a trained doctor and highly placed within the Aum hierarchy. He was tasked with releasing Sarin between the Shin-ochanomizu and Kasumigaseki railway stations. At 7.48 am he prepared to break open his bags of Sarin. At the last moment, the doctor looked around at his fellow passengers. Ikuo was overwhelmed with feelings of guilt and sorrow. Were these not innocent people, people whom he had spent most of his life learning to cure? He looked at the young women and the salary men, oblivious to the horrid fate he could inflict upon them, and was tormented by his conscience.

Not for long, however. Many years of conditioning forced him to obey orders and he thrust the umbrella into the first bag of Sarin. Fortunately for the passengers he did it weakly and the tear was small. The next thrust failed altogether and the second bag remained intact.

Ikuo's attack beat the next four by several minutes.

Toru Toyoda had been up all night with his co-conspirators and the strain was beginning to show. Nevertheless, he boarded his train on time and at 8.01, as it began to slow while entering Ebisu Station, he stabbed down hard on the two Sarin pouches. Even as he left the carriage the fluid was seeping out of the newspapers and spreading onto the floor. He raced up the escalator and within five minutes was being whisked back to Satian 7.

Kenichi Hirose was left at a station in the heart of Tokyo's subway system. This and his decision to deploy the Sarin from a shoulder bag was almost his undoing. At the appointed time of 8 am he found himself wedged against the door of an incredibly crowded commuter train. Not only did he have to ensure that he did not impale any of his fellow travelers on the razor sharp umbrella, Kenichi had to somehow maneuver his shoulder bag onto the floor to access the two Sarin pouches without drawing attention to himself. In the fevered press of the carriage, the two bags tumbled out of their newspaper and onto the floor. Amazingly, Kenichi managed to use his feet to wedge them under the corner of a train bench, where he thrust the umbrella into them just as the train came to a halt at Ochanomizu station.

Yasuo Hayashi was more confident than the bumbling Kenichi Hirose. He had volunteered to release three bags of Sarin on the Hibiya line. As the train pulled into Akihabara Station in the heart of Tokyo's electrics industry, he pierced all three bags. Sarin was soon pouring into the packed carriage as Yasuo made his getaway.

Masato Yokoyama was the fifth and last to make his attack. As the train pulled into Yotsuya Station, he thrust the umbrella into his carry all, but only managed to pierce one of the bags.

Aum Supreme Truth's deadly cargo had been delivered. What effect would it have on the citizens of Tokyo? No doubt Asahara and his intimate leadership coterie were ensconced in their headquarters, tuned into radio and television, waiting for the first reports to come in.

A gas attack with a substance like Sarin doesn't necessarily cause immediate mass panic, hysteria and death. It is more like a creeping and insidious infection that begins with minor symptoms. Gradually people move from a state of mild discomfort to intense debilitating symptoms. As more and more drop, local authorities tasked to help those stricken with the agent gradually realize that they have a problem on their hands and only eventually do they realize there is a full-blown crisis.

So it was with the subway attacks. Some commuters exited the trains with no symptoms at all. Only when they arrived at work did they begin to feel ill, as the Sarin worked through their skin into their circulatory systems. Within the carriages the first thing that many reported was a slightly unpleasant odor. This was often accompanied by stinging eyes and an unexpected hacking cough. Others began to feel nauseous and even bent over double and vomited. One of the strangest experiences many felt was when the Sarin caused their salivary glands to go into overdrive, causing an unexpected foaming at the mouth.

As the liquid sloshed around the floor of the carriages, a slightly acrid smell became overwhelming as it began to enter the atmosphere in a gaseous form. People next to the pierced bags became overwhelmed and almost fell out of the carriages when the train came to the next stop. Nevertheless, the numbers were initially quite small and the train drivers were not aware that anything was amiss. Closing the doors, they proceeded on their route, oblivious to the fact that they were carrying their lethal cargo to the next destination. A small number of people collapsed in the stations and ambulances and medics were quickly summoned.

Soon whole carriages were affected. Rather than one or two distressed passengers getting out, they were emptied wholesale as the commuters, gasping for oxygen, poured out and headed for the escalators in an attempt to reach fresh air as soon as possible. The train drivers, thankfully, became aware that not all was as it should be. Emergency buttons were pushed, claxons sounded and whole trains were emptied of their passengers. Unbeknown to many, Sarin had covered the soles of their feet, lodged in the fibers of their clothes and even settled on skin, where it began to permeate into the blood stream. These individuals would carry the chemical through the stations and up to street level, and even into their places of work. This ensured that many thousands of others felt the effects of the toxin.

With a growing awareness of the crisis, stationmasters began to inspect the different cars. In one carriage several people had collapsed. They thrashed around like fish out of water while the Sarin closed down their nervous systems. Many suffered such severe seizures that, while not killed by the nerve agent, they were brain damaged and entered a vegetative state.

An assistant stationmaster, Kazumasa Takahashi, entered a car and saw a small parcel wrapped in newspaper that was leaking fluid. Donning rubber gloves, he picked up the object and removed it from the car. He then collected other discarded newspapers and used these to soak up the remaining liquid. A colleague joined him and together the two placed the now soaked items into a plastic bag. They took it to their small office and phoned a senior subway official to inform him of the finding. Kazumasa complained to his superior that he was feeling unwell and respectfully requested to take leave. He then collapsed on the floor. Another employee rushed to assist, but found the two men lying entangled in the tiny space. Blood had drained from their faces and saliva foamed out of their mouths.

The two men were soon dead. The first of 12 innocent victims of Asahara's malevolent delusions.

Kamiyacho station felt the full brunt of the attack. More than 50 people lay on its concrete concourse. They jerked about violently; Sarin had destroyed their motor control. Arms and legs suffered extensive bruising and in some cases limbs were broken in the violent spasms. Others tried to stand but were racked by violent paroxysms as they coughed out blood and sputum. One of the first symptoms of Sarin poisoning is impeded vision or even blindness. Those affected tried to flee, only to smash into walls or trip over chairs. Others merely crawled in circles, mewling in pain and terror.

Some sat quietly leaning against station walls, too shocked to fathom the tragedy that had befallen them. Sarin immobilizes the vocal chords. Those who cried out in pain and distress or sought help could only mouth helplessly as froth poured out from their throats.

Hell would soon visit the chilly streets of Tokyo. As the victims emerged from the subways they did not find relief from the symptoms. The nerve agent was already coursing through their systems and the lure of fresh air was an illusion. Distressed civilians poured out of at least twelve stations along the three main subway lines of Hibiya, Marunouchi and Chiyoda. Unaffected residents were shocked to see thousands upon thousands of people boil up from the subway exits to drop gasping, retching and fitting on the streets. The authorities finally realized - they had a crisis on their hands.

Emergency services, police and hospitals were almost overwhelmed by the attack. Citizens lent a hand and made makeshift stretchers to carry the patients to emergency departments, or bundled them into private cars and taxis to get the stricken commuters to medical help as soon as possible.

Even in these secure hospital environments, the Sarin went about its deadly work. A thick cloying gas or a liquid it insinuated itself onto clothing and footwear. Unsuspecting medical workers handled these items and immediately began feeling the symptoms of Sarin poisoning. There were not enough oxygen cylinders and soon hospital corridors were filled with patients gasping desperately to survive. In some institutions basics such as rubber gloves ran out.

Around 5500 people were hospitalized. They did not know it at the time but they were fortunate to survive. Hundreds of thousands could have perished had the stock of odorless, pure Sarin - destroyed on Asahara's orders - been deployed instead of the mixed form. Twelve people died. Many of the injured suffered permanent nerve damage or blindness.

Raids were launched on Aum Supreme Truth compounds throughout Japan. What was revealed stunned Japan and the world. More than 1000 barrels of lethal agents such as cyanide and mustard gas were seized. Under Satian 2 at least 80 barrels covered with the fat and soot of atomized corpses were found next to the industrial sized microwaves. Errant cultists who had drawn Asahara's ire were found, starved of light, food and warmth. Many were only days from death and ready to be microwaved.

Cultists had been forewarned of the coming crackdown and many had fled to cult safe houses. Asahara seemed to have vanished into thin air. It wasn't until sniffer dogs led police to a secret chamber in Satian 6 that he was pulled out into the open. It was no easy task recovering the portly guru. Hacksaws, blowtorches and angle grinders had to be used to cut through numerous bulkheads protecting Asahara and his cache of 100,000 dollars cash and a Kalashnikov with several magazines.

Eventually 350 members of Aum Supreme Truth were tried for a variety of crimes. Despite a bevy of lawyers, Asahara was sentenced to death on 27 February 2004, along with 13 of his top aides. Up until 2018 all of the condemned were kept in the Tokyo Detention Center. In the middle of that year reports were received that some members of Aum were planning an armed breakout attempt for the confined cultists. This was the reason given when seven members were moved to other facilities. However, this proved to be a blind. The Japanese government had executed the cult ringleaders.

Japanese legal custom prevents any capital sentences being carried out until trials relevant to the condemned are completed. In 2016 the last Aum appeals and sentences were concluded, clearing the way for the executions to be carried out at any of the Japanese prisons that house gallows. These include Sapporo, Sendai, Tokyo, Nagoya, Osaka, Hiroshima and Fukuoka.

On the afternoon of 6 July 2018, the Japanese government announced that Shoko Asahara and six of his aides had been hanged. This was despite the fact that his legal representation had sought to portray him as mentally unfit for this procedure. Ever since his trial and sentencing, Asahara had withdrawn from almost all human contact. He did not communicate with the guards and refused to use the toilet in his cell. He wore a large diaper. He did follow commands to take a bath once every three days. The rest of his time he spent sitting silently in his solitary confinement cell, barely recognizable with his shaved head and chin. There were no obvious health or mental problems aside from a skin condition that was typified by rough patches. He refused to speak to family members or legal representation, although he did communicate with the prison doctor.

Asahara would have had no warning of his death. The condemned in Japan are only notified of their death about an hour before their executions. With little ceremony they are hauled from their cells and placed upon the gallows. Their sentence is read and a noose is placed around their neck. Three prison officers simultaneously press buttons to open the trap door so no one knows who was responsible for plunging the inmate to their death.

Reports indicate that there was one priest and several guards present at his execution. It also seems likely that he went to his death dressed in a diaper.

The seven were executed in different prisons around the country and police were out in force to prevent any reprisal attacks from surviving cult members.

Small remnants of the cult still exist in Japan and Russia. They call themselves 'Aleph.' Remarkably close surveillance is carried out on this group and any attempt to charge individuals for courses and seminars is banned.

CHAPTER FIVE

The Family: Horror in Hollywood

Revelation – Book 14

[1] Then I looked, and there before me was the Lamb, standing on Mount Zion, and with him 144,000 who had his name and his Father's name written on their foreheads.

Genesis

The deck was stacked against Charles Manson from the very beginning.

He was born on 12 November 1934 to 16-year-old Kathleen Maddox in Cincinnati General Hospital, Ohio. The father appears to be a shifty individual named Colonel Walker Henderson Scott Sr. 'Colonel' was his given name, but he often used it as an honorific. As soon as Kathleen said she was pregnant the 'colonel' declared he had army business to attend to and promptly vanished. Scott Sr was well known as a local con man who combined shady dealings with intermittent work to pay his way. It appears that Kathleen managed to track him down and was able to extract some state sanctioned child support from the errant father. It is likely that Charles never met his father.

Maddox herself was no stranger to shady dealings. She often acted as a honey trap at local dance halls. Well-heeled men would be attracted by her vivacious smile

Albrecht Dürer released his series *Apocalypse with Pictures* in 1498.
In panel 14 'The Beast' emerges to do battle with 'The Righteous'.

The Children of God during the 1960s and '70s. Behind the smiles was a cult based on fear and exploitation.

David Berg was known as 'God' or 'Moses' by his followers.
He used his cult to promote pedophilia.

Viktor Vasnetsov's *Four Horsemen of the Apocalypse*, 1887. The lamb at the top of the image observes while Death, Famine, War and Conquest wreak vengeance on humanity.

The LeBaron family. Most suffered from a range of mental illnesses.

Joseph Smith, founder of the Mormons.

Roch Thériault moved his cult to the Canadian wilderness so he could freely abuse members.

Joseph Kibwetere. His smile masked an unstable mind.

Charles Manson. The 'son of man' renamed the apocalypse as 'Helter Skelter'.

Sharon Tate. She was in the wrong place at the wrong time when The Family sought to bring on a race war.

The grave of Sharon Tate Polanski and her unborn son, victims of an acid-fuelled delusion.

Vernon Howell aka David Koresh decided that he was the Lamb of God who would unlock the seventh seal and bring doomsday upon humanity.

The leaders of The Movement for the Restoration of The Ten Commandments led their followers to a fiery death.

Shoko Asahara used anthrax, botulism and Sarin in multiple attempts to bring on the apocalypse.

Aum Supreme operatives turned the Tokyo subway system into a deathtrap.

Heaven's Gate members staged a mass suicide to enable them to hitch a ride on a comet.

Marshall Applewhite may have convinced his followers to commit suicide due to his belief that he was dying of cancer. His autopsy revealed that he was cancer free.

before being mugged by Maddox and her brother Luther. One of the young boy's earliest memories may have been seeing his mother arrested for one of these crimes. She was later convicted and sentenced to five years hard labor. Luther got 10 years – all for a grand total of 27 dollars.

Maddox married William Eugene Manson, and the child took his surname. Despite the new relationship, Charles' mother was no role model and the young Manson was shipped between various babysitters and relatives while Kathleen went out on the town. When she was arrested for theft Manson moved in with his aunty and uncle, where he lived for three years.

This trauma had an effect on the young boy. His family noticed that he became moody, he placed no importance on the truth and behind his blank, dark eyes was an increasingly manipulative individual. Frequent visits to his mother, confined behind thick glass walls in the prison visiting facilities, must have been scary rather than reassuring for the four-year-old.

School was no better for the scraggly kid. The other children soon learned that his mother was a jailbird and Manson was relentlessly teased, often reduced to walking home in tears. His uncle did not help things. Seeing that his nephew was acting like a sissy, Uncle Bob made him wear a dress to school.

Upon Kathleen's release in 1942, she resumed her drinking and thieving ways. By this time Charles was acting out. He continually absented himself from school and began shoplifting. Unable to deal with the escalating behavior, Kathleen placed her 13-year-old son in the Gibault School for Boys in Indiana. Young Charles fled from the oppressive regime several times, but his mother always returned him to the care of the Catholic priests in charge of the young delinquents.

At this early stage Manson may have been able to turn himself around with a modicum of love and support. This was not to be. The following years would see him develop a love of sadomasochistic bisexual intercourse and a burning hatred of society.

He fled Gibault and ended up in Indianapolis. Here he burgled stores until arrested and sent to a boys' facility. He teamed up with another boy and together they stole a car and embarked upon a road trip, holding up grocery stores and even a casino on the way. This spree soon ended and once again Manson found himself in custody at the strict Indiana Boys' School. Manson, with his diminutive size, claimed that he was preyed on by other boys and raped repeatedly.

In 1951 Manson again escaped briefly, but was soon in a federal intuition. His file recorded that the young man was aggressively antisocial. It appeared that Manson's aunt was willing to look after him, but just before he was released to her care he was caught raping a boy at knifepoint. Another eight offenses saw him transferred to a maximum-security reformatory, where he would reside until he became an adult in 1954.

The Indiana reformatory in Plainfield was hardly a location that would help the young man mend his ways. Other kids, as old as 21, were quite incorrigible and no doubt taught the younger children many criminal techniques. Manson had to learn to survive in this harsh environment. He would scream and yell if attacked, but if this did not work he would suffer abuse in sullen silence.

Although released as an adult, this freedom did not last long. Until 1967, Manson spent years in federal prisons on charges of fraud, pimping, theft, taking a stolen vehicle across a state line and violation of probation.

On 21 March 1967, the thoroughly institutionalized Manson was released. He actually pleaded with prison authorities to be able to remain in his 'home', but was turned out regardless.

Chucked out onto the street, broke and friendless, Manson had at least picked up one skill in prison – the ability to strum out a tune on a guitar.

Attraction, Initiation and Control

Once released, Manson moved to San Francisco. Here he found a fairly run down flat and paid his way by strumming a few chords and begging for money. He spent most of his time hanging around the fashionable Haight-Ashbury district, which was at the heart of the increasingly popular hippie movement. It was during this time that he seduced Mary Brunner, a library assistant. She was the first recruit to the Family.

Many who encountered Manson during this period noted that he had an uncanny knack of identifying a person's weaknesses, finding out their deepest desires or hang-ups and ruthlessly exploiting that knowledge to bring them into his cult. Drugs, sex, adulation, scriptures – all were devices that he could use. Manson was particularly adept at playing on the fears or desires of young women. They were his most ardent and loyal supporters. He was less successful with men, but used the bevy of young female acolytes as honey traps to attract the muscle that he needed. Endless sex was enough to turn several young men's heads.

Any young lady was fair game for Manson's predatory ways. Dianne Lake was only 14 years old when she fell under Charlie Manson's spell. She was attracted by the drugs and sex, but what she really wanted was a sense of belonging: a family. Dianne was a product of a dysfunctional home – what the young girl really needed was reassurance, love and affection. When she joined the group she felt a sense of liberation. Manson told her to forget about her family, she was needed in the group and there could be no turning back. The 14-year-old gave up her inhibitions and reservations, committing herself entirely to the freewheeling cult.

Mary Brunner was swept into Manson's orbit and became one of his most loyal followers. Her initial reluctance to share the new man in her life was soon broken down and she was soon shacked up and pregnant, sharing her apartment and life with more than 10 other young women who had fallen under Manson's spell. He was increasingly playing the role of guru but had not yet fallen to the destructive urges that would lead to 'Helter Skelter'.

In fact, it seems that in this early phase the cult members had a lot of fun. Before the end of 1967, Manson and eight or nine of his flock piled into an old converted school bus and set off on a drug fueled road trip. The bus had seats removed and replaced by cushions and pillows, making it look like a mobile Ottoman harem. They went north as far as Washington state before turning south and going through Mexico and other south-west states. In what would become standard practice, money was obtained to keep the trek going by sending the girls out to panhandle or turn tricks in the red light districts that they passed through.

Manson became the 'God of Fuck' and acted in whatever role his followers wanted. He was Christ reincarnated, a passionate and skilled lover or a mentor and father figure. Underneath his charismatic surface was a growing preoccupation with death. On their journeys through California, Manson and his followers hooked up with pagan cults such as the Church of Satan, the Process Church of Final Judgment (devotees of Lucifer and Jehovah) the Circe Oder of the Dog and possibly the notorious Four Pi Movement. This latter group graduated from sacrificing and skinning dogs to doing the same to hitchhikers and drifters. The Family adopted some of their practices; there was evidence of animal sacrifice at their later bases.

Soon the mobile cult turned up on the doorstep of Dennis Wilson of the Beach Boys, who had picked up two female members of the cult while they were hitchhiking. He entertained the two women in his Pacific Palisades Mansion on Sunset Boulevard. Manson capitalized on the introduction to the celebrity and soon he and more than 20 of the Family had moved in on a semipermanent basis.

They brought with them a ready supply of drugs, sex – and gonorrhea. Wilson shelled out a fair amount to the local medicos to cure the cult of the STD. The Beach Boy also encouraged Manson in his singing career. He paid for the ex-con to lay down some tracks in a local studio.

It was during this time that a connection was made that would lead to chaos and mayhem. Rudi Altobelli, an industry figure who associated with Wilson, owned a large, sprawling, ranch style home at Celio Drive in the Hollywood Hills. After Manson lost touch with Altobelli, the house was rented out to Roman Polanski and his pregnant wife, Sharon Tate.

Nothing came of Manson's foray into the music industry and Wilson, after his car was trashed by a cult member, sent them on their way. Coaxing the last few miles out of the worn, two-tone school bus, the group relocated to Spahn's Movie Ranch.

The ranch was littered with the detritus of movie sets used to film Westerns in the 50s and 60s. These were all out of commission and the 80-year-old George Spahn now made a living selling horseback rides. He lived in a relocatable home and welcomed Manson's arrival, especially when he sent some of the cult members to clean and cook for him. Lynette 'Squeaky' Fromme, one of Manson's most fanatical followers, continually urged Spahn to make a will out in favor of Manson. Signing such a will would likely also have been signing his death warrant.

The Family did not spend all their time at Spahn's ranch but had several other cult hideouts around Death Valley and on the fringes of town.

It was during this time that Manson began to believe an apocalyptic worldview, taking his followers along for the ride.

The cult environs were far removed from the glory days of living on Sunset Boulevard. Images of the compounds show hard-scrabble ground with stunted desert bushes struggling to survive in the arid environment. Dust and dirt were everywhere and, apart from a dilapidated house with a primitive kitchen, there was not much accommodation. Holes were dug in the ground and covered with a mix of corrugated iron and bits of wood. These were often built removed from the main compound.

When the law finally decided to clean out the cult they had to search for the bunkers, which had been camouflaged to meld perfectly with the desert landscape. Young women were found in these, cowering and hoping to avoid detection. Some slept in the house, while others bedded down in the broken down old bus. This was also the cult's wardrobe; all clothing was tossed on the floor and anybody could help themselves to anything they wanted.

Money was obtained via criminal activities. Cult members would descend from the hills with orders from Manson. Women were instructed to sell themselves for cash. The young men stole Volkswagens and brought them back to the ranch. Here they were chopped up and converted into Dune Buggies, which were then on-sold to unsuspecting purchasers. The members were also involved in illicit drug sales.

At the same time, Manson trained his most loyal followers in the art of the 'creepy crawl.' They would break into family homes in the wealthy parts of Hollywood and creepy crawl around the house. Some small items were stolen, but the main aim was to gain entry, move stealthily around and exit while the family remained asleep and oblivious to the lurking fanatics in their midst.

To go with creepy crawlies there was even more dangerous training. Manson chose his most fanatical adherents and enrolled them into 'murder school.' They were taught the fine art of 'pig sticking.' Issued with razor sharp bowie knives, the young women were told to seize a victim's hair, pull back their head and slash the exposed throat. Another skill taught was the blitz attack, where several members would leap on a target, pin their limbs to the ground and allow the attacker, armed with the knife, to stab the victim in the guts repeatedly, thrashing the blade around to inflict the maximum damage to internal organs.

At the same time, drug-fueled orgies continued under the stars at Spahn Ranch. A constant diet of LSD, pot and smack kept the members – in excess of 50 individuals at one stage – bound to their guru. His increasingly bizarre rants captured the imagination of most of his followers and they fell in with his apocalyptic vision of the future.

Not all were taken in. Several members woke from drug and alcohol fugues to realize that they were stuck in the wilderness with a crazed and increasingly violent group of people. But there was nothing they could do to escape. Removed from civilization, the Family became less like a free love cult and more like an organization that maintained loyalty through the threat or use of violence.

Manson had his 'trusties', the individuals within the group who would be selected to carry out murders and who would report any murmurings of discontent to Manson. The inner circle was something of a closed shop. Recent recruits or those who had not proven their loyalty were often assigned menial tasks and heard only whispers hinting at the terrible crimes the cult was beginning to commit.

After the Tate murders in August 1969, two girls managed to escape by leaving before dawn and going cross-country. They were fortunate to come across some law enforcement personnel investigating the cult. Soon after the fugitives had been picked up, a posse of cult members turned up in their cut down dune buggies, searching for them.

Other members were not so lucky. Those who criticized the Family or tried to leave it were likely to come to a sticky end. Several were killed. While it has not been proven that Manson ordered the murders, there are no other reasonable explanations.

On 30 December 1968, Marina Habe was abducted from outside her home. The 17-year-old's body was recovered on New Year's Day. It is thought that she had ties with Family and this led to her death.

On 17 July 1969 Mark Walts who was a frequent visitor to Manson's camp went missing. He was found the next day with three bullets in his head, injuries caused by a severe beating and tire tracks on his body showing where he had been run over. It is not known how Walts had offended Manson. He may have refused to carry out a murder, leading to his own demise. The murdered boy's brother publicly accused The Family of the murder but nothing could be pinned on the cult.

A female corpse was found at a location north-east of the camp. It was so badly decomposed that she was recorded as a Jane Doe – unidentified remains. While not confirmed, the remains suited the physical proportions of Susan Scott, who had gone missing while at the Spahn Ranch. Some of the clothing was identified as similar to what Susan had last been seen wearing.

Several men were recruited to the Family at this time. Some saw through the diet of drugs and free sex and defied Manson by leaving. If they were wise they cut all communication with members and moved far away.

Those that remained were firmly in the thrall of their leader. His demonic vision had penetrated their troubled psyches. When Manson decided to strike, they would be ready.

Bizarre Beliefs

In 1967 the West Coast of the USA was reveling in the counterculture movement. Opposition to the American involvement in Vietnam was increasing and a whole parcel of new drugs were hitting the streets. Uppers, downers, hallucinogens and pot were freely available. It seems Charles Manson tried it all.

In jail Manson had developed a burning hatred of blacks. This, combined with a fertile imagination, drugs and a hatred of society, led to the outlandish theology that we now know as Helter Skelter.

Tests proved that Manson had an above average IQ and he did a fair bit of reading in jail. He seemed bent on a course of petty crime, until he was released from prison in 1967. He stumbled into the 'turn on, tune in and drop out' culture of San Francisco. Here he found that a plentiful supply of hallucinogenic drugs and average music abilities, combined with a generic religion that pulled strands from Christianity, Buddhism and anything else that appealed, allowed him to begin his own cult.

It is a testament to the amount of drugs that his flock was taking that they swallowed his ideology hook, line and sinker. Manson was influenced by a wide range of thinkers and ideas. These included Hitler, Ron L Hubbard and the Scientologists, Christianity, Buddhism, Black Magic, Hopi Indian mysticism and even the Beatles! He particularly loved the Beatles' 'White Album' and in particular the track 'Helter Skelter'. The discordant vibes and shrill lyrics combined with the unintelligible finale broke into Manson's consciousness. He became convinced that some higher force was communicating through the Fab Four and was appealing to him to bring on Armageddon.

Manson ('son of man' – therefore Jesus, as he thought of himself) used the Book of Revelation to lend his hatred of humankind legitimacy. His interpretation of the text predicted that black people would rise up and attack all of the white people in a world wide race war. Despite the fact that they were only 10 percent of the American population, African Americans would exterminate all of the whites (except for Manson's Family, safely ensconced in the desert). The nascent Black Power movements that were sweeping across the country would then turn against their black brethren until only a remnant survived.

These decimated survivors, due to their supposed racial inferiority, would be unable to run their own affairs and would gratefully welcome the only surviving whites to rule over them.

Manson counted on his musical ability to help bring on the race war. He and some select members of the Family would record a brilliant double album, like the Beatles' White Album, and the sub textual references and hidden sounds would be the soundtrack to these bloody race wars.

Manson's Family, which would increase to the Biblical number of 144,000 adherents, would emerge from a huge golden cavern deep in Death Valley to rule the world. They would have been able to survive the apocalypse because this cavern, which only Manson knew the location of, had a river of milk and honey running through its center, along with thousands of fruit trees that produced 12 types of succulent crops all year round.

Manson, as ruler of the Family, would become the ruler of world. But first he had to provoke the race war.

Armageddon

It is unknown exactly what brought about Manson's desire to initiate Helter Skelter, but the violence escalated midway through 1969. Many suggest that it was Manson's realization that he would never make it as a musician. Auditions held at the ranch in May did not result in a recording contract.

On 1 July 1969 a black drug dealer named Bernard Crowe was shot. Manson had sent 'Tex' Watson, one of his most loyal followers, to raise funds by defrauding Crowe. Crowe threatened to wipe out everybody at Spahn's ranch in retaliation. He was executed with a .22 gunshot to the head and his body was dumped. The news reported that a member of the militant Black Panthers had been murdered. Manson felt he was one step closer to race war.

The need for funds led to the next murder.

Manson blooded his cult with an unusual target: a drug dealing music teacher called Gary Hinman. The musician was known as an easygoing type of guy who often let the stragglers of society stay in his apartment. Sometime before 1969 he had befriended Manson and some of the Family and may have sold them an assortment of hallucinogens. Manson heard that Hinman had come into a juicy inheritance and he decided that it would be better in his pocket than the musician's. On 25 July 1969, Manson sent three cultists – baby faced Bobby Beausoleil, Mary Brunner and Susan Atkins – to go to Hinman's apartment and get the money. Manson made it clear he didn't care how they got it; they could ask for it first, but if the cash was not forthcoming they were to use any means required.

The three turned up to 964 Old Topanga Canyon Road, California and were welcomed by the musician. Things turned sour when he explained that he did not have any ready cash or the means to obtain any. He was held hostage for several days until Manson was called in to break the impasse. The three Family members were not yet hardened killers so Manson had to show them the ropes.

Manson came to the house armed with a sword. Frustrated that no cash was forthcoming he slashed Hinman across the face several times, severing an ear, before instructing the trio to finish him off. After Manson had left, Beausoleil repeatedly stabbed Hinman and the two girls took turns holding a pillow over the talented musician's face. Beausoleil scrawled 'Political Piggy' along with a paw print in the victim's blood on the wall. This was in an attempt to make it look like a Black Panther assassination.

Manson thought this murder might spark a race war, but the only thing it caused was a botched police investigation. This was despite the fact that Beausoleil was apprehended soon after, driving the victim's car and with the murder weapon in the tire well.

No connection was found between the Family and the death. Manson had proven that he could commit crimes with impunity. The Hinman murder gave him the courage to instigate full Helter Skelter.

Manson had the cult members where he wanted them. He had a thoroughly dedicated core of members who would follow his every command. They had all been trained in creepy crawling and were eager to please their guru. On Friday 8 August, Manson announced that Helter Skelter was imminent. It was time to provoke his race war.

At dinner he made his selection. Long-time member Tex (Charles Watson), Sadie (Susan Denise Atkins) and Katie (Patricia Krenwinkel) were chosen as the hit team. The fourth member was Linda Kasabian, who had not been in the cult long enough to get a nickname. (One of the difficulties that faced the police once they began to take a closer look at the cult was the plethora of pseudonyms that all members adopted. Some had as many as four.) While not 100 percent trusted by Manson, Linda had a driver's license and was least likely to draw attention to the murderous group. Manson made an error sending Linda – she later became a key witness for the prosecution.

Manson saw the chosen killers into an old vehicle. He handed a long barreled .22 caliber pistol and three knives through the windows and instructed the three girls to follow Tex's commands. Several days earlier Manson had explained to Tex what he wanted and where the murders were to go down: 10050 Cielo Drive, Hollywood Hills.

It seems that Manson had had a negative interaction with a past tenant of the sprawling mansion. Or perhaps he believed that Rudi Altobelli, the record producer who had refused to back his musical career, still lived there. He was unaware that new people had moved in. The famed film director Roman Polanski and his glamorous movie star wife Sharon Tate were looking forward to raising their first child in the spacious residence. They had inadvertently placed themselves within the path of mayhem and murder.

While Katie and Sadie giggled in nervous anticipation, Manson gave one more instruction: he wanted them to write something 'witchy' on the walls, using their victims' blood.

The cult vehicle proceeded to Cielo Drive without interruption. At the bottom of the estate, Tex grabbed some wire cutters and the pistol. He scaled a short pole and clipped the phone wires. Beckoning to Sadie and Katie, he scaled the fence and began creepy crawling up the drive towards the house.

Just then an ignition sounded and some car headlights snapped on. The team froze, though the beams of light were not concentrated on them. Tex took his .22-caliber long-barreled pistol in one hand and a knife in the other, and stealthily approached the vehicle, a Rambler. Inside the car was a young man who had just recently turned 18. His name was Steve Parent. He had been at 10050 Cielo Drive with the intention of offloading a tape recorder to William Garretson, who lived in the caretaker's bungalow at the rear of the property. Late on the evening of 8 August, Parent had turned up at Garretson's front door to make his pitch.

Parent did not make a sale and he certainly got more than he bargained for. Tex came at him and without warning fired four bullets into the young man's torso before finishing him off by slitting his throat.

Linda heard the commotion. She realized that this was not just a creepy crawly mission and froze. She toyed with the idea of driving off, but a combination of loyalty to – and fear of – the Family made her stay.

The sounds of carnage she heard that night traumatized the young woman. Other neighbors reported hearing glass breaking, thuds and even an occasional scream. However, the houses at Cielo Drive were well spaced and nobody heard enough to warrant a call to the local police. Garretson was oblivious to the mayhem occurring a few feet from his front door. He was listening to music. Nevertheless, he was the police's prime suspect for a period of time as they could not imagine he heard nothing of the violent massacres that occurred.

The three killers broke into the house through a fly wire that Tex cut open. Roman Polanski had recently moved in with his heavily pregnant young wife, Sharon Tate. He was out of town on business, but Sharon was home entertaining some friends.

These four people were to die horribly at the hands of the crazed cultists. They immediately set upon the dinner guests and bloodied their knives. Heiress Abigail Folger sought to flee the house and ran screaming out the front door. She was pounced upon and brought to ground. One of the female assassins then repeatedly plunged her knife into the victim's back.

Folger's boyfriend was next to die. He possibly tried to help his girlfriend, but his brave act was rewarded with several .22 slugs in his back. In a rage, Tex pistol-whipped the innocent man 13 times while another killer, probably the same one who killed Folger, stabbed him 51 times. Both were left to die on the manicured lawn and were found sprawled and bloody the next day by police.

The coroner's reports are clear. The stab wounds were not inflicted on one location of the body while the attackers sought to subdue the victims. They ranged from the face, down the arms, along the torso over the buttocks and onto the legs. These wounds weren't intended to kill as quickly as possible, but to inflict the maximum pain, suffering and humiliation. It's likely that the victims were pinned to the ground by one member while another stabbed them multiple times.

It is likely that the next two victims had a prolonged death. Police officers can often detect when a family member has beaten or stabbed a murder victim to death. Years of repressed anger and hatred boil over into a frenzy of violence. Manson had his killers whipped up into such a hated of society that these killings made even the worst patricide or matricide pale in comparison.

Jay Sebring was a celebrity hairdresser who was at one stage engaged to be married to Sharon Tate. That arrangement fell through, but the two were still close – as evidenced by his presence at Cielo Drive that night. Sebring had something of a murky past and was experiencing financial difficulties at the time of the murders. This was another red herring followed by the investigating police, another delay in their incompetent investigation.

Whatever his past, Sebring did not deserve his horrific death. While it is not entirely clear what happened to him and Tate, it appears they were tormented and tortured for a period of time. The cultists bound Sebring's wrists and tied a rope around his neck, which they then tossed over a beam. The heavily pregnant Tate was then dragged from her bedroom and the noose was also tied around her neck. No one can know the torments the two were subjected to by their drug-crazed killers. Helter Skelter required the killings to be bloody, messy and sadistic – not quiet hits in the night.

Sharon Tate pleaded for her life and for that of her unborn baby. Her killer retorted 'Look, bitch, I have no mercy for you,' and proceeded to stab her 16 times. Sebring was beaten and stabbed before being left dead on the carpet with a towel over his head He was still tied to the now deceased Tate.

Following Manson's orders, the gang then wrote 'Pig' in blood on the doors and splashed blood and gore around the villa. The gang then made their escape.

Just as the horror-stricken Linda prepared to leave, the three bloodied killers appeared beside the car and climbed in.

They stopped several times on their retreat from Cielo Drive. Once was to wash the blood off their faces and change into new clothes. The bloodied gear they had been wearing was tossed over the side of a steep embankment. It was only recovered months later, when some bright journalists who were trying to piece together the course of the crime pointed out their location to the police.

Similarly, the gun and knives were tossed out of the speeding vehicle. The gun was recovered by a young boy, who showed it to his father. The lad knew that any suspicious items should not be handled, so he picked it up by placing a stick into the barrel. The family tried several times to hand the gun into police as a suspicious item. They were fobbed off on multiple occasions and when an officer did finally respond to their prompts he handled the gun without gloves, destroying any fingerprint evidence. The gun went straight into a police evidence lock up without being investigated.

The ecstatic kill team got back to the Spahn Ranch and reported to Manson that the mission had been a success. While they did not brag to other members of the family of their deeds, many overheard how some 'pigs' had been well and truly 'stuck.'

Manson was not finished. Helter Skelter was to be brought about by a succession of killings so similar that the police would put them down to the same gang of ruthless black murderers. This would then lead to race war. The following evening a murder team left to carry out another slaughter, but police didn't link the attacks until months later.

Manson led this second murder spree. On the night of 10 August 1969, Manson pulled over next to a mansion that belonged to a wealthy supermarket owner Leno LaBianca and his wife Rosemary LaBianca. The middle-aged couple had just completed their evening ritual where Leno read the day's papers while Rosemary tidied up the kitchen. The couple were preparing for bed, comfortable in their loving routine.

Manson told his crew to wait in the car. He creepy crawled into the LaBianca house. It is hard to imagine the shock that must have been felt by the couple when the wild eyed, ragamuffin of a guru, who had been getting progressively madder up in the dusty hills above Los Angeles, appeared in their home. He rapidly subdued the couple by waving a gun in their faces before tying them up.

He had a much worse fate in store for them.

The master of creepy crawling returned to his expectant murder team and sent them forth to do his bidding. Once again Tex was the leader.

They set upon Leno first. He was beaten, stabbed and garroted in a paroxysm of orgiastic violence. All of the mad anger, hate and drug-fueled psychosis promoted by Manson was unleashed upon the couple. A large carving knife and fork were rammed into Leno's belly. The word 'war' was cut into his torso while 'Helter Skelter' and 'Death To Pigs' was written in blood on walls throughout the house. Finally, the dead man's head was covered with a hood.

Rosemary did not fare any better. Hearing the agonized cries of her husband, she desperately tried to go to his aid but was pinned to the bed, asphyxiated with the cord from a bedside lamp and stabbed 41 times.

Manson and his team left the scene. They had done everything they could to link the murders – the savage multiple stabbings, the hoods, words written on the walls in blood. What else could they do? Manson even took the pair's wallets and tossed them out of the car in a black neighborhood in an effort to trigger the race war.

The attacks took place in different police jurisdictions and, remarkably, no link was made between the killings.

The cult had not finished. It is estimated that up to 36 individuals may have got in the way of the cult and required removal for various reasons.

Donald Jerome Shea, nicknamed Shorty, was hired by George Spahn to look after the livestock and horses on the ranch when he was not acting as an extra in Westerns down in Hollywood. Shorty always looked after his boss's interests and soon cottoned onto the fact that Manson and his crew were up to no good. He started making moves to get the cult relocated.

Manson was aware of Shorty's attitudes to his Family. Many of the youngest and prettiest girls had been sent to try and recruit the ranch hand, without success. Manson, convinced that Shorty had tipped off the police, decided to sort him out – permanently.

On 28 August several Family members, including Tex Watson, Steve Grogan and Manson himself, took Shorty for a ride. From the backseat, Grogan hit Shorty with a wrench before Tex turned on him with a knife and stabbed him repeatedly. Shorty was thickset and muscular, and managed to put up a decent fight against his six attackers. Eventually he was bundled out of the car, pinned to the ground and stabbed to death. He was buried behind Spahn Ranch and remained there until 1977, when Grogan drew a map revealing the corpse's whereabouts.

In fact the late discovery of Shea's body was indicative of the sloppy police work characteristic of these cases. Since the Tate and La Bianca murders occurred in different jurisdictions, different law enforcement agencies were blind to the fact that they were in many ways identical. Despite the fact that the victims in both crimes were brutalized and stabbed many times, and their blood used to write disturbing slogans, the cases weren't officially connected. Both the LAPD (Los Angeles Police Department) and the LA Sheriff's Department were guilty of appalling oversights.

It was only information from members and the associates of the Family that led to Manson's demise.

On 12 October Manson was arrested for his role in the auto-theft operations, which the authorities were finally pinning on him. There was no proof, or even suspicion, that he had been involved in the two sets of murders. Soon after, Susan Atkins, one of Manson's most devoted followers, was arrested for her role in the Hinman murder. Atkins was determined to tell the other prisoners about what she had got up to at Cielo Drive. Her fellow inmates, Virginia Castro and Ronnie Howard, were shocked to hear of the violent tales and tried repeatedly to inform on their cellmate. The two were prostitutes and drug users with lengthy rap sheets, so the police were initially reluctant to follow up on the information.

A week later there was another break. Al Springer was a motorcycle gang member whom Manson had tried to recruit to do wet work. He had refused and fled after Manson had implicitly threatened him by describing the murders. Springer was a star witness whose testimony, along with that of Castro and Howard, finally woke up the LA Sheriff's Department and the LAPD to Manson's role.

On 18 November, Deputy District Attorney Vincent Bugliosi was assigned to the case. It was his role to bring all of the disparate strands of the investigation together and determine exactly what was going on with the Family. This was an exhausting process and, as Bugliosi describes in his book *Helter Skelter,* when he finally indicted Manson and his murderous followers for murder on 8 December 1969, the case would turn into the longest and most expensive in Californian history.

When the trial began, on 16 June 1970, the key challenge faced by Bugliosi was to prove that Manson was the mastermind behind the killings even though he had not committed them all personally. Bugliosi's argument was actually helped by the cult members who appeared in court to support Charlie. He could silence them with a glance and he could orchestrate protests, sit-ins and other bizarre behavior with a whispered order or a furtively passed note. The most striking evidence of the total command he held, even while incarcerated, was when he carved the swastika in his forehead. Many of his young female acolytes shaved their heads and did the exact same thing. When they all trooped into court with bloody wounds on their foreheads, they proved that Manson had total control over his followers.

Assisting Manson was the defense attorney, Irving Kanarek, whose default position was 'Objection your honor.' Manson was pleased with Kanarek's dogged defense, but was less impressed by the assistant defense attorney, Ronald Hughes. When the latter went on leave, exhausted after the marathon trial, he went missing. Almost six months later his body was found near Sespe Creek, the victim of foul play. Before taking off, Hughes had been increasingly anxious about Manson's attitude towards him. It appears that members of the Family had followed the attorney and executed him in the California wilderness.

Hughes was not the only one to feel Manson's wrath, even while the guru was incarcerated. On 5 November 1969, a distressed young woman called the police declaring that 'Zero' – John Haught, a disenchanted member of the Family – had committed suicide while playing Russian roulette. A shoddy police investigation allowed the suicide ruling to stand, even though it appears that female acolytes had been present.

These machinations came to naught and on 25 January 1971, after a seven-month-long trial, the defendants were found guilty. They were all sentenced to death, then commuted to life in prison after the law was changed to prohibit capital punishment. This did not stop the killings and it is estimated that, in all, at least 49 people died at the hands of the Family during its bloody existence. Manson's first devotee, Mary Brunner, even tried to hijack a plane with the intention of shooting one hostage every hour until Manson and his murderous cohorts were freed.

This all came to naught and on 19 November 2017 Manson died in prison hospital.

CHAPTER SIX

The Movement for the Restoration of the Ten Commandments of God: Ugandan Utopia

Revelation Book 8

6 Then the seven angels who had the seven trumpets prepared to sound them.
7 The first angel sounded his trumpet, and there came hail and fire mixed with
blood, and it was hurled down on the earth. A third of the earth was burned
up, a third of the trees were burned up, and all the green grass was burned up.
8 The second angel sounded his trumpet, and something like a huge mountain,
all ablaze, was thrown into the sea. A third of the sea turned into blood.
9 A third of the living creatures in the sea died, and a third of the ships were
destroyed.
10 The third angel sounded his trumpet, and a great star, blazing like a torch, fell
from the sky on a third of the rivers and on the springs of water.
11 The name of the star is Wormwood. A third of the waters turned bitter, and
many people died from the waters that had become bitter.
12 The fourth angel sounded his trumpet, and a third of the sun was struck, a

third of the moon, and a third of the stars, so that a third of them turned dark. A third of the day was without light, and also a third of the night.

This little-known cult thrived in the heart of Uganda. Three individuals - Joseph Kibwetere, Credonia Mwerinde and the fallen priest Reverend Father Dominic Kataribabo - were able to convince thousands of Ugandans that they were in personal contact with Christ and his mother, the Virgin Mary.

Jesus and the Madonna informed the cult leaders that all who followed the Movement for the Restoration of the Ten Commandments of God would be able to ascend to heaven, while all other humans were doomed to perish in the coming Armageddon. Cult members, estimated to number up to 5000, only had to hand over all of their property to the leadership, stop speaking to each other and resist all sexual activity to earn a place in God's kingdom. By following these guidelines, explained the cult leaders, it was impossible to break the ten commandments!

When the promised Armageddon failed to eventuate, many of the cult's members became disenchanted. There was only one remedy: baptism by fire.

Genesis

A magnificent fraud was perpetrated upon the people of Uganda by the three leaders of the Movement for the Restoration of the Ten Commandments.

The first member of the unholy trinity, Joseph Kibwetere, was a popular man. Born in the village of Ruguma, the young man completed teacher's training in 1955. A Catholic, Kibwetere set an example to his community through his industriousness and good nature. In 1960 he married a woman named Theresa. All seemed to be going well until the newly independent nation held its first elections in the 1960s. A corrupt Protestant-led government subverted the fledgling democracy and the reign of Idi Amin turned the fertile and prosperous land into a hellish police state. After Amin fled, the new government continued to harass and even assassinate high profile Catholics. Kibwetere went into exile. For many years he was denied contact with Theresa and their 16 children. It was no doubt during this time that he formed a dark view of the world.

He also lost his grip on reality. In 1984, Jesus Christ and the Virgin Mary visited Kibwetere and explained that they were charging him with leading humanity back to the straight and narrow of Christianity. Just as God had passed the Ten Commandments to Moses, they were now being passed to Kibwetere.

When a sympathetic government was formed in the capital of Kampala, in 1986, Kibwetere returned to the bosom of his family. He took his vision with him. So fixated was he on the idea that only he could lead Africa to a new spiritual state, and so grandiose were his delusions, that he was subject to several confinements in mental institutions in Kampala. Only a continued course of anti-psychotic drugs could manage Kibwetere's delusions. Later, when with his fellow leaders, he stopped taking them altogether.

The second leader of the cult, Dominic Kataribabo, also began life in promising circumstances. His loving parents put him through an expensive education. Kataribabo proved to be a very bright boy and he soon began training to become a Roman Catholic priest. His photographic memory and proficiency with Latin saw him ordained as a priest in 1957. The Catholic world seemed to be his oyster, but it seems that a number of times he was disappointed with his postings and became resentful of a church that was not able to recognize his worth.

The ambitious priest was sent to a minor seminary where he became increasingly embittered. He also became viscous and unpredictable. No doubt frustrated at his humble posting, Kataribabo began to take his anger out on his students. The slower learners came in for particular attention and their teacher would oscillate from benign paternalism to vicious verbal and physical attacks. A minor infraction would set Kataribabo off – a whole class was expelled thanks to one individual's small act of defiance.

Nevertheless, the young priest established a good reputation with his parishioners. He set a good example in piety and ensured that his flock received spiritual nourishment as well as food and water. Kataribabo had one other strength that made him perfect for administering to superstitions villagers: he believed that with prayer, fasting and a rejection of sin he could send evil spirits packing. Ugandan traditional belief systems held that minor ailments or strokes of ill fortune were caused by evil spirits or witchcraft. Rather than dismissing these fears out of hand, Kataribabo respected the parishioners' beliefs.

Through hard work and disciplined self-control, Father Dominic was able to transfer to Loyola Marymount University, a prestigious Jesuit College in Los Angeles, where he earned a doctorate in theology. In this role he performed pastoral duties including the hearing of confessions. No doubt the many and varied ways in which the residents of Los Angeles were able to break the ten commandments was something of an eye opener to the young African whose roots were in Ugandan village life.

When he returned to Uganda, Kataribabo was sure he could secure a prestigious appointment at Makerere University, Kampala – the country's premier institute of higher learning. Such an appointment usually led to a clear run to an appointment as bishop.

It was not to be. Despite his ambition, or maybe because of it, Father Dominic found himself posted to a teacher's college. The ambitious young man swallowed his pride and accepted the posting, but before he could take up the role another shock eventuated. Kataribabo was given another posting – he would return to Rugazi, his hometown. This humiliation placed the young man as far as possible from the tree-lined avenues of Kampala or the dynamic hub of Los Angeles. It is clear that rather than accepting the post with humility, the ambitious priest became disenchanted with the Roman Catholic Church. Perhaps the Marxists were right, he may have thought, perhaps the church was an anachronistic institution removed from its parishioners and any real spirituality.

Thus the disillusioned priest was well primed when he encountered Joseph Kibwetere, who spoke of the corruption engulfing the church and the ability of people to flout the ten commandments without any real consequences. The priest was so disenchanted with the church hierarchy that he was able to disown the Pope as God's representative and accept that the manic school teacher and the young sex worker, Credonia Mwerinde, were the vessels chosen by Jesus and Mary to renew the decaying church and bring about the spiritual renewal of Uganda and even the world.

Kataribabo was not the only priest to jump on the Kibwetere/Mwerinde bandwagon. Father Paul Ikazire and Father Kasapurali also despaired at the state of the church and felt that the two prophets would be able to rekindle the embers of faith.

The final figure in this triumvirate of false prophets was Credonia Mwerinde. It seems this woman was always looking out for number one. Despite coming from a staunchly devout Catholic family with the means to provide their daughter with a good education, Mwerinde decided that writing and reading were not on her to-do list and dropped out after four years of primary education.

Even at an early age Mwerinde employed deception to get by. From her early adolescence to her late teens she entered six marriage contracts, but canceled them all when she tired of her prospective mates. She was described even at this early age as difficult and cantankerous, with the morals of the farmyard. No doubt some of the engagements were broken off when her fiancés found out about her infidelities.

In her early twenties, Mwerinde embarked upon a career as a sex worker. This lasted for several years until, tiring of the lifestyle, she returned to her home village of Kanunga. No doubt her reputation preceded her, but that made no difference to the five men who married Mwerinde - all stormy marriages ending in divorce. Mwerinde was not made out for a life of domestic drudgery at the beck and call of a man in a traditionally patriarchal society.

She developed two key skills during the late 70s and early 80s. Mwerinde ran a pub and became involved in local politics. It was in this latter role that she discovered a talent for public speaking; her emotive use of language was a powerful tool for swaying public opinion at large party rallies. Mwerinde tried to use her political connections in several extortion attempts, but even a notoriously corrupt judge saw through her scheme and chucked it out of court.

She was viewed with mistrust by her neighbors, which was exacerbated by some botched attempts at sorcery. A potion administered to her brother-in-law in an attempt to stop his wandering ways resulted in the poor fellow vomiting until he died.

Even with her virtual ostracism from her fellow Kanangians, Mwerinde managed to find husband number six. He too owned a pub. It began as a prosperous affair, but once he handed it over to his wife to manage it soon went bankrupt. It appears that she was drinking the profits. Mwerinde's husband accused her of reverting to her sex work in the back of the bar and the marriage descended into an acrimonious shouting match.

Mwerinde developed a unique strategy to save her marriage. In 1988 she began to experience visions of the Madonna at a local holy site. She pleaded with her husband to come to Nyabugoto rock and see the miracle for himself. She explained that she had been witness to revelations since 1986. Once he saw the Madonna, Mwerinde said, he could sell his remaining assets, hand them over to his wife and lead a life devoid of distractions, filled with holy enlightenment. Husband number six smelt a spiritual rat and divorced his wife in 1988.

This may have been too much for Mwerinde. She took herself from the hostile community of Kananga to Western Uganda and joined the entourage of another prophetess, Gaudia Kamushwa. The two became firm friends and both had visitations on an almost daily basis.

Soon others were flocking to what became known as the Gaudia Cult. Ursula Komuhangi, Mwerinde's younger sister, was among the new adherents and she too began to have daily revelations.

Joseph Kibwetere saw his opportunity to ingratiate himself with the new prophets, and, with his wife Theresa, he hosted the two sisters in their comfortable Ruguma home. Here Kibwetere, Mwerinde and Ursula joined forces and founded the Movement for the Restoration of the Ten Commandments of God. Kibwetere assumed the title of Prophet while Mwerinde was named the Programmer. Her daily communications with the Virgin Mary allowed her to pass on actions, or 'the program,' to Joseph.

The next task of the leaders was to appoint twelve apostles. Jesus Christ began to reveal his will to Mwerinde. He explained that previously he had anointed twelve male apostles, but that had been a mistake. This time he would appoint members of both sexes. Their role was to lead his chosen church against the wiles of Satan, to enforce the ten commandments and to drive out evil spirits and devils from poor possessed Ugandans. Mwerinde, Ursula and Theresa were chosen, as was Father Dominic Kataribabo, who had been attracted to the new cult. He readily accepted his role despite being contacted by the bishop, his friends and family, and other priests he had trained with. Alternating entreaties to abandon the cult and threats of excommunication if he refused did nothing to dissuade the priest.

Kataribabo took the decisive step to join the new church. He was told to leave his parish and that he could no longer administer the rites of the Catholic Church; he was in essence defrocked. Despite this, Kataribabo continued to wear his priest's garb in the following years and administered the sacraments to members of the new church. His appearance added an air of credibility to the cult leadership and both Mwerinde and Kibwetere soon began to wear clerical gear. Joseph Kibwetere was not content wearing the clothes of a humble priest; as the prophet of the new church he decked himself out in a bishop's regalia. He wore a purple cassock with the traditional black sash around his waist.

While not wearing a bishop's miter, he did seek to rival the Christian church by proving his immortality. One day Kibwetere's wife Theresa was informed that he had died. His funeral party was already on the way to bury the corpse. When his wife asked to view the body she was turned away. Suspicious that some sort of spiritual shenanigans were under way, and fed up with the cult's intrusion into her private life, Theresa reported the matter to the police. They forced the coffin open and found it full of rocks. Kibwetere had faked his own death and intended to appear three days later – proof of his divinity would be established for all time.

Although not all of the 'divine manifestations' came off as planned, the charismatic cult began to attract followers from all over Uganda. Their combination of traditional teachings and divine revelations were a potent mix.

Bizarre Beliefs

Many Ugandans must have been delighted to hear such a strong message coming from their prophets. The Madonna did not deign to visit only one of the cult leaders but all of them – repeatedly! There could be no doubt what the Movement for the Restoration of the Ten Commandments of God stood for.

Credonia Mwerinde received her first 'blessing' on 14 June 1989. The Virgin Mary declared that she had a message for all who lived on Earth. Regardless of race or gender, all who lived on the Earth could receive her blessing. Christ wanted to contribute his two cents and declared that even Muslims and pagans could be saved. The holy pair had returned to Earth and wanted to tell all humans that by following Mwerinde's teachings they would be saved from eternal damnation.

Mwerinde was transported to heaven by the blessed pair and there she was able to witness a divine quarrel. God declared that all of humanity had turned from his teachings and as a result He was determined to destroy each and every person on Earth and even the planet itself! Jesus and Mary were shocked to hear that the divine thunderbolt would soon be heading earthward and the Mother of Christ knelt in front of God, pleading for mercy. God declared that since humans had shown such disrespect by crucifying Jesus He would not give them a second chance. The Madonna, seeing the urgency of the situation, prostrated herself in front of the holy throne, wailing and weeping for humanity. Thankfully, as Mwerinde explained, Jesus stepped in and asked his father to give humans a bit of leeway if he could speak through a new representative on Earth.

Finally, God relented. As long as individuals listened to his message He might just allow some lucky folks to survive. But, declared God, He had already begun punishing wayward humans with the lethal effects of AIDS and there were a whole lot of other nasty tricks he was willing to unleash on unbelievers. For those who repented, He could give an instantaneous cure to the 20th century scourge.

He would allow the Madonna and Christ to communicate through Mwerinde in a last ditch effort to save humanity. In the ensuing months the two divine personages had much more advice for their chosen one.

Most cults seek to encapsulate their message in written form. The Movement for the Restoration of the Ten Commandments was no different. Dominic Kataribabo, with his extensive training in the Catholic church, was best suited to the task and he produced the cult's seminal work: 'A Timely Message from Heaven: the End of Present Times.' Emblazoned with a crucified Christ on its cover, this became the fount of most sermons preached to the captivated cult followers.

The first duty of any who sought salvation was punctual arrival at church. The Madonna was obviously something of a dilettante and she instructed that the first order of church business should be the absolution of sins by the presiding apostle. Any members who ambled into church late would not receive the blessing. Alcohol consumption was frowned upon; a drunkard broke all ten commandments with one drink.

Other rules of behavior were laid down. Prayer should be practiced with other believers. Extramarital sex was a definite no-no. Sex before marriage was off the table and none should try to attract the opposite sex by wearing miniskirts or by behaving in a coquettish manner. The 'Timely Message From Heaven' went into great detail on this topic.

The 'Message' returns time and time again to the importance of providing tithes to the church. The worst-case scenario was a regular small stipend, but in an ideal world all of a cult member's goods should be signed over to the leadership. A member was required to work for six days of the week. The seventh day, Sunday, was a day of rest – from work at least. Each member was expected to return to their hometown and family. Here the devoted followers were to convince their relatives and friends to join the church. Or at least give a donation.

By these strictures the members of the Movement would cleanse Satan from their soul. When Christ or the Madonna possessed the apostles they railed against Satan and his minions, who were everywhere. God had given his son and Madonna a limited time to convert humanity. The world as it was would end on 29 December 1999.

Dominic Kataribabo made that most fundamental of mistakes. He came up with an exact date for the end of days.

A gloomy picture was painted of the coming Armageddon. AIDS was the first visitation from an angry God. The pain and distress that the disease was causing was merely a foretaste of the coming crisis. Soon a violent wind would arise from the East. Even the finest mansion would crumble before its fury. Crops would be leveled and the mightiest trees would be tossed about like matchsticks. To finish the destruction there would be swarms of huge locusts that would block out the sun and eat any remaining crops. In His infinite wisdom and fury, God would make these locusts poisonous; any who ate them would die a horrific, lingering death. Some might seek to deny the Lord and hoard food, but He would send a horde of nasty little pointy-toothed demons into their larders to spoil the food and even snatch sustenance out of the mouths of babes. Humanity would descend into a cannibalistic orgy. They could not eat beef or drink alcohol; all beverages would be tainted by the Lord and turned into the most lethal poison.

Snakes would then emerge from the bowels of the Earth – some the size of ocean liners would stretch over the globe. Smaller snakes would breed in fantastic numbers. Rather than being docile and shy, the avenging serpents would become incredibly aggressive while their venom would become 100 times more lethal. Their skin would transform from smooth scales to sharp needles and they would cover so much of the land that no one would be able to walk without stepping upon them.

An angry God would then deliver His grand finale – a real showstopper. A violent earthquake would tear apart the continents. Mountains would become valleys and valleys would be thrown up to become mountains. Clouds would become heavy and leaden, they would fall from the sky and squash the air from unbelievers. Hell on Earth would descend. Darling nursing infants were to be replaced by jaguars feeding from the breast. Water would turn into poisonous blood. During this time only the 'redeemed', the members of the Movement for the Restoration of the Ten Commandments, would survive. They were to be housed in safe houses called 'arks' built on cult land. On the 29th all unrepentant sinners would vanish. The redeemed would shelter in their arks for three days and three nights of absolute darkness. Stars were to be erased and the inky blackness would be so complete that no artificial light would cut through its murky fog.

After three days the 'redeemed' would wake to a perfect world. It was to be absolutely flat with abundant crops, perfect children playing happily outdoors with no predators, sickness or dangers of any kind. Each cult member would have a house with electricity and running water. None would argue, children would be obedient and, since there was no sickness, there would be no need for hospitals or doctors. A holy highway would connect heaven and earth. Silver vehicles would be on permanent standby so that any who chose to could whiz upstairs and have a chat with God, Madonna, Christ and the angels.

With such spiritual riches on hand, how could anybody in their right mind reject the teachings of the divine Mwerinde?

Attraction, Initiation and Control

Thousands were flocking to the Church of the Movement for the Restoration of the Ten Commandments of God. Years of civil conflict, government mismanagement and corruption had led to a disenfranchised peasantry barely able to get by on their small plots. Whatever taxes were extorted from the people were secreted away by the fat cats in Kampala. At the same time, hundreds of fringe religious movements sought to use the old tribal remedies or superstitions blended with Catholic or Muslim orthodoxy to try and lure the disenchanted into their clutches.

What set the Movement for the Restoration of the Ten Commandments of God apart from other cults was the presence of three ordained priests, even though they had been defrocked. The trio continued to wear the garb of the clergy and administer the sacraments. Many found the combination of charismatic message given by the 'revelations' and traditional Catholic practices to be irresistible.

The leaders of this cult had one more ace up their sleeves. The Madonna, who no doubt had a fair knowledge of how cults were organized, had taken a personal interest in the initiation process for new members. She had revealed the program in great detail to one of the apostles.

The Virgin Mary ordered that prospective members first had to be clothed in spiritual armor to fight the temptations of the devil. They were required to turn up at one of the learning centers that were popping up around Uganda on a Monday or a Friday. These were the Christian fasting days and the Virgin Mary explained that Satan was scared of people who were fasting. The aspirants therefore were required to turn up with an empty stomach on the chosen days at 8 am, before embarking on an eight-hour day of education. Rolls were taken and Mary would punish any who were late in the afterlife.

The first session instructed on spiritual hygiene. All frippery was to be removed. Hair was to be shaved off the head and from the pubic region. Nail polish and makeup was forbidden, as were deodorants or strong soaps. Artificial scents were the work of the devil. Once the correct appearance had been achieved, the aspirants were schooled in spiritual cleansing.

The seers explained that the Virgin Mary detested individuals who were obsessed with worldly wealth. Money and property were chains that would drag non-believers down to hell. They should be surrendered to the cult coffers immediately. Many took the message to heart and sold off all their worldly goods. Families were impoverished and even wealthy Ugandans fell for the con. One prosperous farmer sold off an immense herd of cattle and donated the proceeds, thousands of dollars worth of cash, to the cult coffers.

For the next ten weeks of training, each of the ten commandments was dealt with in detail. Initiates were urged to examine their own past and detail to their classmates how they had lived in the sink of depravity. Along with this emotional purging were fiery speeches and sermons where the pure teachings of the Madonna and Christ were repeatedly thrust upon the aspirants.

Once the seers deemed that the new recruits were sufficiently indoctrinated, they were invited to be reborn into the caste of God's chosen people. Only they would survive the three days of darkness. Amidst much wailing and beating of drums the cleansed initiates shed their worldly clothes, ate a concoction of human blood mixed with burnt hair and, finally, donned their cult robes. These simple garments became their everyday wear and the color was determined by how much wealth they had donated to cult coffers.

For particularly fervent (or physically attractive) initiates there was another ceremony. Omukago is a traditional Ugandan practice where two individuals cut their palms and join hands in a symbolic mixing of blood. This symbolizes an eternal bond. If one of the twelve disciples took a fancy to the initiate, they joined with the chosen individual by performing Omukago. This elevated them to the kingdom of God for eternity. AIDS was of course ravaging central Africa during this period, making Omukago a particularly dangerous procedure. But if the Madonna had ordered it, who was to complain?

Once the initiation ceremony had been completed, cultists were encouraged to sell the last of their worldly goods and relocate to one of the cult compounds.

In 1991 the cult was given a large tract of land in Kanungu by Mwerinde and Ursula's father. The group relocated to the prime patch of fertile ground. Using funds donated by members, a church was soon erected on the land, as well as two long dormitories, one for men and one for women.

Soon a place unlike any on Earth developed. Every aspect of life in the compound was strictly regulated. Simple, flowing robes were worn by all members. The top echelons of the cult were allowed to wear white, floor length robes and white veils if they were female. The clothes were very similar to a nun's habit. Kataribabo and the other two ex-priests continued to wear their black suits with white collars, borrowing the prestige, without membership, of the Catholic hierarchy. The lay members who had contributed significant sums of money when joining the organization were allowed to wear green robes. The majority, the poor peasants who had flocked to Mwerinde's messianic vision, were only permitted to wear a long black robe – very uncomfortable garb for the menial tasks they performed. These robes had to sweep the ground; the physique had to be covered lest the evil of sexual attraction filter into the sacred compound. Underwear was strictly forbidden. Confused reasons of hygiene were given for this rule but it in reality it was a cost cutting measure.

The reason given for this strict dress code? When the last trumpet sounded, heralding Armageddon, heavenly angels would descend to Earth to carry the true followers of the ten commandments to heaven. Their work would be cut out for them in this task, but the faithful would stand out from the rest of humanity in white, green and black robes, allowing easy identification by the heavenly host.

One other aspect of life in the Kanunga compound set it apart. As the devotees scuttled about their daily business, not one word was spoken. Those who spoke risked breaking any of the ten commandments so it was best if all were silent. Only the wealthiest benefactors were excluded from this rule.

A complex sign language was developed. The members could of course speak when performing the rituals and prayers, or when they begged for absolution from the cult leaders. There was another carrot held out to the cult members to ensure silence: by maintaining silence they too might be privileged and hear Jesus or Mary as they went about their daily chores.

The followers had chores aplenty. As well as surrendering all of their worldly possessions, the members of the Church of the Ten Commandments spent their days in a camp dedicated to hard labor and prayer. The day began at 4 am when the cultists were subjected to a morning service that lasted for up to four hours. Led by one of the ex-priests, the followers were given the blood and body of Christ. In this case the wine did turn to blood. Or at least it was replaced by sheep's blood. Some say that as the cult was radicalized, human blood was given out in the pre-dawn light. Whatever the actual substance, the parishioners were told that if they tasted blood they had begun the process of ascending to heaven.

The cultists then began their daily chores on the estate. They toiled in the tropical heat like an army of black robed ants. Clearing weeds, shifting dirt, carrying water in large buckets, sowing, hoeing, planting and harvesting. A range of animals were tended to including fowl, cattle and goat. Ten-hour working days were the norm, all in absolute silence.

The 'disciples' were not entirely devoid of feeling. Their subjects were allowed 20 or 30 minute breaks during the working day. However, since idle hands do the devil's work, there was always a disciple on hand during these rest breaks to preach the latest revelations delivered to the leaders and instruct the members regarding the painful death that awaits unbelievers in the coming holocaust. After hours and hours of backbreaking labor, the cultists were treated to an austere dinner. Thin gruel was served up with lots of jugs of holy water. Meat was off the menu for everyone except the leaders.

At the front of the compound was a retail outlet that became known in the region for its abundant and competitively priced supply of meat, eggs and dairy products. None of the income from the shop went into the pockets of the workers. The farm manager, an ex-policeman known as Kananga, was always on hand to make sure that visitors took positive reports to the outside world.

After dinner there was another lengthy sermon and prayer session. Credonia Mwerinde, one of the priests or Joseph Kibwetere were sure to preside over these. Their latest missives from the Madonna or Christ were shared with the exhausted flock. These were no gentle discussions or calm dissertations. Cultists were treated to fire and brimstone harangues, guaranteed to keep them subservient and loyal. The exhausted workers went to bed at midnight, grateful for the reassurance that they were already, through their labors and piety, guaranteed a role in the future chastisement of mankind.

Whispers also began to arise claiming that cultists who were disloyal and had sought escape were intercepted by Kananga. They were still at the compound, it was said, buried at the bottom of disused latrine pits.

As the exhausted laborers staggered off to their uncomfortable pallets, the leaders of the church were able to view their domains with satisfaction. The farm was generating wealth beyond their wildest dreams. The followers were obedient and hardworking; even if they had doubts there was no means to express them. The Madonna and Jesus were never going to cease communicating the desired revelations to the leadership.

There was, however, one hiccup. With the founding of the Movement for the Restoration of the Ten Commandments of God, Mwerinde decided that it was important to provide for the future needs of the new kingdom. She instructed Kibwetere, the educator, to set up a boarding school to prepare her flock's children for the coming salvation. Subjects such as mathematics, history, geography and English were, according to the programmer, tools of the devil. A new syllabus was required. Obeying the wishes of the Madonna and Christ, a splendid new school – the Rescue Place for the Virgin Mary Primary School – was opened amidst much fanfare. Many politicians, keen to be associated with the thriving new church and intent on getting a free meal, were present, along with local brass bands, to welcome the new institution.

The gloss wore off fairly soon. As with most cult institutions, the role of the Rescue Place for the Virgin Mary Primary School was to isolate its pupils from the rest of society, indoctrinate them and subject them to soul breaking privations. At 7 am the pupils had to report to a parade ground clothed in their simple tunics. The first period of the day would be spent in repetitive prayer. Many of the students were groggy from spending a difficult night sleeping on bare concrete floors without blankets.

After morning prayer, the children were given a thin corn porridge, which was also dished up for lunch. In between classes that preached loyalty to the cult and a deadly fear of AIDS, the students spent hours laboring in the cult fields and plantations. Some tended the large fields of maize, beans and bananas, while others spent their day gathering firewood, cleaning and performing other manual labors. Children were harshly punished for questioning the cult's teachings and the entire academic curriculum revolved around the prophet's and the programmer's interpretation of the ten commandments.

Not surprisingly, reports of malnutrition, dysentery, malaria and respiratory illnesses began to filter into the surrounding communities. Government inspectors were horrified at the conditions and the curriculum imposed upon the pupils of the Rescue Place for the Virgin Mary Primary School, and in 1998 the Department of Education shut it down. It was felt that a school which taught one subject – the inevitable coming of the end of the world – did not really satisfy the demands of a modern curriculum.

Despite this setback, things were going well. The cult leadership had no reason to think that anybody would interfere with the rivers of gold streaming into the church treasury. The one catch was the date given for the coming Armageddon, 29 December 1999. This one error led to the destruction of the cult and a fiery death for almost 1000 people.

Armageddon

As the exhausted cultists collapsed onto their uncomfortable beds, they would have had little solace for their tribulations. Mwerinde had declared that fornication was the ultimate sin, even if it was between husband and wife. Families had been split up, with men in one dormitory and women in the other. Children were removed from their parents altogether. If the filial bonds were particularly strong, the family members would be shunted off to different encampments. Sex between husband and wife was forbidden and a severe beating was on the cards if they were discovered in the act.

There were no such strictures for the leadership. Among the virtues they preached were austerity, moderation, celibacy and abstinence. They talked the talk but did not walk the walk of Christian piety. While overworked subordinates sat through the evening sermons before collapsing into an exhausted sleep, the sounds of increasingly rowdy partying could be heard from the disciples' compound. These quarters were well away from the huge dormitories of the followers.

Parties were held with throbbing disco tracks, dancing, flashing lights and huge trays of roast goat and beef along with a liberal supply of alcohol. The parties degenerated into drunken orgies. Father Dominic Kataribabo was bisexual with a preference for young men. He surrounded himself with attractive young cult members. Occasionally, particularly attractive cultists would be summoned to the dormitory and treated to several evenings of debauched excess. The following morning, they would be ushered into the presence of Estate Manager Kananga. He would threaten all kinds of punishments to the kith and kin of the member should she or he ever blow the whistle on the depraved activities.

Soon rumors of cannibalism began to spread. Included in the platters of meat, according to the whispered accusations, were human body parts. Combined with the alcoholic punch was infant blood. One cultist was promised that she would be promoted to the inner sanctum and allowed to leave the days of agricultural drudgery, if only she would offer up her infant to the night's celebrations. She refused and was one of the few individuals to escape. Mwerinde was seen staggering out of the evening revels. Her white robes were stained with alcohol and blood, her lips and chin covered in the red liquid. The representative of the Madonna and Christ looked more like a sated vampire than a religious leader.

The wild parties conducted by the leadership and the harsh lifestyle of the cultists seemed to intensify as 1999 came to an end. With good reason - all were convinced that Armageddon was coming. Unbeknown to the members of the church, this date would signal the approach of the final bloody end of the cult.

The cultists must have relished the idea of the coming apocalypse. They would be released from their daily drudgery and privation and enter a celestial kingdom of pure and everlasting joy. As the date approached, particular attention was paid to bringing the estate and its chapel up to a pristine condition. Tropical flowers were used to decorate the buildings and every surface was scrubbed clean.

The entire compound went to sleep on that last night dreaming of the new age. On the 29th they arose. Nothing unusual had happened. As the hours ticked by it was clear there would be no end of the world. On the 30th the sun still rose and set. The cult leaders scrambled to adapt: there had been a tiny miscalculation; 3 December 1999 was going to be the first of the three dark days.

As the new millennium was ushered in around the world, the members of the Movement for the Restoration of the Ten Commandments awoke to find that, rather than an impenetrable darkness that canceled out even the brightest of lights, the sun was rising in the sky. Outrage met this development. Such was the intensity of emotion that even the most stringent rule, the rule of silence, was broken. Men and women stormed out of their dormitories and marched in an angry mob to the cult leaders' compound. Those in the green robes, the ones who had contributed the most funds to the Movement, were particularly strident in their shouts of betrayal. Many demanded that all of their money be returned immediately. A steady stream of people packed up their meager possessions and left the estate.

The leadership had anticipated this. No doubt cursing Kataribabo for giving a date for the new age, Mwerinde appeared to her flock. An apparition had appeared, claimed the programmer, and explained that the end of the world would now happen between that sunny morning and 31 December 2000. This was soon backed up by the Prophet Kibwetere. He announced that he had spoken to Jesus Christ, who explained that the generation would now end before 2001.

The more optimistic or fanatical gave the leadership the benefit of the doubt. Some even saw it as a God-given opportunity to recruit members of their families to the cult so they could enjoy the new kingdom too.

Many were not so accommodating. The calls for restitution became more forceful, as did the calls for a more specific date. Such was the challenge to the leaders' authority that they came up with a scheme to limit dissent. Those who were most vocal in their opposition would be summoned to a personal rendezvous with either Jesus or Mary at one of the four cult learning centers. The more compliant were told that the Madonna would reveal herself on 17 March 2000 at the main compound in Kanungu. The leaders knew that this was just a Band-Aid to maintain control. A longer-term solution was required.

This longer-term solution involved mass murder.

In January 2000 members of the cult noticed members of Interahamwe, a paramilitary group, hanging about the cult learning centers and minor compounds. They stood out. Rather than wearing cult robes, the young men wore tattered jeans and dirty T-shirts. They had a vicious cast to their eye. The Swahili-speaking men were refugees from Rwanda. Interahamwe can be roughly translated as 'hit man' – stateless individuals who hid in the lawless places of Central Africa and the Congo. Participants in countless atrocities in Rwanda and adjoining countries, for a small payment they would commit any murder.

Dissident members were summoned to cult centers in Western Uganda to have their one-on-one meetings with the Madonna. As the enraptured cultists entered the small chapels, they expected to be bathed in a celestial glow. Instead, rough hands pulled them to the floor, slashed their throats and collected their blood. Some were strangled or beaten to death. Rude trenches had been dug behind the centers and the lifeless bodies were tossed into them. Any blood that had been gathered would be used in cult ceremonies.

At least those who dared to question the murderous triumvirate's teachings were given a relatively quick death. Kataribabo, Mwerinde and Kibwetere had something much worse in store for the true believers. In rural cult compounds, chapels were converted to arks in preparation for the March date laid down by the Madonna. Thick blinds were installed, as were strong locks covering doors and windows. Kanungu was still the largest compound and farm and it was to this location that most cultists were summoned.

The leaders wanted to make sure both past and present members were accounted for. Newspapers and radio ads called for ex-members to come back and meet the Madonna by 17 March. New recruits were also sought. Some ex-members heeded the call. One fellow sold his house and land for a pittance and explained to his shocked neighbors that he would not need any wealth or assets where he was going. He was right, but not for the reason he believed.

Kataribabo, the ex-priest, took an active hand in the planned holocaust. He was driven into Kasese by his chauffer and purchased 40 litres (10 gallons) of sulfuric acid and 60 litres (15 gallons) of paraffin. No doubt the townspeople of Kasese wondered what a priest wanted with such chemicals, but the respect paid to a clerical collar would have discouraged any intrusive questions.

By the time Kataribabo arrived back at Kanungu with his deadly cargo, over 500 people were assembled and partaking of their last supper. Rules had been dispensed with and they gorged on beef, goat and unlimited bottles of Coca Cola. The apostles were present and they urged their flock to have a second, third or even fourth course. After all, the next morning the new age of plenty would arrive – they would have no need for earthly sustenance. On the evening of the 16th the cultists retired to their crude pallets; no doubt many found it difficult to sleep due to excitement about their imminent meeting with the Madonna.

In the morning the believers followed apostles up to the chapel, which had been converted into a secure ark. Children, pregnant women and young men, all freshly shaved, bathed and with clean robes, made their way into the ark to wait through the three days of darkness. The doors and windows were securely bolted to ensure no devils entered and the blackout blinds ensured not a skerrick of light penetrated into the space. The cultists began singing hymns.

At midday on 17 March, farmers tending plots adjoining the Movement for the Restoration of the Ten Commandments compound heard an almighty explosion. A plume of black smoke was observed boiling out of the Kanungu compound and desperate screaming could be heard. Residents from adjoining villages were soon streaming towards the chapel to witness the sturdy building engulfed in flame.

Agonized cries from adults and infants summoned the observers to help, but such was the heat than none could even approach the building. The tin roof burnt like dry tinder and the entire building collapsed in upon itself. Without fire extinguishers there was nothing the stunned observers could do.

When the fire died down only blackened ruins remained. The cultists were charred beyond recognition and most of the corpses seemed to be gathered around the windows as if they had tried to escape. One figure was identifiable: adjacent to the door was a large man wearing a white clerical collar around his neck. Clasped to Father Kataribabo's chest was a baby. In his other hand was a doorknob. It appears that the conflagration had been so fierce that he had not been able to escape. Perhaps in a last gesture of mercy the fallen priest had tried to save one innocent soul.

Over the next two days the Kanunga compound echoed with cries of bereaved family members and the retching of convict laborers. The local lock-up was emptied by guards carrying Kalashnikovs and the prisoners were marched to the ark in single file. Here they were ordered to dig large trenches and bury the charred bodies. Many bodies were intertwined and swollen, making burial difficult. Violence was needed to keep the unwilling prisoners working. Many were serving short sentences for minor tax violations and the manner in which they were forced to work amidst the horrific scene was surely an abuse of their human rights. Many bore psychological wounds after this ordeal, but in the short term they had more pressing concerns – they were not allowed to wash even their hands after performing the labor.

Along with the convicts came hordes of locals seeking to profit from the tragedy. Looters carried off the livestock, religious icons and anything else that was not nailed down. Rumors began to spread alleging that there was a large horde of buried cash. When night fell, avid treasure hunters descended on the plantation, looking for sites where the soil was disturbed. What they found was not gold but decomposing flesh. The fire on 17 March was, it appeared, merely the climax of a murderous spree that had been going on for months.

Father Dominic Kataribabo had been particularly active. Maybe he felt he had to make amends to his fellow leaders since he had made the catastrophic blunder of giving a firm date for the apocalypse. It also became clear why he needed the acid he had bought along with the paraffin before the fire. At the fallen cleric's sugar estate in Rugazi, 73 corpses were dug up from a mass trench. Acid and decomposition made identification almost impossible. He had concealed under his bedroom floor another 81 dead cult members. Hauled from the mass grave with shovels and flung on top of a pile of corpses, the body of one of the young children found in Rugazi barely surfaced before it was unceremoniously thrown back into the dark earth and re-buried. Like most of the others, her name will never be known. Her last minutes will remain unimaginable.

The children pulled from Father Kataribabo's garden and from beneath his home may have been drugged and strangled at one of the other remote sights before being trucked to their graves. Local intoxicants, herbal sedatives and discarded bottles of poison suggest members were weakened and drugged before being killed.

At the town of Rushojwa, a cult learning center had been the scene of more than 80 murders. All had been strangled and stabbed before being buried in a banana garden out the back. At Kampala, 55 corpses had been stacked in the garage. All had been poisoned. It seems that after buying the chemicals Kataribabo had invited members to a banquet. Reports of a few who left early mentioned that the priest had insisted on serving all of his flock himself. No doubt he had laced their drinks with some lethal substance. Police pathologists found it impossible to determine exactly how many had perished, but there were more than 1000 confirmed deaths.

The Ugandan press had a field day reporting the slaughter. It soon emerged that there were many warning signs. For years people had reported to the police that family members had joined the cult and had never been seen again afterwards. The police much preferred to receive kickbacks in the form of food or cash rather than examining the movement too closely. It was unwise to push the police too much – after the atrocities of the Amin years, few were willing to trust them anyway.

There were other rumors. Reports of bloody orgies involving human sacrifice began to surface. It turned out that Friday was a particularly dangerous day to be a child in the cult – that was when they were most likely to be sacrificed. Also emerging was an understanding of the hold Credonia Mwerinde had over the locals. It was believed that she was a powerful sorceress. If any earned her ire, she only had to level a malevolent evil-eye in their direction and they would find their crops, marriage and children cursed for eternity.

The last reported sighting of Kibwetere and Mwerinde was made by a lad who snuck out of the ark on the evening of 16 March 2000. He knew that he would be fasting for three days and wanted to fill his belly first. He later claimed that he saw the two load up a van and drive off. Some reports have Kibwetere dying of AIDS, but even as late as 2014 a claim surfaced that he was hiding in Malawi. Rewards were put up for information leading to the arrest of the entire leadership, including Ursula Mwerinde, Joseph Kasapurari and John Kamagara, but to date none have collected.

CHAPTER SEVEN

The Church of the Lamb: Mormon Assassins

Revelations Book 6

[10] They called out in a loud voice, 'How long, Sovereign Lord, holy and true, until you judge the inhabitants of the earth and avenge our blood?'

Emerging from the harsh borderlands between America and Mexico came one of the most vicious cults in modern history. Originally set up as a seemingly harmless break away from the Church of the Latter-day Saints (Mormons), the Church of the Lamb was taken over by Ervil LeBaron. LeBaron came from a long line of mentally ill individuals. While his ancestors saw visions, heard voices and were possessed by largely benign delusions, LeBaron used his fantasies to build a quasi-religious criminal empire that required all unbelievers to suffer 'blood atonement' – death at the hands of his fanatical assassins. LeBaron's lonely death in a jail cell did not end the killings. It seemed as if he could reach out of the grave and continue a bloody harvest of his spiritual enemies.

Genesis

Most people know Mormons as those polite chaps who wander the streets in immaculate white shirts and neat narrow ties, seeking to spread the Mormon way to unbelievers. The Church of Jesus Christ of Latter-day Saints likes to present this clean cut and wholesome image to the world and it would much prefer us to forget their violent history. Unknown to many, the Mormon Church was founded on blood, madness and megalomania.

Joseph Smith (1805–1844) had his first messianic experience at the age of 17. He was kneeling in prayer when Moroni, an angel of the Lord, appeared, bathed in light, to have a chat with the American youth.

Many of Joseph's neighbors were quite surprised that the teenager had been chosen for a divine role. He was known as a bit of a character, who liked to get up to all kinds of mischief with the local lads. All agreed that he had the gift of the gab and could spin quite a yarn.

And he spun quite a yarn with his revelation. According to Smith, each believer in his new faith had a direct link to God (as long as they were white and male). They were all 'saints' in the new church. The greater the wealth the individual possessed, the greater his saintliness. When Judgment Day came each saint would be seated next to God on His celestial throne. This was all heady stuff and soon spiritually ambitious and financially successful men were flocking to the church.

In 1831 Smith declared that Western Missouri was to be the new promised land. God had told him that he was to found New Zion and await Judgment Day. All others would perish in the inevitable cataclysm that was foretold in Revelation.

For some reason the native Missourians weren't too happy when hordes of Mormons arrived on their doorstep. In 1833 things turned violent and anti-Mormon mobs set about the new settlers. Smith formed an army, called the Danites, and began answering in kind. The Danites were also used to attack dissidents within the church – a precedent that would echo down the years.

The church moved to a new location and its numbers began to swell. Smith decided that since he was infallible the Danites could destroy any who challenged his divine vision. This vision included polygamy (43 women were 'sealed' in the prophet's bed), the raising of an army of 100,000 men to conquer Texas and a proclamation that he alone was the one true king of the Kingdom of God. Some moderates within the church were troubled by Smith's increasingly strident claims, but any who dared resist his growing power were silenced by a violent Danite mob.

Surrounding state militias were anxious about the increasingly lawless sect within their midst and marched on the heart of the Mormon empire. They shot Joseph Smith dead on 27 June 1844.

Brigham Young succeeded Smith as the new ruler of the church. Young emulated his predecessor and declared that the Great Salt Lake basin beyond the Rocky Mountains was to be the New Zion. In 1847 the cult arrived at the new destination and became the dominant power in what was later the state of Utah. Like Smith before him Young proclaimed himself to be the One True Prophet, the Lamb of God and the Chosen One. Brigham Young created another innovation: blood atonement. Those who sin against the church cannot be redeemed on Earth by their actions. But if they are killed on the order of the Chosen One, their blood atones (pays for and cancels) their sins. Simply put, any who are damned by their actions can be sent directly to heaven if they are assassinated on the orders of the leader of the Mormon Church. A sinner could only be saved in the eyes of the Lord if his blood was spilled by somebody more righteous. It was actually an act of love to dispatch a heretic to the afterlife.

Brigham Young sent his cronies to every Mormon household. They were armed with a questionnaire of 26 queries. Each had to be answered truthfully. Some were fairly harmless and dealt with personal hygiene. Others asked about the level of tithing. The most important ones asked if the individuals had ever spoken ill, or had bad thoughts about, his leadership. This set off an extraordinary wave of bloodletting known as the Mormon Reformation. The purification sought by Brigham led to many deaths as suspect Mormons were subjected to blood atonement. The violence culminated in a slaughter of 120 pioneers in Mountain Meadows in southwest Utah. This was too much for the federal government, which dispatched troops to the area in 1857. This intervention, combined with the opening up of the railway, led to the decline of Mormon control of the region.

In 1877 Brigham Young died. He left a legacy of a large flock of hardworking and honest Church of Latter-day Saints. He also left a legacy of violence that could be appropriated by any Mormon who claimed to be the Chosen One.

One such man was Alma Dayer LeBaron. Born on 15 March 1886 in Tempe Arizona, he was bought up as a devout Mormon. Much to Dayer's chagrin, the Church of the Latter-day Saints had sought rapprochement with the American Federal Government. After the turmoil of Brigham Young's and Joseph Smith's rule, the leadership felt that a more moderate approach was required if the Church of Latter-day Saints was to get along with neighboring communities.

In 1890 the fourth leader of the church, William Woodruff, issued the 'Manifesto,' which submitted to federal laws banning the practice of polygamy. To escape this prohibition many Mormons divorced their first wife before marrying another woman, then continued a de facto marriage with the original wife or wives. Alternatively, if a Mormon was determined to live legally married to all of his wives, he could pick up his chattels and move across the border into Mexico.

In 1923 Dayer LeBaron had a series of visions that told him several things. Firstly, God wanted him to marry the maid who had been helping his wife (and mother of their eight children) around the house. Secondly God, who was speaking through the spirit of Dayer's grandfather, commanded him to lead the Mormon priesthood and wear the Crown of Celestial Glory.

In 1924 the monogamous members of the church hounded Dayer and his two wives out of Utah across the border into Mexico. While fleeing, Dayer and his wife Maud conceived their ninth child: Ervil LeBaron. He was born on 22 February 1925. Maybe the dark days of the forced exodus planted a seed of discord in the unborn child's soul. Whatever it was, he proved to be a narcissistic and psychotic individual who was able to turn Mormon theology into an instrument of death and destruction that stretched across decades of misrule.

The family arrived in the Mormon bastion of Colonia Jurez. Unbeknown to Dayer this community which had once thrived on polygamy had turned against the practice with a vengeance. The LeBaron children were mercilessly bullied at school and the civil authorities considered it their duty to turn the citizens of the town against the new arrivals. The Mormon Church excommunicated the family.

This persecution had an effect on the children.

There is an old saying that 'the apple does not fall far from the tree'. Nothing could be truer for Dayer's family. All three of his daughters would suffer delusions of grandiosity or paranoia. Of the seven LeBaron boys, six claimed to hear voices, five would have divine hallucinations and four claimed to be the new Lord's Prophet, taking upon themselves the mantle of Joseph Smith. Dayer and Maud's fourth child, Lucinda, spent most of her days chained by her ankle to a small hut.

In 1944 it all got a bit too much for Dayer. The ongoing persecution for his divinely inspired beliefs was ruining the lives of his children and his wives. Thankfully for the persecuted clan the patriarch had a revelation that he was to move the entire family to a remote windswept hardscrabble parcel of land on the Sierra Madre Valley, about a hundred kilometers from Colonia Juarez. Not much was on the land. A couple of tin shacks vied with a rough adobe house in a desolate wasteland of cacti and sand. Colonia LeBaron was intended by Dayer to become the hub of God's community on Earth.

Just down the road, Dayer's son Ben set up another ranch. He too claimed to be a leader of the church, with a total following of four adherents. Ben took himself pretty seriously and assumed the titles of the One Mighty and Strong, the Elephant Strangler, the Bull Catcher, the Eighth Priest, the World Champion and, finally, the Lion of Judah. Ben proved that he fit these titles by doing hundreds of push-ups, roaring like a lion, and thrashing any of his small flock who showed disrespect.

Ervil became a devotee of his older brother and began to proselytize for his cause. He produced pamphlets proving that Ben was the chosen one, all the while living in a poor shack on the ranch. He adopted Ben's practice of shambling around the countryside dressed in rags and talking to himself.

In 1951 Dayer died. Ben manipulated the situation so that he became heir to the family's claim to divinity. The Kingdom of Ben did not last long and its membership soon fractured.

Ben's younger brother Joel received 19 revelations in one day during 1955. Each revelation had been delivered by one of God's true messengers. These included Adam, Abraham, Moses and Jesus Christ himself. All the messengers agreed on one thing: Joel was to be the new Mighty and Strong, destined to be the Lord's twentieth prophet. His ministry was to be known as the Church of the Firstborn and the Fullness of Time. Joel nominated his younger brother Ervil to be his second in charge or 'Governor General.' Ervil soon proved to be a powerful propagandist, attracting followers to the new faith, and at first the two brothers worked together as a powerful team. New adherents from as far away as France began to join the church.

Joel had invited a viper into his nest. Ervil's character began to sour. His lust for power led to the blood atonement of his brother. And like their true prophet - Jesus Christ - Joel seemed to walk willingly into his death.

Joel impressed his flock with his outward humility. He lived simply, in threadbare clothes, and was averse to using tithes to feather his own nest. While absolutely convinced of the righteousness of his mission, Joel preferred to use reason and gentle persuasion that allowed followers to find their own way to him and his vision. Even today Ervil's brother is remembered for his saintly nature.

While Joel was an effective operator in the spiritual realm, he was much less successful in the real world. In attempts to build his wealth, Joel undertook a succession of costly business ventures that came to naught. Not only were his financial decisions bad, but so was the decision to remove himself from Colonia LeBaron in pursuit of elusive riches, while giving his brother Ervil the responsibility of running the cult property in his absence.

Ervil was given the role of 'Church Patriarch' in 1961. This gave him the power over all of the 'angels' within the church and allowed him to receive and interpret the word of God through revelations. On a more mundane level Ervil was also in charge of rationing, work allocation and, most disturbingly, the church funds. He decided who would work in the broiling Mexican sun eking meager crops from the hardscrabble soil and who got the cushy jobs in the kitchens and store rooms. The Patriarch ensured that his food was always of a higher quality than the rest of the hardworking flock.

Unlike his brother Joel, Ervil was not reluctant to spend the tithes. He outfitted himself in fancy outfits, complete with elaborate boots and a wide brimmed Stetson hat, helping him to add to his bevy of wives. While the rest of the organization made do with battered pick-up trucks, Ervil was seen visiting the cult properties in a shiny new sedan. His manner was dictatorial and, using the oldest trick in the cult leader's handbook, he would overcome any opposition with long, loud, humiliating harangues that, while unintelligible to most of the church, prevented anybody from challenging his logic lest they appear foolish.

Complaints were launched against the increasingly autocratic Ervil and in the early sixties some long time members left. Joel largely ignored these protests and let Ervil get on with his own agenda. This agenda became increasingly preoccupied with increasing his harem of wives. One of the Patriarch's duties was to assign pairings and arrange marriages. Ervil was able to use his position and his many revelations to ensure that the comeliest women moved straight into his bed. Ervil eventually had thirteen wives 'sealed' to him. Their offspring would form the basis of his holy hit squads and would cause much terror and bloodshed further down the track.

By November 1969 Joel could no longer ignore his brother's increasingly autocratic behavior. Ervil began intimating that he was the true prophet and only a blood reckoning would see him take his rightful position as head of the Firstborn Church. His increasingly strident calls for Armageddon alienated many members, who decided to up sticks and leave Colonia LeBaron.

Joel sacked Ervil. Rather than reflecting on his loss of privileges and accepting his demotion with humility, Ervil decided that Joel was Satan and it was his job to remove him. He began a campaign of destabilization against his brother. This involved penning lengthy diatribes condoning violence and an unceasing campaign to attract church members to his side. Joel excommunicated his brother but took no further action. His closest adherents were shocked at the prophet's fatalism in the face of this increasing danger.

On 20 August, Ervil ordered three of his closest followers to kill his brother. The hit would take place in broad daylight in the town of Ensenada. Joel was lured into a vacant house by two of his sibling's adherents to pursue a spiritual discourse. While the three were talking, Dan Jordan, Ervil's chief lieutenant, arrived at the house. He got out of the pickup, walked up the drive and into the house. After a brief greeting the three men set upon Joel. Two of the men held him down while Ben beat him senseless with a kitchen stool. Cries of 'Shoot him' echoed down the street. This was followed by two rapid gunshots before quiet returned to the sleepy Mexican street.

Unbeknown to the killers, Joel's son Ivan had been waiting in his father's Buick and had witnessed the whole thing. The killers came down the drive. At first Ivan thought he too was going to be shot, but the killers proceeded to walk calmly along the street, in full view of a Catholic church congregation waiting for Sunday service. They jumped in a white pick-up truck and drove off.

Ivan got out of his father's car, looking for assistance. None was forthcoming. He walked into the house to find his father lying on the floor. Joel was on his back with his arms above his head and blood running down the side of his face. Police soon arrived. The following investigation revealed what had happened. Joel had been wrestled to the ground, where his arms were pinned to the floor. His mouth was forced open and a pistol barrel was placed in his mouth. The first shot probably grazed out through his throat. The second shot destroyed the brain of the Prophet of the Church of the Firstborn of the Fullness of Times.

Ervil's first hit had reflected the Biblical story of Cain and Able. He had used fratricide to seize control and none would impede his apocalyptic vision.

Bizarre Beliefs

Building on the earlier writings from the Church of Latter-day Saints, Ervil and Joel had cooperated in August 1956 in creating the Firstborn Church's theological opus: Priesthood Expounded. This bestowed authority on the leader of the church and explained the laws by which those who truly lived in the Kingdom of God were to abide.

Strict adherence to the Ten Commandments – 'The perfect laws of liberty' – was required so that the Kingdom of God on Earth would be established. Once this happened Jesus would return to Earth, seize total political power from all governments and full spiritual authority over every faith in the world and rule benevolently for all eternity.

Any who committed treason by engaging in murder or adultery would have to pay for their sins by execution. But Priesthood Expounded went even further. Any who defied the 10 laws or sought to set up an alternative government could pay blood atonement. There was an urgency in the brothers' message. They saw that all of Earth was ruled by sinners and soon it would be engulfed in fire and fury. The United States surely had it coming as it had subverted the will of Joseph Smith and turned

God-fearing Mormons away from the true way of life. Joel and Ervil saw that Colonia LeBaron would attract a gathering of believers who would be the only survivors of the coming apocalypse.

As with all cults, the selfishness and blind egotism of the holy vision was extraordinary. At its founding the Church of the Firstborn and the Fullness of Time had five members. Two brothers – Joel and Ervil – two sisters – Alma and Floren – and their mother would be saved. Everybody else on Earth could burn in hell.

By the early 1960s the church had attracted a large following. When Ervil seized control he radicalized the ideals of the group. While Joel had been satisfied to draw converts to him through his theology, Ervil placed much greater emphasis on the role of the leader. In doing so he was hearkening back to the more strident beliefs of Joseph Smith and Brigham Young.

Drilled into every believer was the idea of the leader's infallibility. None could question his authority without questioning God's. Ervil was able to argue that God spoke to him every day through vivid visions and pronouncements.

One more slice of Mormon history allowed Ervil to turn his followers into a killer cult. The early leaders cultivated a 'them and us' attitude. Those who were against the teachings usually utilized violence to attack the church. Therefore, the act of accumulating arms, undergoing paramilitary training and following 'combat orders' was a means of fulfilling the Prophet of the Church of the Lamb's lawful rule on Earth. Theology gave justification for murder.

While Joel had never really dealt with the 'perfect law of liberty' idea that any individual could be killed for breaking the commandments, Ervil had no reluctance to use violence. During the years after his sacking as the 'Patriarch' he used holy pronouncements to distinguish his theology from his brother's. The key difference was this attitude to violence. He claimed that as all of the Firstborns were the Lord's Chosen People, it was up to them to help bring on the apocalypse and prepare the way for the rule of the church through an active program of violence. A regular feature of Ervil's fiery sermons was the repeated question, who would bear arms for the Lord and kill His enemies? Every government leader, soldier, civil servant and policeman of every nation on Earth were operating in direct contravention of God's law – and could, therefore, be assassinated.

Ervil was becoming increasingly paranoid and the slightest provocation could send him into a paroxysm of rage. He would often enter a manic state and could go for three or four days without sleep. He would squint and pinch his furrowed brow and eyebrow for hours at a time while working through spiritual conundrums. He would work for hour after hour typing out his theological tracts, which were in essence repetitive diatribes harping on about one or two key points. Ervil's sermons lasted for hours; he often collapsed at the culmination of the exhausting harangues. Or else he would suddenly slip into a trance-like state and stare into the distance before snapping back to reality and picking up where he left off.

Ervil's paranoia extended to a conviction that other organizations, such as the Catholic Church, saw him and his ragtag batch of hardscrabble Mormons as a real threat to their global supremacy. He was constantly on the lookout for [illegible] squads and, like Mao Zedong, constantly moving between a choice [illegible] d compounds, Ervil made sure he varied which wife he slept with [illegible] antly moving between residences. He refused to sit near windows or [illegible] o a door.

[illegible] period when Ervil was moving against Joel, he and his followers were [illegible] uishable by their willingness to display firearms on their person. He was keen to deploy a shotgun in the cab of a pickup truck or a holstered six shooter. Ervil and his followers became a menacing presence in the cult's compounds. Many men and women were attracted to this macho militancy, including his loyal right-hand man and enforcer, Daniel Ben Jordan.

In 1972 Ervil released his first two tracts. The first, in July, was co-authored with Daniel Ben Jordan and was entitled 'Priesthood Revealed'. The second, one month later, was 'Message to a Covenant People'. These two opuses were an amalgam of messages from the Bible and Joseph Smith all cooked up into an unpleasant hash that had a clear intent: to place Joel in the role of Satan and justify violence in pursuit of his overthrow. Nevertheless, even after Joel's assassination, the violent theology within these tracts remained the basis of Ervil's leadership. Ervil was God's top representative on Earth. Any who did not recognize this were deserving of extreme punishment. Doubting his authority was likely to result in a whirlwind of pain that was the due of all unbelievers, culminating in a bloody death. However, any who repented and willingly accepted God's True Prophet would have their sins forgiven and the death penalty rescinded.

Once Ervil had removed his brother there was little standing in the way of his increasingly delusional message, despite the fact that he stood trial in 1973 and was sentenced to twelve years in prison for his role in Joel's murder. The verdict was overturned in February 1974 and Ervil walked out a free man.

In the following years Ervil continued to pump out theological manifestos with impressive sounding titles such as 'Hours of Crisis – Day of Vengeance'. Despite the fact that they often exceeded one hundred pages, their basic precept could be boiled down to one or two key ideas. All of humanity had to submit to Ervil's authority or else a blood atonement was on the cards. This became the basis of a criminal enterprise that spread through the American south and into Mexico.

Attraction and Control

Many have compared the exploits of Ervil and his offspring as resembling the Mafia: a close-knit family carrying out a range of criminal activities that exploited those who were not privy to the organization's beliefs. At the head of the family was Ervil, who ruled through vicious subordinates.

Ervil had a strange magnetism. Not only was he able to call on the family ties that bound many of his flock to him, but his powerful presence could overawe even the most reluctant subjects. He had charisma. When he spoke, there was an almost supernatural light in his eyes, something that could hypnotize people with a glance.

While many heard Ervil speak and were turned off by his repetitive message – there was no messiah there for them, just the mundane – like all cult leaders he didn't mind if the majority escaped, as long as he netted one or two new disciples to add to his flock. In many ways those he attracted were preconditioned. Having spent years in the Church of Latter-day Saints, they would all have been exposed to both the moderate interpretation of the Book of Mormon as well the fundamentalist strains that permeated the community. It must have been a spiritual and psychological relief for many of LeBaron's followers to commit themselves wholesale to his world view.

Ervil's continued success in adding to his harem added to the perception of his priestly status. He did not hesitate to reward his followers with grandiose titles such as 'First Counselor to the President of the Kingdom of God' along with spiritual gifts such as the 'crown of eternal life'. More prosaically, he could hand out cash rewards when they were called for. The greatest reward he could dispense to those he wanted bound closely to his church was marriage to one of his many daughters.

When Ervil attracted a patriarch to his cult, the new member invariably bought his family along for the ride. As a consequence, should an individual seek to leave the evil influence of LeBaron they would be forced to cut ties with their loved ones. Most of these loved ones would have been well and truly indoctrinated. Children were withdrawn from school, isolated from mainstream society and forced to work in the cult's electrical chop shops.

Ervil enforced obedience using classic cult techniques. Long-winded sermons that echoed his strident writings could continue for hour after hour. The same message delivered with minor variations broke down any remnant of resistance and encouraged group-think to be practiced by the members. Disobedience in any form would be met with thunderous condemnation and each member of the group would reinforce this message.

Along with the unrelenting theological assaults, Ervil ensured that his flock were half starved, exhausted and poverty stricken. In the many electrical repair shops and garages that the cult operated, even young children put in days that could be 16 hours long. Families were split up and often children slept, ate and lived in the business premises, sleeping on makeshift cots in grim storerooms. They were not paid and were given subsistence rations. Any children who misbehaved would cop a beating. Women were engaged in the shop front, servicing clients, while men were exhausted by 24-hour callouts.

Those who did not live on the business sites did not fare much better. They were crammed into overcrowded one, two or three bedroom houses. Several wives and up to 15 children could be crammed within one residence. They were instructed to look neat, keep quiet and not draw any attention from the neighbors. Ervil always told his subordinates to rent the homes in respectable neighborhoods. The last thing he wanted was an intrusive police presence sticking their noses into his business.

By maintaining a low profile, even if they were trawling dumpsters for food, child protection services would not be alerted to the dreadful conditions many of the cult's offspring were experiencing.

While Ervil and his closest lieutenants knew where each of the church's outposts were located, and the personnel or assets within, there was little communication between the different branches. This cell-like structure meant that Ervil could maintain control of the smaller groups, conspiracies could not be hatched against him and, in case of problems with the law, few would be able to testify against the cult's nefarious activities. If there were any problems, individuals could be shuttled across the border or across state lines and removed from their support networks.

Ervil's key lieutenants played another important role for the cult leader. While the leader could keep his charismatic hands clean from the crimes, he ordered his hard-edged enforcers received much of the blame from the Church of the Lamb members for the dreadful conditions they endured. Daniel Ben Jordan was particularly hated. Members saw him as perverting the essential godliness of their prophet. In a refrain exploited by cult leaders as diverse as Hitler or Koresh, the members lamented 'If only the leader knew.' At the height of the killings, even Ervil's victims thought the bloodshed was all a misunderstanding and believed that Jordan, not LeBaron, was behind the orders to kill.

The other key ingredient to the success of the cult was its essentially criminal nature. A fear of the law kept all members in line.

The church's appliance businesses had flirted with the edges of the law. The utilization of children as bonded labor and the conversion of commercial spaces into primitive accommodation facilities must have broken a hundred municipal and state regulations, but it could be argued that they were not criminal in nature. Ervil recognized the burgeoning success of the first auto and appliance stores and decided to spread a chain throughout the southwest. These new stores became centers for auto theft on a grand scale. Auto and appliance repair shops were established in many cities including Indianapolis, Jackson and Dallas. In each of the cities was a dedicated labor pool of wives and children forced to work long hours. Specialist carjacking teams roamed between the different shops, targeting upmarket SUVs and pick-up trucks. These specialists took vehicles at all hours of the day and drove them to the Church of the Lamb yards. Within 48 hours the re-sprayed and re-registered vehicles were ready for on sale for a tidy profit.

Also on hand were legal specialists. If a member was caught red-handed and hauled in front of a judge, a church member would be there to get them out on bond before whisking the offender over a state or federal border to freedom.

The businesses performed a more sinister purpose. They were used to stockpile weapons. Pistols, rifles, and even automatic assault rifles were hoarded as the members of the church began to prepare for the upcoming conflict that was prophesized in the Book of Revelation.

Ervil expected, and obtained, instantaneous obedience to his every whim. Whether it was getting an order of fried chicken in the dead of night or procuring firearms for a hit, he could count on 24-hour obedience. Underpinning all of these techniques was the ultimate threat of blood atonement.

Armageddon

Joel LeBaron was the first of many deaths ordered by Ervil.

Any member of the Church of the Lamb who refused to follow the new teachings and give unbending allegiance to Ervil's will was likely to meet an untimely and particularly unpleasant end. Some members were gunned down in a hail of automatic fire; others were beaten to death. Some knew nothing until a 9 mm slug smashed into the back of their head. The most common form of bloodshed was when an individual who had been slated for blood atonement was lured out into the Badlands of Mexico or Texas, shot in the head and buried out in the wilderness, never to be found. Thanks to the vastness of this harsh environment few of these bodies were ever recovered, so it is almost impossible to determine exactly how many died. The people chosen to carry out these killings had been extensively trained in their art.

Dean Vest had a rather specialized skill set. He had emerged from his service in the Vietnam War with two things: a large steel plate holding his skull together, and an intimate knowledge of modern weaponry. He became Ervil's military advisor and trained members of the cult in marksmanship, the manufacture of firebombs, surveillance techniques and all of the other necessities of modern warfare.

Ervil dispatched these killer squads with all of the sophistication of a military operation. Various groups would be ordered to a given location and dispersed into motels, where they were instructed to blend in and maintain a low profile. On the day of an operation they would rendezvous, carry out the assigned attack, and disperse to all four points of the compass to avoid pursuit. Some attacks are well documented.

Ervil no doubt presumed that all of the members of Church of the Lamb would immediately come into his messianic fold as soon as Joel had been exterminated. This was not the case and large elements of the congregation recognized him as the tyrannical madman that he had become. Adherents in Colonia Le Baron swung behind the youngest brother, Verlan. Ervil realized that Verlan too had to be eliminated. He received intel that his youngest brother was stationed in the cult settlement of Los Molinos.

This large settlement, which had been founded by Joel, was located approximately 220 kilometres (140 miles) south of Tijuana and north of the Baja Peninsula in Mexico. The orderly town of 200 souls contained some families who supported Ervil. They engaged in surveillance over a period of time, trying to work out who were the strongest supporters of Verlan and how they could take Ervil's rival down.

On the night of 26 December an attack was launched. Although Ervil was moving between several safe houses in America, he had made it clear to his hit squad what was expected. It didn't matter how many Firstborns the team had to take down, as long as they got Verlan.

As night fell, a small convoy came bounding down the rutted road into Los Molinos. Each vehicle was packed with Ervil's supporters (and three of his children) heavily armed with rifles, machine guns and Molotov cocktails. As the trucks made their way through the outskirts of town they dropped off personnel at prearranged locations. A couple of boys too young to fight, including one named Isaac Salido, were dropped off on a hill overlooking the village. They would see some serious fireworks that night.

At 9.20 the attack began. A three-story house burst into flames when several Molotov cocktails were tossed through some windows. The unsuspecting residents of the town rushed to the scene, rescued the inhabitants and formed a human chain to douse the flames. Some of them climbed up to the higher floors to help with the fire fighting effort.

A shot rang out. A young man fell from the top floor, blood pouring from a wound in his leg. A fusillade followed as four other attackers fired into the crowd. They were sitting ducks, illuminated by the flaming building, and soon people were falling left, right and center as bullets and buckshot slammed into the residents. At least 12 were wounded and fighting for their lives. The shout 'Ervilistas' echoed through the town when people realized what was happening. Unwounded people disappeared into the darkness as the hit squad emerged from cover and advanced, still firing, towards their victims. The 16-year-old who was first hit was crying piteously for his mother. It did him no good. He received a fatal shotgun blast of pellets into his chest.

When Ervil's soldiers realized that Verlan was not among the wounded they initiated phase two of the attack - they would draw him out with mayhem and murder. Climbing back into their pick-up trucks, the squad spent 20 minutes roaring around the once peaceful settlement of Los Molinos.

Molotov cocktails were tossed onto buildings and anything that moved was hit by a fusillade of gunfire. Particular attention was paid to the house of one of Verlan's wives. Molotov cocktails were thrown onto the roof and every window was shattered by intensive gunfire. To no avail. Verlan's wife and children had taken shelter in an irrigation ditch as soon as the firing started. Verlan was in Nicaragua at the time of this pointless attack.

By 10 o'clock the shooting was over. Two-dozen homes were damaged or destroyed, 13 people were wounded and two were dead. Everyone knew who had launched the attack but there was little that the Mexican authorities could do other than send armed guards to protect the Firstborns from further assaults.

Soon after, another killing was carried out. A feature of Ervil's bloody rule was his willingness to use his wives and children as assassins. Noemi Zarate had apparently offended the Firstborn leader by threatening to report the group's activities to the authorities. Whatever the reason, Ervil was convinced that she was troublesome and needed to be taken care of.

Two of his wives, Vonda and Yolanda, took Noemi for a drive in late January 1975. They headed to the foot hills of the San Pedro mountains in a 1970 blue Dodge. When an isolated spot was found, the mood suddenly shifted. Vonda ordered Noemi out of the car. The confused woman was shepherded to the rear of the vehicle before Ervil's tenth wife raised a .38 revolver and fired a volley of shots into her head. The two women then bundled the body into the Dodge's trunk, scuffed out the blood stains and drove deeper into the Mexican wilderness. After two hours digging their victim was buried in a grave that remains hidden to this day.

The next victim was another Mormon who believed that he had a direct connection with God. Bob Simons did not have a devoted following like Ervil LeBaron, but he did have some things that Ervil envied – a beautiful wife and a 65-acre ranch. He also had the temerity to challenge the Prophet's authority. Ervil decided that Simons had to be atoned. He called some of his most dedicated soldiers to a briefing in one of the cult houses in Salt Lake City. Ervil concocted a sophisticated plan to eliminate Simons. Lloyd Sullivan, Eddie Marston and Mark Chynoweth were given the task.

Simons was particularly devoted to the ideal of converting indigenous tribes to the Church of Latter-day Saints. Lloyd Sullivan turned up at Bob's ranch and delivered the great news that there were five Indian chieftains who were willing to hear the word of the Lord from the rancher on 23 September 1975. A fair amount of preparation had gone on in the preceding weeks and Simons was well primed. He willingly went along with Sullivan and the two men set off for a rendezvous at twilight.

It proved to be a fatal rendezvous. Chynoweth and Marston had spent several hours digging a grave out of the rocky soil at a prearranged site near a distinctive rock known as the Indian Marker. They then hid in bushes at the side of the road waiting for their mark to turn up. The murderous pair did not have long to wait. Sullivan drove up to the marker and both men got out. There was no sign of the expected five chieftains. Sullivan left the car to relieve himself while Simons got out to have a look around. As he was peering into the distance, the two assassins emerged from their hiding place. Marston snuck up behind the target, raised his 12-gauge shotgun to the back of Simons' head and pulled both triggers. Nothing happened. He had left the safety on. Chynoweth raised his .357 Magnum to do the job, but Eddie managed to release the safety and gave Simons both barrels. Simons' head exploded and his poleaxed body fell to the ground.

The three men carried the corpse 15 metres (50 feet) away and, after taking his wallet and cash – even Ervil's most trusted men were kept short of cash by their leader – they tossed Simons into the prepared grave.

The three men returned to the safe house where the hit had been planned. After several hours driving the trio were met by a welcoming committee that included Ervil, over the moon with their triumph.

Dean Vest was the next to go, brought down by the diminutive Vonda White with a pistol shot to his guts.

Ervil's propensity for making grand sweeping statements knew no bounds. Not only did he declare that every branch of the Church of Latter-day Saints would bow down to him and acknowledge that he was the true successor to Smith et al, but he also declared that every believer had to pay him a minimum of 10 percent tithing. As soon as they could earn more money, a tithe of 50 percent or more was appropriate, given that he was in direct communication with God. Ervil would leave no stone unturned in his quest for cash.

Dean Vest, the former Navy veteran who had done so much to train and arm Ervil's acolytes for the coming showdown, was in possession of a fine boat worth at least $10,000. For several years Ervil had been asking Dean to sell his vessel and tithe 50 percent of its value to the church coffers. An increasingly disenchanted Vest refused and it seemed that he was preparing to leave the organization, taking his expertise, and his boat, with him: a sin in the Church of the Lamb's eyes.

This developing situation caused Ervil some anxiety, but fortunately God interceded. One night the Lord revealed that the only thing that could save Dean from sin was a blood atonement. This logic demonstrates a new innovation in Ervil's thinking. Previously blood atonement could only be used for those who had committed a sin. Now it would be used to prevent individuals from committing a sin. In effect Ervil had given himself and his followers a carte blanche to take out any individual on the most meager pretext or the smallest suspicion of incorrect thought.

Ervil explained that God's revelation was actually a compliment to Dean. Since Dean had risen so high in the New Kingdom, God was determined that Dean should not fall into apostasy by doing a runner. It was a blessing from the Lord that he would be washed clean in his own blood.

Ervil concocted a plan, devilish in its simplicity. His tenth wife, Vonda White, had already proved her loyalty dispatching Noemi Chiselthity and by happenstance had recently moved to San Diego, where Dean Vest was currently residing and working on his boat. The two had an excellent relationship and Ervil perceived that Vonda would be able to lure him to his assassination. There was one problem: Vest was a hulking ex-Navy man trained in the art of self-defense, while Vonda was a diminutive, heavily pregnant woman.

No problem, thought Ervil. He selected from his arsenal a .38 Colt with a snub barrel; it had some stopping power but would not be too hard for Vonda to fire. He modified the pistol so that it had a quick release trigger. In June 1975 Ervil drove to San Diego to deliver the gun and detailed instructions as to how to carry out the hit.

On 16 June 1975 Dean Vest walked into the clutches of his killer. It's hard to imagine a less likely assassin. Vonda had often served up a home cooked dinner to the man and he had been a frequent visitor to Vonda's two-story house in 439 East Eight Street, helping out and playing with the six children who lived there with Vonda and another of Ervil's wives, Linda Johnson. He considered the two women to be friends and he often camped on the lounge room floor.

Vest was in something of a panic on the 16th. His wife and daughter had been in a minor traffic accident and he had booked a flight to Seattle to check that they were OK. He had stored many of his possessions at East Eight Street and when he arrived he asked Vonda to help him pack some.

As far as Vonda was concerned this seemed to prove Ervil's suspicions. She doubted that Vest would return once he was united with his wife. She had to act. She shooed the six children upstairs and instructed them to lock themselves in the back bedroom and to stay as quiet as mice until she came and fetched them. She pulled the Colt .38 out of her dresser, placed it in her apron pocket and walked downstairs.

Dean had finished packing his car and was ready to drive to the airport. Vonda begged a favor before he left. The washing machine had been playing up and she asked him to check if there was a loose wire. Dean agreed to help and spent some time trying to find a fault. There was nothing wrong and he came into the kitchen to wash grease from his hands.

Vonda struck while he stood at the sink. She had placed a surgical glove over her right hand and silently drew the pistol from her apron pocket. Vonda approached the large man. When the pistol was less than an arm's length from his back, she pulled the hair trigger. The first shot smashed into Dean's left side, above the belt line and into the liver. Her victim straightened up and turned to the right before the second shot slammed into his lungs and broke open his circulatory system. The horror that Vest felt as blood gushed in torrents from his mouth and the wounds in his back can only be imagined. He spun around while collapsing on the floor, spraying blood around him like a pinwheel. Vonda desperately tried to step out of the way but tiny droplets hit her white canvas shoes and trousers. Dean did a full circle and collapsed facing the sink once more. Vonda, careful to avoid the spreading pool of blood, placed the .38 just behind the stricken man's left ear and pulled the trigger a third and final time.

Ervil's training had not been wasted on the diminutive assassin. She had already wiped the bullet casings of fingerprints and she did the same with the pistol when she deposited it onto the floor next to her victim. In the upstairs bedroom she washed any gunpowder residue from her hand and put her apron in the washer. She disposed of the surgical glove before calmly calling the local emergency hotline.

When detectives arrived at the scene there was significant evidence implicating Vonda. The victim was obviously close to the killer, indicating it was someone he knew. There were blood spatters on the pregnant woman's clothes and in her bedroom was a half open box of surgical gloves with some of the contents scattered on the floor as if they had been put on hastily.

Once the lead investigator began to interrogate the members of the household, he came up against a blank wall. The women readily admitted that they were involved in a religious war with a breakaways sect of the Church of the Firstborn. Vonda claimed she had been upstairs when the shots were fired. The investigators tried to find a chink in this story by questioning the children, but they were so well versed in subterfuge that even the youngest backed their mother's story. With too little for an arrest they had to let the women go, cautioning them not to leave the state. Of course as soon as they were released the two families decamped to Denver, Texas, where they were rewarded by Ervil. Vonda was made an 'elected lady' and would be able to take her place sitting next to Ervil in the new Celestial Kingdom.

Nevertheless, the San Diego authorities knew that Vonda was the killer and that she was part of Ervil LeBaron's increasingly notorious sect. They would continue to push for a resolution in the case.

After these murders there was a lull in the bloodshed. Ervil had other matters to deal with. The pause did not last long and in 1977 another blood atonement was called for.

Rebecca Salida's story is a sad one, not only because of her painful end but as an illustration of the life lived by Ervil's flock. Her death also demonstrates Ervil's capacity for ruthless violence – she was his daughter.

Rebecca was the offspring of the cult leader and his third wife, Delfina Salida. She was a kind-hearted girl, and during the early 1970s lived in squalor when cult finances were at a low ebb. She helped Delfina raise the large brood.

When wealthy Victor Chynoweth joined the Church of the Lamb, Ervil sought to bind him, and his money, closer to the cult by offering Rebecca as Victor's second wife. The 15-year-old Rebecca did not have any say in the matter, but Victor leapt at the chance. As soon as she had been 'sealed' to his household, he set about impregnating his bride. Soon a boy was born, but he brought the young mother no joy. Victor's first wife despised the younger and prettier addition to the family. Victor largely ignored Rebecca except when he required sex. The baby was all but removed from Rebecca's care to be raised with children from the first marriage. Rebecca became moody, difficult and overweight. She engaged in petty theft in the local stores.

Deciding that they'd had enough, the Chynoweths dispatched Rebecca to Dallas. As far as they were concerned, Ervil could handle his troublesome daughter. She was given a position at Budget Appliances, but continued her difficult behavior. When Rebecca realized she was three months pregnant with her second child she began to indulge in fantasies of taking both her children, fleeing the cult and establishing a loving and caring household free from the baleful influence of her father and his deadly minions.

As in any cult, expressions of dissent led to isolation, suspicions and monitoring from the other members. Rebecca found that none of the church's cars would be made available to her, her finances were stripped and whenever she was on the phone, a cult member would be sure to be listening in. She threatened to go to the authorities and tell them everything that went on in the church. As a daughter of LeBaron she was privy to all of the inner workings – a serious threat indeed.

Rather than giving emotional and physical support to help his child get through the difficult time in her life, Ervil received a revelation from the Lord. His 17-year-old daughter had to die. Ervil informed Rebecca that her wish had been granted. She would be driven to collect Victor Jr and the little family would then be taken to Mexico, where she could establish a household and wait for the birth of her second son. Just before she left, Rebecca told her younger brother Isaac the excitement she felt. She also confided to the young man that she was aiming to take her children out of the cult.

Eddie Marston and Duane Chynoweth were given the task of driving the new mother to her happy future. They were also given another task. Both men repeatedly set up a small tent on the concrete floor of a warehouse and Eddie was learning rope tricks. The two were instructed to take Rebecca on a detour on the way to the airport.

In April 1977 the three piled into Ervil's new LTD. At an isolated spot outside of Dallas the two men climbed into the backseat on either side of Rebecca. Duane pinned her down while Eddie took his rope and proceeded to strangle the 17-year-old. He could not exert enough pressure and after several minutes of agonizing struggle passed one end of the rope to Duane. The two combined forces, pulling from each side, to gradually asphyxiate the young woman. They tossed the body in the trunk and drove back to Dallas to report a successful completion of the mission.

Remarkably, rather than feeling sorrow or shame at the part he played in his daughter's death, Ervil reveled in it. He drove the car around for several days, with the rotting corpse of his daughter still in the trunk. He even showed it off to some of his followers.

Several days later he could hold on to his trophy no longer. Eddie and Duane were instructed to buy several bags of ice, place them around the decomposing corpse and dispose of it. Here the second part of Ervil's diabolical plan came into play. The two men drove their nauseating cargo across the Oklahoma State Line, into a secluded park, and set up the tent. The floor sheet had been removed and the two men used the cover of the tent to dig a large grave for their victim. Once it was dark the two men removed the body from the trunk, carried it up the hill to the tent and buried it. After tamping down the soil the site was covered with branches and stones. Rebecca's body has never been found.

The two assassins did not get much of a reward from Ervil. He went through them in a white-hot rage. Some of Rebecca's blood was on the internal mats and in the boot of his car. There was Oklahoma soil on the tires, bumpers and wheel wells. It was these basic slips, Ervil complained, that could give the law the clues they needed if they ever caught up with the assassins. Ervil replaced the LTD with an identical model soon after.

More hits followed the killing of Rebecca. Despite the elimination of their military expert, these attacks displayed a breathtaking level of skill. The individuals chosen to carry out the hits were remarkable for their ordinariness. Well dressed, polite and entirely nondescript, they blended in with the general population. Wigs and padded clothing were used for the actual hits. Police received reports of curly headed overweight women as perpetrators; after the killings had been carried out these disguises would be dumped, allowing the perpetrators to disappear. Support teams used scanners to follow police responses and the assassins crossed state lines straight after the crimes.

The police were increasingly aware that LeBaron was responsible, but it was almost impossible to pin anything on him. He had moved to Mexico, so they could not even bring him in for questioning.

Ervil's downfall came from a most unlikely source – one of his previously obedient wives turned on him.

Delfina Salido LeBaron was Ervil's third wife. They had been married since 1950. She gave birth to 10 children, including Rebecca and Isaac. When Rebecca first disappeared, she had been willing to believe the fiction that she had moved down south, but as the months and years went by Delfina became increasingly concerned about her daughter's fate. By 1977 she was getting frustrated with life in the cult and particularly disliked being shuttled around at the whim of her husband. When she learned of the role that her husband had played in the execution of her daughter, Delfina became, in the eyes of the cult, unmanageable. It was decided that she was to be atoned.

Fortunately for Delfina, she realized that two of Ervil's assassins were planning to eliminate her. She was left in a cult house while the pair went to a warehouse to gather some equipment. This no doubt included firearms, a tarpaulin and a spade.

As soon as they left Delfina grabbed her daughter and what little cash she had before fleeing. They proceeded to a Greyhound terminal at Dallas and bought tickets to Mexico. A tip off led to a federal agent taking the pair off in El Paso and on 11 June 1977 Delfina and her daughter were led into the office of a prosecuting attorney in Salt Lake County. For the next several days she told all that she knew about the inner workings of the Church of the Lamb and in particular Ervil's role in the killings. Soon she was joined by her son Isaac, who despite his young age had attended most of the meetings where Ervil gave his orders for atonement.

With the names and dates provided by these and other informers, a net was cast for some of the killers. While many were released after an unsuccessful prosecution, Vonda LeBaron was found guilty and sentenced to a lengthy jail term for the murder of Dean Vest.

Ervil stayed in Mexico until he was arrested and delivered to American authorities on 1 June 1979. He had been arrested with his fifth wife, Lorna Chynoweth, on 25 May and between this time and his delivery to the FBI he had endured a severe battering. The Mexicans were not concerned with legal niceties such as a formal extradition and it seemed that they wanted to get the troublesome cult leader out of Mexico as soon as possible.

Ervil, despite his beatings, was still full of his own importance. He made several crucial mistakes in the first interview with American law enforcement. He politely explained that he was the 'True Prophet' who had returned to Earth to usher in the millennium and become the leader of the Kingdom of God. The policemen, Ervil explained, were in fact committing criminal acts by impeding his mission in the name of the American government, which was in fact an illegal organization. He went on to explain that in his role as the Chosen One he had penned all of the tracts issued by the Church of the Lamb in the last decade.

By confessing to this Ervil placed himself clearly in the sights of any future prosecutor. It could now be claimed that it was Ervil who incited blood atonements. Had he had the foresight to claim even joint authorship with his lieutenants, LeBaron could have shifted the blame onto others.

The One True Prophet had always managed to hold sway over his disciples through the force of his personality and by the threat of atonement. Once in custody, supporters began to fall away. Despite letters and phone calls pleading for money to fund his defense, little was forthcoming. By the time he went on trial, on 12 May 1980, his support base was rapidly diminishing.

The number of people willing to testify had increased. Once again Isaac was a key witness for the prosecution. By now the young man had been involved in several years of litigation against various cult members and the strain was beginning to show. He also admitted that his evidence, damning in its totality, was likely to earn him a death sentence. Isaac's premonition was correct. After the trial he committed suicide, although the circumstances of his death indicated that at least two of the people he testified against may have helped him on his way.

Forty-three prosecution witnesses testified against the fallen prophet. The defense had few resources to call upon and wisely did not ask Ervil to testify. Despite his neat appearance and open countenance, the jury saw through his mask – after three hours of deliberation, Ervil was found guilty of first-degree murder and conspiracy to commit murder on 28 May 1980. Soon after he was sentenced to life in prison.

Ervil did not adjust well to his new life. More and more of his supporters used his incarceration as an excuse to move out of the cult's orbit. More and more refused to take his collect calls or answer his letters. During his confinement, the Chosen One demonstrated behaviors that would now be associated with bi-polar disorder. He would go for days moping in his cell and refusing to communicate with guards or fellow prisoners. Periods of manic activity would follow where Ervil tried to recruit his cellmates to the Church of the Lamb and he would receive visitations from the Lord promising the imminent destruction of the prison walls and his ascension in the coming Armageddon. He'd pace for hours, mumbling, exclaiming and pulling at his eyebrows in a gesture that his followers knew well.

During these manic phases Ervil began to write a new tract, the Book of New Covenants. While many supporters had given up on Ervil, he had not given up on them. From his cell the Prophet ordered some of his last fanatic followers, his son the stone-cold killer Arturo among them, to visit the fallen members and use the threat of violence to bring them back into the fold. This backfired on him and the prison authorities threatened to cut him off from all external communications.

As the severity of his sentence sank in Ervil, at times, gave in to despair and engaged in self-harming activities. He thrust his head into a toilet bowl and even asked the governor to execute him – not for the crime of murder but because he had given in to temptation and masturbated. The governor could of course not carry out Ervil's wishes, but the march of time did. In the early hours of 16 August 1981 his body was found stretched out on his cell floor. The Chosen One had exited this mortal coil.

It was not the end of the story. Ervil LeBaron had left two legacies. The first was the Book of the New Covenants, which had been smuggled out of prison by his daughter and son-in-law, Lillian and Mark Chynoweth. The second was a network of wives, children and grandchildren who still saw themselves as soldiers of the Church of the Lamb.

Ervil would reach out of the grave and the killing would continue.

In his dying days Ervil had ensured that he finished his last tirade – the Book of New Covenants. The Patriarch knew that his influence had diminished greatly since his incarceration. He was also acutely aware that some of his once loyal 'Swords of the Lord' were using this as an opportunity to slip away from him. Four of his toughest soldiers came in for particular mention – Dan Jordan, Mark Chynoweth, Duane Chynoweth and Eddie Marston. Mark had of course helped carry out the final writings of the 'One True Prophet' and many years later he would regret this act. All four were named by Ervil as 'sons of perdition' and 'apostates' who were sentenced by 'The One Mighty and Strong' for blood atonement.

At first the four had little to worry about. They used the skills learnt in the appliance repair business to set up profitable enterprises well away from any church compounds in the suburbs of Texas. They considered themselves well rid of Ervil's family and his deadly cult.

For many years it appeared they had made the right call. Just as ravening jackals fight over a corpse, so Ervil's sons, daughters and wives fought for supremacy within the Church of the Lamb. These were not harmless manoeuverings within a largely benevolent establishment but bore a greater resemblance to clan warfare within the Mafia. Individuals were hacked to death, shot in the back of the head, murdered after being dragged out of bed into a compound courtyard, battered to death with a tire iron, or even strangled or asphyxiated when a plastic bag was placed over their head.

An 18-month infant was murdered by his father through suffocation, merely because the baby had a problem in its digestive tract. As in many coups it was not just one person who would be killed; clutches of adults and children would fall all at the same time as different factions sought to clear out unreliable family members.

Finally, by 1977 the internal factional bloodletting came to an end. It was time to fulfill Ervil's last covenant. Tarsa LeBaron, the eldest daughter of Ervil and Lorna Chynoweth, and her brother Aaron gained total control. Tarsa was the brains of the operation and was proof that the apple does not fall far from the tree. She was able to deploy her father's charm when necessary, could talk anybody around to her way of thinking with an inexhaustible hectoring style and would, if these other methods did not work, turn a deadly baleful glare onto any who did not follow her reasoning; through the threat of violence she would end up getting her way. Tarsa used the Book of New Covenants as a weapon. She convinced several followers to carry out hits in the purges by pulling quotes from the turgid prose.

Tarsa turned her attention to the four apostates. In 1987 Aaron declared that it was time to unite the church and destroy the sons of perdition.

Daniel Ben Jordan was the first to go. The one-time enforcer had settled in the town of Bennett in eastern Colorado. He turned up in the town in 1982, bringing his twelve wives and 50 offspring with him. He opened up a thriving home appliance business but it seems his real income was generated by welfare fraud. Jordan used his vast brood to harvest welfare checks from a multiplicity of state authorities as he shuffled wives and children across state borders to claim assistance.

Daniel had been named a son of perdition when he reported Arturo's proselytizing attempts to the authorities. By 1987 it seemed that his inclusion in Ervil's hit list was just a distant bad dream. Then, in August, a large posse of LeBaron children turned up on his doorstep. The group was in urgent need of shelter and food. They were desperate to escape the bloodletting in the cult and they called on Daniel to help them. The inner workings of the Church of the Lamb had been well hidden and Ervil's former enforcer had no idea that Tarsa and Aaron were now in firm control. Daniel had only heard of the terrible bloodletting and welcomed the teenagers into his house. Next day they were acting as unpaid labor in his business - working 16-hour days for rent and board.

In October of 1987 Jordan went on a hunting expedition. He was unwilling to leave Ervil's children behind, fearing the mischief they could cause. He decided to take them with him to the Manti-Le Sal National Forest in central Utah. It was the last bad decision he would ever make. On Friday 16 October Dan Jordan left the campsite to answer the call of nature. At 2 pm a 9 mm bullet entered the front of his chest. Immediately afterwards another slug tore into his right temple. Dan had been facing his attacker, but when his cold body was found by another hunter at 4 pm he was in no position to name names.

Investigating police came up against a wall of ignorance. Even though the campsite had been full of Dan's and Ervil's family members, nobody had seen anything suspicious.

The cat was out of the bag. The Church of the Lamb was back in the news and Mark Chynoweth, Duane Chynoweth and Eddie Marston knew they were back in the sights of the Avengers for the Church of the Lamb.

All three men were respectable upstanding citizens in the eyes of their local communities. They dressed well, had well behaved children and ran appliance repair stores with a reputation for honesty and efficiency. The three men had used the profits from these businesses to purchase comfortable houses in which to raise their children. Duane Chynoweth, who had picked off church members in the attack at Los Molina, lived in a perfectly maintained house in the suburb of Spring Branch, Houston. A few kilometers away in the same suburb, his brother Mark did the same with his several small children. Not too far away, in the town of Irving, Texas, Eddie Marston, who had helped strangle Rebecca LeBaron, lived with his girlfriend in a small apartment behind his shop.

The neighbors had welcomed the Chynoweths into their communities but in 1987 and 1988 they noticed something odd. The families began receiving telephone calls at all hours. When they answered there was only a deathly silence on the other end of the line. Strange cars began to turn up in the peaceful streets. They would take many turns by the Chynoweth residences and sometimes they even stopped and the driver took photographs of children playing in the yard. School friends began reporting to their parents that there were firearms scattered in their playmates' houses and shotguns leaning against the hallway walls. By June 1988 the houses had been turned into veritable fortresses. The children were no longer allowed to play outside and all doors and windows were securely locked 24/7.

This was for naught. All three would die in a succession of hits that resembled a scene out of *The Godfather*.

Duane Chynoweth probably thought that 27 June 1988 was just another day. He may have registered that it was the anniversary of the bloody death of Joseph Smith in 1844, but if so it made no difference to his working day. Just before 1 pm he received a call at his store offering him a used washer and dryer for sale at a bargain price. He agreed to the deal and made an arrangement to pick up the two items at a Rena Street address at 4 pm At 3.50 Duane pulled out of his store with his eight-year-old daughter, Jennifer, in the cab. He drove his pick-up to the address and once there backed it up into the drive ready to load the two appliances. While looking out his rear window, Duane did not notice a black Silverado that pulled up, blocking the drive.

Getting out of the vehicle was a man in a business suit. Thinking it was the seller, Duane was in the process of exiting the cab when the approaching man pulled a .357 Magnum from his jacket. One shot slammed into Duane's chest. He crumpled to the ground and two more shots were fired into his head. Seeing her father's blood splashing over the pick-up, Jennifer began to scream. Until then the assassin had not taken any notice of the eight-year-old. She wedged herself into the corner of the cab and continued to scream. The killer placed one shot into her open mouth and another into her head as she slumped forward. The innocent girl's brains splattered all over the rear cab window. Jennifer had been atoned for her father's sins. When police arrived soon after they realized that the pair had been lured to a vacant house. Somebody had removed the 'For Sale' sign that had stood for several weeks.

Eddie Marston received a similar call that day. He too was offered an appliance at a knock down price and asked to collect it from a house on the west side of Irving at 4 pm. In exactly the same set up, he attended the house and while backing up the drive a car had driven up before disgorging an assassin. Eddie was shot several times and, although still alive when police attended the reported shooting, he soon died in Parkland Hospital.

Back in Dallas, the hit on Mark Chynoweth went less smoothly. Just after 4 pm a customer was shocked to find the former cult member sprawled in his office chair.

He had received multiple gunshot wounds from a .45 automatic, but the killing was much less efficient than the other two. Bullets had been sprayed around the office and there was no clean coup de grace. Nevertheless, Mark was in no condition to report his killer. As with the other two hits, there were few witnesses. It later turned out that the killer was Heber LeBaron.

These murders became known as the four o'clock murders. They had been ordered by Aaron and Tarsa. The killers managed to evade trial for almost five years. Finally one of the participants, Cynthia LeBaron, realizing that she had been slated for blood atonement, decided, with her brother Richard, to roll over. Richard was the trigger man for the murder of Duane and his daughter. In 1993 Heber LeBaron was sentenced to life for the murder of Mark Chynoweth. Doug Barlow was similarly sentenced for the murder of Eddie Marston. Patricia LeBaron, who drove one of the killers, was also sentenced to life in prison without parole.

Federal and state authorities arrested many of the other members of the cult for theft and larceny of motor vehicles, essentially breaking the economic base of the group.

In 1995 Aaron was arrested in Mexico and in 1997 he was sentenced to 45 years for his part in the four o'clock murders. However, it wasn't until the arrest of Tarsa LeBaron in May 2010, while hiding in Honduras, that the last of the cult leaders was convicted. Given a three-year sentence for her role in the murders, she was the last in Ervil's long and vicious line to suffer imprisonment for blood atonements.

But is the story of the Church of the Lamb finished? It is impossible to be sure.

CHAPTER EIGHT

The Little Ants: Green Apocalypse

Revelation Book 11

[18] The time has come for ... destroying those who destroy the earth.

Roch Thériault was an unlikely messiah. Pretty much an ordinary fellow during his late adolescence, it is possible that an illness rewired his brain to turn him into a megalomaniacal cult leader. He managed to gather a ragtag group of impressionable youngsters into the wilds of the Canadian wilderness. Thériault fused the teachings of the Seventh Day Adventists with a desire to get back to nature and co-exist with the environment, but soon these ideals disappeared and the drunken tyrant brutalized followers at his manipulative mercy.

The isolated community became Thériault's sad little fiefdom. Chances are they could still be there today if it was not for one weakness – his fondness for the bottle. The avuncular leader became a raging, violent bully when under the influence of drink and perpetrated such violence that the authorities could not ignore his crimes.

Unlike many other cult leaders, he was abandoned by most of his disciples as soon as the law caught up with him. Thériault was beaten to death in prison in 2011, abandoned by all who once worshiped him.

Genesis

Roch Thériault was born on 16 May 1947 to Hyacinthe and Pierrette. The Thériaults were descended from settlers from the west coast of France, who made their way to Port Royal on the shores of Nova Scotia in the 1640s. Although the French settlers were successful farmers in the fertile river valleys in this south-easternmost province of modern-day Canada, they suffered greatly during the wars between France and Britain in the 1750s. Hyacinthe was descended from members of the community who were chased out of their prosperous lands to the harder and more unforgiving terrain around Quebec.

Roch's father was a product of these rough beginnings. Fiercely proud of his French heritage and a devoted Catholic, he and his wife were determined to have a large brood brought up to hold conservative values. Roch was the second of seven children and the entire clan was expected to work hard on the family's small acreage while their parents went into town to earn intermittent wages.

During his trials Roch made much of his abusive childhood and seemed to relish telling stories of the beatings that he received at the hands of his father. It is likely that he was angling for 'extenuating circumstances' to justify his vicious acts and that there was no basis for these claims. Teachers and students who associated with the Thériaults recount that the children were well turned out with full lunch boxes and cheerful demeanors. It seems that the family was loving and the parents were bon vivants who enjoyed good food, wine and public displays of affection.

Roch proved to be a bright student who loved reading all sorts of literature and would often bed down with a good book after doing his chores. He was something of a tearaway who enjoyed adventures in the surrounding wilderness areas and was always ready with an amusing yarn to entertain friends and family. Nevertheless, there was a touch of the devil in the young man. He was a born manipulator who could stir up trouble with ease. He disrespected authority and became adept and blaming others when coins or cigarettes were stolen.

Hyacinthe had one abiding passion that was to play a large part in his son's psychological development. He was a fanatical believer in the 'White Berets.' This was a blend of right-wing hatred of 'Jewish bankers,' corrupt politicians and grasping capitalists, combined with a perceived need to bring Canadian society back into the fold of conservative Catholic views. As a staunch Catholic and fierce nationalist, Hyacinthe was determined to raise his children to fear and respect God.

What Roch did fear was the Sunday Mission that was forced upon him and his siblings. Each Sunday all seven children would dress up in their finest gear, don their own tailor-made white beret and head out in the family car to proselytize for their father's cause. It must have been excruciatingly embarrassing for the young ones. Hyacinthe would knock on an innocent householder's door. When the owner appeared, the children would fall on their knees, berets and all, and recite a prayer. A collection box would then be held out to the bemused resident and the clan would move on to the next mark.

Roch loathed these expeditions with a hatred that only the young can muster. His friends teased him mercilessly and for ever after he was moved to anger whenever he saw a priest or a Catholic icon.

Nevertheless, the young man developed into a very attractive personality. Dropping out of school at 14, he earned a wage doing odd jobs. He hated taking orders but was a keen worker as long as he was left to his own devices. He was surrounded by friends and could enter a pub and instantly get everybody there rolling around at his comic antics. Roch was a natural born showman with a great sense of humor. He had no trouble attracting lots of girls, who flocked to his warm sensuality.

Things were looking good for Roch when he married a woman named Francine in 1967. The two had several years of wedded bliss and, like Roch's parents, the couple proved to be very fertile.

In 1970 that all changed. Before this time there was no indication that the well-built young man was destined to turn his charm and charisma to evil purposes. Thériault was struck down with agonizing stomach pains. He was forced to undergo several operations that removed large parts of his stomach. There were complications from these attempts to cure duodenal ulcers – he developed dumping syndrome, a condition that led to chronic pain. For the rest of his life Thériault would consume alcohol and pain relief medicine in ever-greater quantities.

Many of the young man's associates noticed that these troubles 'broke' him. He became selfish and demanding. Living in a constant state of hypochondria, he became obsessed with medical procedures and considered himself an expert on surgery – something that would have dire consequences later in his life. Thériault became reckless, uncaring and obsessed with sex. He also became delusional. While trying to take over the local council he blackened his name by dishing out bad checks. Throwing in a job with the fire department, he tried to make cash by selling handcrafted beer mugs in pubs and hotels. He was soon bankrupt and alone. Francine left him after their house was repossessed.

Thériault didn't seem to mind – he had turned his attention to religion.

Bizarre Beliefs

The Seventh Day Adventist Church relies on continual proselytizing to maintain and boost their numbers. They got more than they bargained for when Roch Thériault came into their orbit.

When the Millerite movement collapsed in the wake of an unfulfilled prophecy, few remained to keep the fire of imminent apocalypse burning. One exception was Ellen White, who had a nice interpretation of events. Judgment Day had occurred, but it had only happened in heaven. The Heavenly Sanctuary had been cleansed and the Lord had turned his attention to humanity but was yet to act on his judgments.

White's teachings led to the establishment of the Seventh Day Adventists in Michigan in 1863. She produced huge amounts of theological literature and 53 books. Her tips for leading a successful spiritual life included an abhorrence of wigs – they led to insanity – and a fear of masturbation, which apparently caused thousands of death each year. On the other hand, White did recognize that the wearing of tight corsets did physical damage. Many of her teachings came about while she was in a trance state. It seems that if White was diagnosed today she would be declared an epileptic.

The Seventh Day Adventists, with White at the helm, expanded on Miller's apocalyptic vision. The faithful would not ascend in a bloodless event. A world dictator Antichrist would arise and do battle for seven years with the forces of righteousness. The Seventh Day Adventists, who believed that the Sabbath was on a Saturday and preached that 'Dunking' was required for baptism, would lead the fight against the Beast. After seven years of battle Christ would return to Earth and smite the Antichrist. This would be followed by the resurrection, where all worthy individuals living and dead would be raised and granted a life of immortality. The Book of Revelation was the wellspring of this holy vision.

The Church of the Seventh Day Adventists did, and still does, many worthy activities. They believe in a pure life without alcohol, drugs or the consumption of meat. One of the most powerful fundraisers for the Seventh Day Adventist Church is their anti-smoking workshops. Before e-cigarettes and nicotine patches these workshops were some of the most successful resources for individuals who sought to give up smoking.

The Adventists were usually successful in the missions that they undertook. Missions were continually moving into new territory, offering health foods, anti-smoking courses and, of course, a warning of the coming apocalypse.

One such mission turned up in Thetford Mines in early 1977. They had prepared the way with flyers, handbills and posters. At the first meeting, sitting in the front row, was a prematurely balding young man. He had deep blue eyes and a clear complexion. Roch Thériault was a seeker and he found his mission that cold Canadian winter's night.

Thériault attended every meeting sponsored by the church and within two months he had agreed to be baptized. Soon 'Brother Thériault' had given up smoking and drinking. He also had an interest in the coming apocalypse and particularly enjoyed the tales of mass slaughter and mayhem that would strike the unbelievers of the world. Thériault took little notice of the teachings of Christ.

The Adventists made much of their money by selling literature aimed at healthy living. Some were vegetarian recipe books while others were tips on how to give up smoking. Thériault was given responsibility for several regions and he soon began to excel. Bringing with him the enthusiasm of a new convert, Thériault used his natural charisma to inveigle thousands of dollars worth of sales – 40 percent of which he pocketed at an agency fee. Another money-spinner was the five-day anti-smoking courses offered by the church. The young man soon had hundreds of recruits turning up to the evening seminars.

That was not all. The leaders of the Adventists saw that Thériault's attractive demeanor and folksy charm was perfect for recruiting young, disenfranchised seekers to the Church. Thériault took to this task with a will and soon there was a group of adherents, mainly attractive young women, who hung on his every word. Thériault was a charismatic preacher and his desire to see the coming apocalypse entranced his followers. Like many charismatic preachers, Thériault dwelled upon the horrors of the coming doomsday scenario. He talked of the world's problems in the late 20th century. Wars, pollution, nuclear accidents and the rise of dreadful dictators - all of these were harbingers of the coming devastation. Soon, said Thériault, the fallen, the dogs, the idolaters and the wicked would be tortured by plagues of locusts, smashed with giant hailstones and plunged into lakes of fire. Only those who followed the way would be saved and taken up to live next to God for a thousand years.

Thériault's virtuosity in recruiting individuals to the church was recognized by the local Adventist organizers. His innovative approach and fantastic money making abilities gained official recognition. However, those closest to him noticed that he was becoming increasingly self-important. The school dropout pronounced himself more intelligent than those around him and came up with a fantastical backstory that placed him well above his fellow man. He had been a member of the Knights of Columbus and God had, according to Thériault, given him the power of hypnotism over his fellow man.

Early concerns were well founded. Thériault was emerging as a guru. He attracted a large group of disenchanted young people, many of whom slept on his lounge room floor, and began to establish a hold upon them. He urged them to drop any educational goals - they would not be needed in the coming apocalypse - and he harangued them into believing that only he could truly interpret the Bible's meaning.

He used his young followers to make extra money. Several businesses were set up. They were initially quite successful thanks to the free labor provided by Thériault's young followers and the trusting local tradespeople who extended him easy credit.

The Adventists were too late to realize the snake in their midst. Not only was he attracting followers to his own little sect, he was also blackening the church's good name. Those who had extended credit in the form of goods and services to his Adventist-backed business soon found it increasingly difficult to call in their debts. Finally, the Church of the Seventh Day Adventists formally cut any ties with Thériault and his followers.

Thériault didn't mind. In early June 1976 he loaded his little sect – 12 women, 6 men and 2 children – into a truck, a bus and a car and headed into the Canadian wilderness. They left their debts, and a lot of anxious parents, behind them. They also left a canvas bag at the side of the road. This contained all of the formal identification documents of the cult's members. Bank books, driver's licenses and any other ID was left behind. Thériault had decided to take his followers off the grid. With good reason, according to Thériault.

There was good news and bad news.

The bad news was that on 17 February 1979 the Seventh Angel was going to launch the apocalypse. All unbelievers would be crushed by stones falling from heaven. A great earthquake would follow and all of man's works, his cities, his parliaments, every building that sought to elevate man above God, would be dashed to the earth. Those that survived this cataclysm would be destroyed by raging floodwaters.

The good news was that God had appointed Thériault to be his personal emissary on Earth. All he had to do was remove his flock beyond civilization and return to nature. All of the trappings of civilization were to be abandoned and the group was to re-establish contact with Mother Earth by engaging in sustainable and self-sufficient farming practices. After the cataclysm Thériault would lead them out of the wilderness, where they would found a new society that would last for a thousand years.

The little band of travelers only had to live amidst pure unspoiled nature, gain self-sufficiency by working the land and listen to the word of God's one true representative on Earth. What could go wrong?

Attraction, Initiation and Control

Thériault was unusual among gurus in that he did not seek to dominate a large flock of followers. Once he had attracted a small following that never exceeded two-dozen souls, he was content. Like all good cult leaders he was able to pick out the 'seekers'; those who were lacking direction or those who came from a troubled background. By inviting them into his select club Thériault was able to make them feel special. He was able to turn himself into an emotional crutch that they could not do without.

One of his earliest followers was Gabrielle Lavallée. As a nurse she had seen her fair share of troubles. Many years after the experience she was able to discuss how Thériault had managed to ensnare her.

Like most of Thériault's flock, Gabrielle was at a crossroad of her life. Despite the fact that she was a recognized nurse with a successful career, she was battling with depression and a feeling that all she touched turned to dust. At the time the theory of 'recovered memory' was popular and Gabrielle suspected that there was a history of abuse buried deep within her childhood memory. When she first attended the Seventh Day Adventist Church she noticed Thériault. He had an immediate impact on the young woman.

With his uncanny ability to pick the easy marks, Thériault focused his entire attention on Gabrielle. He turned the full wattage of his charismatic visage upon her; it seemed to Gabrielle that he was looking straight through her feeble defenses and into her innermost being. The young woman was mesmerized. She wanted to place her entire trust within the hands of the dynamic teacher. It seemed as if God was talking through him.

Other attractive young women fell under his spell. Not only did he seem to have a tremendous grasp of the scriptures but he was able to communicate their intent with wit, humor and a terrific enthusiasm. As their numbers grew, his followers began to reject all outside influences while a group belief system took hold. One of the first things that Thériault did was tell his new followers to abandon all worldly goods. The few members that did have any assets or cash handed them over to Thériault. Individuality was to be frowned upon and soon the entire group was wearing shapeless and bland ankle length frocks.

This psychological dependence became a physical dependence when they trekked into the wilderness in July 1976. The 18 young Quebecers followed their master on an exhausting journey into the heart of the Canadian wilderness. Leaving their vehicles in the village of Saint Jogues on the Gaspe Peninsula, Quebec, the small band trekked for days to find the promised land. It was finally found near the strangely named Dry Lake (Lac Sec), four hours walk from the nearest bush track and 22 kilometers (14 miles) from the nearest town. There was a small hillock amidst the scraggy brush. Thériault named it the Eternal Mountain. It was in this godforsaken place that he would set up his alternative society. This jail that Thériault erected would not have any metal bars. The psychological barriers that he set up would be just as effective.

Other cults often broke down an initiate's resistance with pointless busy work. Not so Thériault. If the small group was to survive they had to work. They had arrived in July and had only a few months to build shelters before winter set in. The first mammoth task was to move a huge assortment of tools and power equipment to the site – four hours from the cult's transport. For several days the youths lugged these materials as well as camping equipment through the rough brush to the new promised land. At 5 am they would rise from their camp beds to fell timber, dig foundations, pour concrete, dig a well and build several wooden huts from scratch. Thériault provided the plans and the carpentry expertise. Apart from that he did little.

Thériault always had access to food and alcohol, but his followers were on what could be considered starvation rations. They were forced to give up breakfast lest the meager cult supplies dry up.

By September the first cabin had been built. While rough around the edges it did at least have a wood stove in the kitchen area, a fireplace and a large central area for the followers to congregate. At the front of the cabin, closest to the fire, was a raised throne. This became the seat of 'Moses', as Thériault named himself. The rest of the cult were given Biblical names. Within this dank, cold and rough kingdom, Moses began to break down the last vestiges of his followers' resistance.

Night after night he would sit in front of the hall lecturing upon the evils of the world, its decadence and its impending demise. He adopted a set of splendid red robes, grew out his beard until it reached his chest and wore a diadem bestowed upon him by his most enthusiastic female worshipers. Each member was encouraged to expose their character flaws and weaknesses. Troubling incidents from the past were examined in great detail and blown out of all proportion. These tales served as proof that all those who remained in civilization – including the families of the cult members – were evil.

The exhausted and malnourished cultists became dependent on their leader. They were worked too hard to have any time to think things through. All blessings came from Moses. If he approved of an act they would get greater rations. If they expressed disenchantment or complained they would be informed upon and given the worst tasks, such as cleaning the primitive latrines or chopping wood. This was a gradual process. One family saw through it and left, but most became dependent on Thériault. Through a haze of exhaustion and malnutrition, they began to see him as a divine figure.

Everyone who knew Thériault was aware that while he had only limited formal education he made up for this with cunning and a tremendous ability to manipulate people. This was exacerbated within the new Kingdom of God. His followers were split into two groups: those who had earned Moses' favor, and those who displeased him. The lower class had no rights, were rarely allowed to speak and were often subject to cruel punishments. The other group received better food and their bedding was closer to the hearth, but they knew that the slightest misdemeanor would result in demotion to the lower class. Conversely, the act of snitching on a fellow cultist could lead to rapid promotion back into the favored group.

The best way to enter into Thériault's good books was, if you were one of the female members, to sleep with him. When the cult moved into the wilderness Thériault had banned all sexual activities. He soon began to prey on the women, who became in effect his harem. Those who put extra effort into massaging the guru's back or performing sexual acts could be spared from laboring in the clearings, where the group tried to extract meager crops on which to survive.

The Bible was used as justification. He annulled any previous marriages and declared that, like King David or King Solomon, he deserved a harem. The book of Genesis gave him the right to lord it over all of the females, as their role was to ruled by men. While the rest of the group toiled in the fields, a woman would be invited into the guru's bed. He made it clear that their role was to please him. They were not allowed to kiss him on the mouth and had to bring him to orgasm by fellatio, masturbation or intercourse. As well as satisfying his carnal attitudes, the women had to satisfy his ego. They soon learned that an easy way of gaining Moses' approval was to write long rambling love letters extolling 'Pappy's' many virtues.

He did not only exploit the women in bed; he exploited them financially. While he made great outward show of abandoning civilization, at least $1400 in welfare benefits flowed directly into his account. Cultists were sent into town on a snow mobile and here they purchased everything that Thériault wanted. After a year or so, the ascetic lifestyle had worn thin for Moses and he made sure that he had a larder stocked with potato chips, beer, whisky, prime cuts of meat and everything else that he desired.

Thériault loved beer. He began drinking to excess. He changed from being a benign, guru-like figure to a delusional bullying madman. He would stay awake all night lecturing and preaching to the sober audience of his followers. Should they nod off or lose focus on his wise words, God's representative on Earth would explode into a furious rage, seize a piece of timber and beat his victim in front of the terrified flock.

Members would be forced to stand outside, naked, in the snow for hours at a time for minor transgressions such as stealing a pancake. Those subject to the most horrible humiliations felt that they could not strike back – to them, that would mean they were striking God.

In late 1979 Thériault began to inflict permanent physical damage on his followers. One woman spoke of leaving the compound. Even though Thériault would make wheedling apologies after his drunken outbursts, Maryse Grenier could see the violent behavior escalating. Thériault would have none of it and ordered Jacques Grenier to remove one of her toes with an axe. Jacques was of course horrified by this order and initially refused. When Thériault threatened to chop off all of the young woman's toes, her husband reluctantly cut off his wife's little toe. The first step had been taken. Jacques became Thériault's enforcer.

More violence was to follow. Thériault crossed the line from delusional prophet to vicious bully, targeting the most vulnerable in his cult. An infant named Samuel died. There are several versions of what caused the young boy's death, but it is likely that he was beaten by Thériault after he had botched a surgical procedure to circumcise Samuel. Another member may have been involved in the death. The young boy's mother was too numbed by Thériault's tyrannical rule to put up a protest when the tiny corpse was incinerated.

Thériault tried his hand at another surgery soon after. Guy Veer joined the cult in 1980, after several stints in a psychiatric ward where he was treated for depression. He may have played a role in young Samuel's death and Thériault decided there had to be a reckoning. He set up a mock trial for the disturbed young man. The membership wrote on ballots that they agreed with their leader's punishment. Veer was to be castrated.

Veer was led to the kitchen bench in the communal hall and held down by the cultists. Some pinned him to the table while others held his legs wide apart. Equipped with a rubber band, some tweezers, a razor blade and a magnifying glass, Thériault performed the surgery while Gabrielle illuminated the proceedings with a penlight. It was fortunate for Veer that the trained nurse was present, as his scrotum became inflamed and turned purple.

Thériault was not finished with Veer and continued to bully and brutalize the cult's eunuch. Eventually Veer made the lengthy trek into town and reported the death of baby Samuel and his own abuse at the hands of Moses. The authorities acted and soon the compound was razed to the ground and the key actors in the two violent atrocities at the Eternal Mountain were in police custody.

On 29 September 1982 Thériault and some of his closest followers were found guilty of a range of charges.

Many parents felt that they would now have a chance to sever the hold that Thériault had over their children. It was not to be. Through phone calls, letters and audiotapes Thériault made sure that his followers stayed loyal.

When Thériault was released, in February 1984, he had learned from his mistakes. No longer would he be prey to the attention of Quebec authorities. He would re-establish his cult far removed from any prying eyes.

His true evil nature asserted itself. While 'Moses' swore to his followers that he would no longer drink and abuse them, he was no doubt planning to initiate a new rule of terror well away from the strictures of society.

Armageddon

In April 1984 Thériault and his trusty enforcer set out in a battered pick-up truck and went in search of a new promised land. Thériault was determined to escape the watch of the Quebec authorities and set off on a cross-country anabasis deep into the heart of Canada. After traveling more than 1000 kilometers he and his companion arrived at the tiny town of Kinmount.

He must have seemed like manna from heaven to the local real estate agent. All he wanted, Thériault explained, was a parcel of land well removed from any electricity, roads or infrastructure of any kind. The realtor had plenty of these lots, which were useless for anything but duck hunting or cattle grazing. They took Thériault out to a 200-acre property just near Burnt River. It was several kilometers from any road, had a small cleared area and a large copse of maple trees. There was not even a track through adjoining farms to the property.

Perfect. Thériault placed a deposit, signed the contract and headed back east to pick up his followers. Despite the fact that 'Moses' was asking them to start from scratch in the hardscrabble lands of the Canadian wilderness, most followed his call. On 2 May 1984, three men, nine women and 10 children disgorged themselves from their vehicles and began work on the new utopia. Most of the women considered themselves to be Thériault's wives. Most of the children were Moses' offspring.

Midges and blackfly made their lives miserable. Nevertheless, they had it down to a fine art. Soon there were crops in the ground, and a smoke house for the abundant catfish found in the local waterways was built. A two-story compound gave shelter from the cold and Thériault had his own sleeping quarters, complete with a tub so that he could get a nightly 'rub down' from one of his wives. It was not unusual for Thériault to have intercourse with one of his wives while the others rubbed his back.

Initially the new settlement had a positive feeling. It seemed that everyone was pulling together to create a new sustainable society. Everybody toiled to get crops started and several businesses were set up. Bulk purchases of produce were made and it was sold through roadside stalls in the region. The new camp had a state-of-the-art oven allowing the production of top quality baked goods that found ready customers in surrounding markets. It was at this time that the sect christened itself 'The Little Ants' or 'The Ant Hill Kids' thanks to their industrious ways.

As the challenges of setting up an economically viable settlement were met, and as the routine of daily life became established, Thériault got bored. He began to drink again.

With this final move Thériault had his followers exactly where he wanted them. In a bush block removed from any infrastructure he was truly the master of his domain. Pesky social workers and police often found the property difficult to find, let alone access. A maze of unsigned fire tracks came off the rough mountain roads and no doubt Thériault made sure that any signs or indicators of the cult presence were removed whenever possible. This move was not necessarily driven by conniving logic. Thériault was becoming increasingly paranoid.

Not only did the distance from infrastructure make it difficult for the authorities to keep track of the members, it also made it near impossible for his following to escape his bullying ways. This was not enough for Thériault. He prohibited any of his followers from leaving the compound on their own, even for an hour or so. Each individual was told to report on even the slightest suspicions that a member was contemplating flight. Thériault's paranoia was communicated to his flock. Many turned up to Thériault with fabricated or inaccurate accusations. Whether there was any truth in the claims was irrelevant – punishment was bound to follow. Even the slightest misdemeanor, such as not giving the leader the best loaf of bread or failing to complete a task the way he liked it, could result in a snitch having a word in the leader's ear.

The greater the informing on other devotees, the greater devotion they showed to Thériault. As well as constant snide backstabbing, Thériault established a primitive class system. Some members were designated slaves. To them went the worst jobs: cleaning toilets, carrying water, chopping wood.

Thériault became the dispenser of all that was good in the world. Extra rations were provided on the cold winter nights and those who were particularly favored could sleep in his bed or stay at his side during the communal meals. One of the greatest privileges was to be rewarded with his leftovers, or even a bottle of beer from the private stocks kept under lock and key. Thériault could turn the full power of his charismatic charm on an individual and transform the lucky recipient into putty in his hands. It only had to happen once or twice, but that was enough to bind them to him and make them desire more. Praise given in public and in front of the less favored became a valuable tool of manipulation. New rubber boots or a nice jumper could make the difference in the harsh environment the cult existed in. All largesse came from the one source.

From the same source came unimaginable pain. Those who broke the 'law' were sentenced to jumping naked into frozen streams. Others were beaten with rods. The favored members of the time often carried out the discipline under Thériault's supervision.

Like many cults leaders, compliance did not lead to a lessening of violence but instead drove Thériault to ever-greater atrocities. His violent methods were as simple as the rough conditions his followers lived in. He would use anything at hand. When 'Pappy' became angry, he instructed his followers to seize the offender and pin them down to a bench. He would grab anything at hand – knives, cleavers, skewers – and proceed to torture and maim. Fingers and toes were lopped off, teeth were extracted and skin was torn from flesh. Followers demonstrated their belief by maiming each other. Some broke limbs with sledgehammers while others shot at each other with shotguns. Feces, rats and bugs were forced down unwilling throats for the tiniest misdemeanor.

One of Thériault's favorite punishments was to order the perpetrator to lie naked on the cold floor of the shack. He then urinated in their mouths and over their head. At other times he ordered one cultist to defecate on the floor before commanding another to lick their unwiped anus and smear the feces over their face.

Such was the control that Thériault had over his adult followers that they derived a perverse satisfaction from the cruel punishments he dished out. In their minds they had sinned and 'Moses' had seen through their wickedness. In his wisdom and full of love, Thériault had given an appropriate consequence and cleansed them of their sin. In the topsy-turvy world of cult life, punishment meant love. The most important thing in life was to get attention from Thériault.

Thériault was of course a classic manipulator. After dishing out a particularly brutal punishment he would reverse roles within the group and elevate the individual that he had just punished over the other members, giving them a temporary authority.

This constant state of fear had perhaps the greatest effect on the children. When social workers did manage to get within the cult compound they were greeted by a unique group of youngsters. Outwardly the scenes seemed normal, with adults going about their business while the children moved around with serene smiles on their faces. But after an hour or so it dawned on the visitors that something was wrong – the children didn't laugh, or play, or cry or interact with their parents in any meaningful way.

Even the toddlers knew that drawing attention to themselves through boisterous behavior was likely to earn a whipping. One social worker visited the school. A group of children under five sat coloring in for hours on end, without making a sound or moving from their chair. One two-year-old sat amidst a plethora of toys. He did not move, too afraid to even touch a toy, let alone play with it. They were like little terrified zombies.

No wonder. It was made clear to all within the cult that the children were Thériault's. Parents were not allowed to take an active hand in raising their children. Any who took too great an interest in their offspring would soon find themselves being informed upon and punished. To prove the point, Thériault used the children to punish their parents. There were many incidents where children slapped, kicked and hit their parents in full view of the rest of the congregation. No humiliation was spared the errant mother or father – they received the punishment while on their hands and knees, tears coursing down their faces. This was nothing compared to what Thériault could get up to. In his foul moods he would attack the children, throwing them against trees or tossing them into the lake.

Just as children were conditioned by Thériault, so were the parents. When the local child services threatened to take away the children and place them in foster homes unless their mothers left with the children, none would leave Thériault, fearing the impending apocalypse and too scared to sever their emotional dependence.

Once he had taken his people into the wilderness, his bullying nature came to the fore. With no civilized restraints Thériault unleashed a reign of terror upon the cult members. He later remonstrated with himself, explaining that it was alcohol that led to his excesses, but he used it as an excuse for his brutality, his murderous inclinations and his incipient necrophilia.

After each drunken outburst Thériault would plead for forgiveness from his followers and promise to mend his ways. This contrite state usually lasted as long as his hangover and his violence continued to escalate. The subservience of the Little Ants grew commensurate with the savagery inflicted upon them. Finally, Thériault turned his hand to murder.

Thériault had always favored his own offspring. He had divided the children into two groups: the chosen ones and the slave children. He took a particular dislike to a five-month-old baby named Eleazar. The infant was the son of Gabrielle and was born with a slightly deformed eyelid. Thériault maintained that this was the mark of

Satan and continually beat the tiny child. He repeatedly swore when in the presence of the infant and complained that they would all be better off with the child dead.

Irate at some perceived slight from the child, Thériault ordered Gabrielle to place the baby outside in a wheelbarrow. She did so at 9.30 am on 26 January 1985. It was minus 10 degrees Celsius (14 degrees Fahrenheit) that snowy morning. At 10.45 Thériault allowed the young nurse to check on her child. Eleazar had turned blue in the cold. Using the commune's two-way radio, an ambulance was summoned to rendezvous on one of the fire tracks near the camp. The baby was rushed to the local hospital but was declared dead on arrival.

Thériault was not held responsible for this death and the tragedy was put down to cot death. Local childcare protection agencies were not convinced that it was a harmless mischance. In a military-like operation the local social services, using all-terrain vehicles, descended on the commune and seized the remaining children. All of the adults chose to remain with the increasingly violent guru.

One of Thériault's obsessions was with surgery. Considering himself above the common man he believed that he was an expert on all things medical. He had a collection of surgical manuals and would use any pretext to operate on one of his followers. Along with Jacques the other remaining adult male within the group was Claude Boaz. Thanks to some minor infraction he was ordered to tie a rubber band around one testicle. By the time it was taken off several days later the young man's testicle had become swollen and painful. It was the size of an orange and was turning blue and black.

Thériault decided to operate. Boaz was having none of it and hid in a communal hut. Thériault, thoroughly drunk, jumped in the commune's jeep and repeatedly rammed into the hut until it threatened to collapse on the terrified Boaz. As he came out, other members seized him, took him into the hut and pinned his arms and legs. Thériault took a razor blade, sliced open the scrotum and removed the offending organ with his grubby fingers. He then took a red-hot iron and cauterized the wound. Boaz staggered off into the forest with blood streaming down his leg. He was fortunate to survive with one testicle intact. Solange Boilard was not so fortunate.

Solange was one of the first recruits to Thériault's orbit, when he was still proselytizing under the aegis of the Seventh Day Adventists. She had held out longer than the other girls against the leader's sexual approaches and was initially able to stand up to his wild pronouncements. By 1984 she was one of his staunchest supporters and was treated as Thériault's head wife. She kept the commune's books and acted as Thériault's chief lieutenant.

Solange's health began to deteriorate under the dreadful conditions that they were living under. In the autumn of 1988 her condition worsened and she found it difficult to hold down solids.

Thériault decided that Solange had a liver problem and that he would operate. He summoned all of the remaining cultists to help. He began by laying Solange on a table covered with a plastic sheet and a woolen blanket. Thériault believed in the medicinal properties of enemas and had a device that held a mix of water, olive oil and molasses. He spent half an hour trying to insert a rubber tube into Solange's rectum. While the others stood and watched she lost control of her bowels, shedding urine and feces over the operating table. Undaunted, Thériault continued.

The next stage of the surgery was to soften up her kidneys. Thériault punched the young woman violently in the stomach several times. A new tube was then inserted through Solange's nose and the cult members were ordered to blow into the tube. While performing this bizarre ritual Thériault made a 12-centimetre (5-inch) incision into her belly, below the right ribs. He then proceeded to pull out pieces of intestine, which were cut out, along with slabs of fat. The conscious woman was silent during the procedure. Thériault assured her that she was now cured and told her to get up and walk around.

Had a medical practitioner been present he or she would have realized that Thériault had handed his wife a death sentence through acute peritonitis. This is when digestive chemicals leak into the abdomen through wounds in the intestine, leading to acute inflammation of the peritoneum. After several days of agony Solange died and was buried behind the cult's dormitory.

Thériault was not finished with his murdered wife's body. He had the corpse exhumed. The coffin was uncovered and the uterus and kidneys were put in a jar. She was then reburied, but not for long. The now rotting copse was exhumed and a hand drill was used to lobotomize her prefrontal cortex. The top of the skull was cut off so that Thériault could masturbate over her rotting brain. These exhumations continued for several weeks, each time another body part removed by the increasingly deranged Thériault, who claimed that God was commanding him to carry out these macabre acts.

It was too much. In a rare show of defiance the Little Ants demanded that Solange's remains be cremated. Before this final act he had a rib removed and this, along with his other possessions from her corpse, were used to make a necklace.

Remarkably Thériault was not to pay for this crime for several years. The catalyst for his downfall would come with the defection of Gabrielle Lavallée, the nurse.

After Solange's death Gabrielle became the focus of Thériault's ire. He treated her mercilessly. Gabrielle had already endured unimaginable torments at his hands. She suffered from a prolapsed uterus but, despite pleading with Thériault to allow a doctor to have a look at it, he refused and tried to treat it himself. One 'cure' was to thrust a pinecone into her vagina and strap it in with leather. Another method he tried was to tie the prolapsed organ with tape in the vain hope that it would wither away like a constrained testicle. Once, complaining that Gabrielle was 'mouthy' he grabbed a pair of pliers and tore nine teeth out of her jaw bone.

On 26 July 1989 Thériault went too far. Fearing that she would run from the commune, the intoxicated leader used a hunting knife to pin her right hand to a table. She stood there for 45 agonizing minutes while the drunken Thériault and three other stunned cultists looked on. Thériault took a curved carpet knife out of his toolbox, took it up to Gabrielle and began carving chunks out of the flesh of her right arm. Soon he tired and asked the other members to finish the job.

Such was the control that he exerted over his flock that they did not dare question him as pieces of flesh were hacked off until the bone of the upper arm was exposed. Thériault pulled out the knife, lay the butchered limb on the table and, with several whacks of a cleaver, severed the arm. It was taken outside and burnt. The stump was bound with twine and dipped in a saline solution. Several days later Thériault decided that he had to cut away bits of the stump as it was infected. He also cut off part of Gabrielle's breast so that it would 'attract' the infection.

For some unexplained reason he beat her on the top of the head with the blunt side of an axe. Two days later he cauterized the stump with a red hot metal bar but was so drunk that he dropped it several times, inflicting agonizing burns to her stomach and buttocks.

Gabrielle decided that if she was not to end up as a desecrated corpse like Solange she would have to flee. On 16 August 1989 an exhausted and fly blown victim of years of brutality turned up at York County Hospital.

Thériault had gone a step too far. He was arrested after an exhaustive manhunt on 6 October. On the 24th of that month he was charged with the first-degree murder of Solange Boilard. This was downgraded to second degree and Thériault was sentenced for a short custodial sentence. Prosecutors were not satisfied and as the true stories of the horrific events at Burnt River leaked out it was decided that he was too dangerous to be released into the community. On 18 January 1993 he was given a life sentence.

Thériault's half-baked ideas have had no long-term impact. All that remains of his time at the helm of his cult are mentally and physically scarred individuals. After sentencing, Thériault sought to appeal several times before declaring that he never wanted to be released anyway. He got his wish.

On 26 February 2011 the 63-year-old was stabbed to death by a cellmate named Matthew Gerrard MacDonald. MacDonald was a lifer and had nothing to lose. He took exception to Thériault's holier-than-thou attitude but reports claim he was particularly upset that most of his cellmate's crimes had been aimed at women and children. He made no attempt to hide his crime. With a prison shank MacDonald launched a blitz attack on Thériault and repeatedly stabbed him in the neck. There was no attempt to conceal the crime and everything was caught on CCTV. Once his victim had bled out, MacDonald walked up to the guard station, handed his knife to a guard and said 'That sonofabitch is done for. He's all sliced up, here's the knife.'

MacDonald pleaded guilty to second-degree murder and was given another life sentence.

CHAPTER NINE

Heaven's Gate: Alien Intervention

Revelation Book 11

3 And I will give authority to my two witnesses, and they will prophesy for 1,260
days clothed in sackcloth.
7 And when they shall have finished their testimony, the beast that ascends out
of the bottomless pit shall make war against them, and shall overcome them,
and kill them.
11 And after three days and a half the Spirit of life from God entered into them,
and they stood upon their feet; and great fear fell upon them which saw them.
12 And they heard a great voice from heaven saying unto them, Come up hither.
And they ascended up to heaven in a cloud; and their enemies beheld them.

A San Diego police patrol car was instructed to proceed to a rented mansion in the hillside suburb known as Rancho Santé Fe on 26 March 1997. The call out was an 11-45: San Diego code for suicide.

The pair moved through the unlocked door into an immaculately clean two-story mansion. If they were experienced troopers they would have recognized a particular scent: the smell of human flesh about to turn foul.

Throughout the mansion, lying peacefully on bunk beds, were a collection of dead bodies. The call sign 11-45 was inaccurate. There was not one suicide but 39. They were all dressed in black trousers and shirts with white socks and brand new Nike runners. Two had plastic bags placed over their heads and 37 were covered with purple shawls. On closer inspection it became clear that approximately half had been dead for several days. Their flesh was beginning to swell and corrupt in the San Diego heat. The others were fresher and still displayed symptoms of rigor mortis.

The group belonged to Heaven's Gate. They had decided to follow their master to a new plane of existence. This was a mass suicide that had its roots in a unique interpretation of the Book of Revelation. Marshall Hepplewhite, who was one of the founders of Heaven's Gate, was facing his own personal Armageddon. He believed that he was suffering from incurable cancer and was determined that he would not ascend to the next level of existence on his own. Hepplewhite was going to take as many people as possible with him.

Genesis

Marshall Herff Applewhite's upbringing was more apple pie than mass suicide. He was born on 17 May 1931 to the Presbyterian minister Marshall Herff Applewhite Sr and his loving wife Louise. He had three siblings. The family moved around frequently, following Marshall Sr to his various ministries, and was seen to hold conservative values.

Marshall Jr became religious from a young age. While still a young man he followed the conventional path of a brief stint as a draftee in the army and a marriage to his sweetheart Anne Pearce. The young couple soon had two children. He earned a bachelor's degree in philosophy before earning a master's degree in music at the University of Colorado. During this period, he developed a fascination and love of musical theater – perhaps this was an early indication that Marshall Herff Applewhite was not quite as clean-cut and straight-laced as he first appeared.

A strict religious upbringing combined with increasingly powerful homosexual urges produced the unique cult leader that Applewhite eventually became. So strong were his urges, and so deep his guilt, that Applewhite neutered himself and some of his followers in the quest for a pure faith.

Herff was a popular young man throughout his years of education. Friends from that period remember him as a cheerful character with a fine sense of comic timing and piecing blue eyes. It appears he did not take himself too seriously and would often play the fool with funny walks and humorous impersonations. He was quite charismatic and was able to perform in amateur theater quite credibly; by all reports he had an excellent singing voice.

Some individuals who are struggling with self-image or sexual confusion seek to deal with these issues by overachieving and maintaining a furious pace. It appears that Applewhite sought continual motion by serving as president of many voluntary organizations. He was persuasive and intelligent, and his popularity ensured that he was seen as a born leader. As a young man he was handsome and attractive, not the gaunt and fanatical looking leader who appeared in videos urging the entire world to commit suicide. He could not maintain the facade for ever.

Cracks began to emerge. Following his father to a new church every two or three years meant that Applewhite had to leave friends behind. He perhaps sought to overcome the pain that this produced by building more superficial relations with people, becoming adept at manipulating individuals so that they would rapidly accept the newcomer in their midst. He soon developed a knack for gauging and satisfying the needs of individuals.

Life with the Presbyterians had another damaging effect on the passionate young man. Applewhite Sr believed that sex was for procreation, not pleasure. It should be completed in as simple a manner as possible. Homosexuality was a sin. It was punishable by the foulest tortures that Beelzebub could devise.

Applewhite Jr compensated through a passionate pursuit of music. While his loving wife stayed home raising his children, Applewhite played several starring roles in amateur productions through Colorado and Texas. He was the choir director at the prestigious St Mark's Episcopal Church in Houston and sang for the Houston Grand Opera.

His pursuit of a musical career led to his undoing. Applewhite became a music professor at Houston's University of St Thomas. Solo lessons were too much of a temptation and he found that he could not keep his hands to himself. He embarked upon an affair with a much younger man and soon there were whispers and rumors circulating through the university halls. This was not the first time Applewhite had strayed and it appears an earlier position had been terminated for the same reason. His wife knew there was something up and the couple divorced in 1968.

Scandal is never a good thing in educational institutions and in a bid to cover up the affair the university fired their music professor, citing emotional issues that were impacting his health and performance. To add to Marshall's troubles he was given a lead role in a professional musical production, but was forced to resign, as his vocal scale was insufficient. This was too much and it would appear that he had a total psychological collapse that necessitated a period of recovery in a hospital for the mentally ill. Debilitating panic attacks combined with heart problems required a range of medicines. He was also determined to fight his homosexual urges.

It seems that Applewhite was under so much pressure that he experienced a heart attack. That was not all that he experienced. While knocked out and in recovery the man, who by now was in his mid-forties, witnessed his first visitation. Two figures dressed in white visited the ill man and suggested that he was perhaps the most recent reincarnation of Jesus Christ.

It is around this time that he met the other figure who would - indirectly in her case - lead to the mass suicide of the members of Heaven's Gate. Applewhite had an instant connection to Bonnie Lu Nettles. At 44 years old the trained nurse was locked in an unhappy marriage with two disabled daughters. She was developing a rich fantasy life to escape the drudgery of her everyday existence.

In the early 1970s she began dabbling in spiritualism. Nettles attended many séances, poured a small fortune into consultations with mediums and fortune-tellers and eventually formed a spiritual connection with a long deceased 19th century monk named Brother Francis. The two often communicated and Nettles was informed that she would soon meet a mysterious tall man with a fair complexion and mesmerizing eyes.

Lo and behold, in 1972 she met Applewhite and there was an immediate spiritual attraction. Nettles conducted an astrological reading for her new friend and found that their fates were closely aligned. It was the first recognition of 'synchronicity' - the fortunate merging of two disparate events that would play such a key role in the cult's fortunes.

The two realized that they were on a mission from God. Nettles would be the sage, he would be the speaker. On New Year's Day 1973 they left the past behind and embarked upon a journey of spiritual discovery.

The two fed upon each other's fantasies. There is a psychiatric syndrome known as folie à deux. This occurs when one partner draws the other into a shared system of delusional beliefs. These then build with mutual reinforcement. The mish-mash that the pair came up with included material from the New Testament, some Eastern religions and even *Star Trek*.

Bizarre Beliefs

In many ways Heaven's Gate lives on. Their website is still maintained by diehard members determined to preserve the wisdom of Applewhite. It is rather dated and filled with 1980s iconography. It is remarkable though in that it contains the last messages laid down by the cult just before the mass suicide.

The theology propounded by Applewhite is quite simple. Two thousand years ago, aliens who had ascended to the next level of spiritual attainment realized that many humans were ready to evolve beyond the constraints of their bodies. These 'vehicles' were wedded to mammalian impulses and prevented the spirits within from moving to a new spiritual plane. A guide was sent to prepare selected members for ascension to the new plane and it inserted itself in the readymade 'container' that we now know as Jesus. The new plane of existence is what we mortals refer to as heaven. This vehicle called Jesus knew its role. It had to gather around it a group to be harvested. By accepting his teachings and renouncing all that tied them to an earthly existence, this group would be able leave their vehicles behind and ascend to the next level on spaceships crewed by similarly enlightened beings. Jesus' role was to help others metamorphose into higher beings – he was the guide who would provide passage through Heaven's Gate.

Fortunately for us, the message continues, another vessel had been chosen in our time to do the same as Jesus. Applewhite, or 'Do – The Present Representative' as he was now known, was the latest reincarnation of Christ and it was his job to harvest willing acolytes who would leave their primitive vessels behind and ascend to the new level.

But this was no easy role, according to the Present Representative. All around the world were 'Luciferites' who were determined to lead people astray. Governments, the media, education, employers, producers and retailers were all part of a giant conspiracy aimed at ensuring that most of humanity were bound by their mammalian urges. These evil 'discarnates' were constantly attacking the true believers and reinforcing the norms of society.

Do was giving humans one last chance to ascend to a higher plane. They must be quick though; this was the last chance until a new age at least 2000 years in the future. The window was briefly open. Any delay in leaving the vehicles behind might make them too late. Heaven's Gate would soon close.

This rather bizarre theology did not arise out of nowhere. It had been gestating since that first meeting between Nettles and Applewhite. He had experienced visions nominating him as a new Christ – she had been told in a prophecy that she would meet a new messenger. They had found each other just as their previous lives had unraveled. The misfortunes and tragedies of the past were actually God's plans for the pair. The two became inseparable. While traveling they meditated together, prayed and thrashed out their new reality. After six months the pair experienced a powerful revelation. They realized that they were 'the two' prophesized in Revelation. Chapter 11 of the text taught that two witnesses would be placed on Earth to teach God's will. After fighting the Beast the two would die. Three days later their physical bodies would be reanimated with God's energy and they would ascend to heaven in a cloud. The cloud was, according to the pair, an intergalactic spaceship.

Applewhite was to be Jesus and Bonnie was his guide. Once they had gathered a school of adherents they would all be collected in a spaceship and become immortal androgynous beings. At this early stage it was presumed that their living bodies would be collected. This event was known as 'The Demonstration' or 'The Harvesting'.

It is unlikely that the two enjoyed a sexual relationship. Applewhite was constantly struggling with his sexuality and the two firmly believed that all worldly pleasures such as family, friends, good food and good sex were all impediments to moving from the vehicle and onto a higher plane of existence.

The pair spent several years traveling and seeking to spread their message, but their theology was greeted with scorn. This led to an apocalyptic flavor developing in their thinking. Satan was a former member of the next level who had turned against God. He produced millions of evil spirits who possessed human vessels and encouraged them to satisfy base desires. These powerful forces were leading to natural disasters, war and pollution – surely signs, the pair maintained, that Armageddon was on its way.

In 1974 the two received further proof that Satan was working against the pair. Applewhite was arrested for credit card fraud and theft of a rental vehicle. He spent six months in jail. This proved to be a blessing as he used the time to write a pamphlet extolling his vision. After his release this pamphlet swayed a group of 24 'seekers' who were also preparing for ascension in Los Angeles. The organization had recently broken up and in another 'synchronicity' they attached themselves to the pair.

With a new flock to attend to the leaders renamed themselves and Bo and Peep. They gave their sect the name Human Individual Metamorphosis (HIM). From this solid core they attracted up to 200 members by conducting lectures throughout many states. Numbers fluctuated over the years and unlike most cults there was no effort to hold members against their will. In fact one group was sent to set up a base camp in Arizona but never heard from the leadership again and eventually dispersed. In 1976 the pair renamed themselves Ti (Nettles) and Do (Applewhite) and with their supporters actively sought a spaceship to take them to the new level.

Their theology also altered to take into account those who became disenchanted with the cult. The true members, those that would be harvested during the demonstration, were actually neophyte members of the next level who had been planted by the extra-terrestrials in human bodies. Their parents were no more than vessels, test tubes as it were.

In 1985 the cult took the first step towards becoming a suicide cult. Nettles died. In 1983 she had an eye removed due to cancer. This was just an outward sign of a cancer that was ravaging her body. Her doctor informed her that she had a limited time to live. She and Applewhite disbelieved the diagnosis. They were 'the two' and would ascend to heaven together. This delusional thinking came to an end in June 1985 when the aggressive cancer destroyed her liver and other organs. Ti was no more.

Applewhite was not dismayed. She would be reborn in three days, just as Revelation 11–12 prophesized. When this did not happen Applewhite had her vehicle cremated and the ashes scattered over a lake in Texas. As with all good mystics Applewhite was able to do some quick thinking to explain the new circumstances to his followers. Ti had in fact ascended to the next level, he explained. Her work on Earth was done. The physical container was not necessary. Even now Ti was communicating with Do and helping him in the preparations to carry the students to the next level.

Most of the members were satisfied with this explanation, although some left. For those who stayed there was an important change in their thinking. It was possible to discard the vehicle and the soul could carry on to the next level without it. Suicide was now sanctioned in the revised theology.

In 1988 Applewhite almost died of tick fever. He began to work on the theory that his body was merely a suit of clothes that he wore while tending the garden. Applewhite went further. In 1993 the sect was renamed Total Overcomers Anonymous. They were to overcome the imminent recycling of the world when all of civilization was destroyed. Not only humankind but all of life as we know it would vanish. Only those who had evolved to the next level would survive.

The cult began a media blitz to spread the new apocalyptic message. Videos were sent to New Age stores and ads were taken out in UFO magazines. No expense was spared and there was even a full-page ad taken out in *USA Today* at a cost of $30,000. This told in graphic detail how 'weeds' had taken over the 'garden' and the entire world would soon be 'recycled'. Despite these blitzes, numbers in the cult stayed static.

A new problem arose when Applewhite's health began to decline. The most dedicated members could not imagine life without Do. The 'class' began to discuss how it might be necessary for them to move on. Suicide became a realistic goal. Drowning and gunfire were options that were discussed, but these were seen as too violent. By the mid-90s the group began to refer themselves as Heaven's Gate. The scene was set for mass suicide.

Attraction, Initiation and Control

From the years 1975 to 1997 Heaven's Gate, in all of its different forms, may have had up to a thousand members. Few remained for the long haul. The regime placed upon them by Nettles and Applewhite was harshly monastic and few could maintain the required enthusiasm. Those who did not show the correct level of commitment were frequently moved on by Applewhite himself. They were given train tickets, a warm hug and an invitation to return if ever they did decide to recommit.

The recorded 'Earth Exit Statements' are quite remarkable in that they show a passive and defenseless manner in the members. They all talk of a deep alienation from mainstream society. These were the types of people Nettle and Applewhite sought to attract. Unlucky in love or money, unable to fit in with their more robust peers; all sought some kind of personal transformation. That Ti and Do offered eternal life was another attraction.

The cult operated on the principle that the further a net is cast, the greater the likely catch. In lecture halls up and down the west coast of America, meetings were held where the two delivered their counterculture message. They would then leave the hall and some of the more persuasive members of the class stayed behind to recruit.

Once an individual had decided to join the organization they had to sever all ties with their previous lives. They could go for years without contacting friends and relatives. All personal possessions were sold off and the proceeds put into the cult coffers. To give Nettles and Applewhite their due, they never used the money for their own personal pleasures but put the funds towards building 'spaceship bases' or renting cult buildings and paying for necessities. If a member chose to leave they were often reimbursed.

Another source of revenue was a web design business, which the cult specialized in. This allowed the members to generate income without personal physical contact with the outside world.

And that was the key to the new world that members entered - removal from society. They were to see themselves as an elite crew of intergalactic travelers. Do was the captain and Ti was the admiral. They had to train themselves and demonstrate perfect discipline, just as a crew on a naval ship were expected to. But they were training for life on board an approaching star ship.

In a remarkable 'synchronicity' Thomas Nichols - the brother of Nichelle Nichols, the actor who played Lt Uhura in the original *Star Trek* series - was a member of the Heaven's Gate Away Team. He died during the suicides.

Once within the class their lives were strictly regimented. They had to remove themselves from humanity altogether. They were not allowed to listen to music, read, take drugs or engage in sex. They developed an androgynous look, wearing shapeless garments and sporting plain haircuts. Applewhite knew that sex had distracted him from a fulfilling lifestyle and he had himself castrated, along with six other males within the group, to eliminate this temptation.

Nettles and Applewhite took it upon themselves to teach their flock how to perform as a highly functioning next level crew. The rented mansion was called a craft. Within the craft strict protocols were used to imitate life on board a spacecraft. Members were given precise parameters about when they could have breakfast, how many times they could pass a knife with butter over a piece of toast, when they could use the 'bath chamber' and when they could sleep. While lying in their bunks each member had to lie with their hands above their waist on top of their blankets; lying on their stomach was a definite no-no. Private property was non-existent. Individual identities were suppressed. At one stage facemasks were worn while within the craft.

The crew had to check in with 'Central' once every eleven minutes. Here they were asked to reflect on their experiences for the day and ask themselves how they could serve the community better. Just as citizens of Maoist China were asked to make criticisms so were the members of the class. Any human preconceptions were challenged and if a member reverted to a mammalian habit such as whistling or doodling they would be called on it by their peers. When in the outside world, members were required to complete journals discussing the human behaviors that they saw around them.

Helping the members clear their minds was 'the tone.' Students would concentrate for hours on the ringing of a tuning fork, excluding all other thoughts. Another rule was to reduce all talk to the barest minimum. For days, all communication was considered unnecessary and they could only say 'yes,' 'no' or 'don't know,' if they had to answer a brief question. Otherwise, small handwritten notes were used. Another activity was watching for the 'Demonstration.' All night vigils were maintained as members kept a look out for Next Level Activity – the spacecraft that were to pick them up.

With the death of Nettles, Applewhite felt that his position needed support. He presented each of the members with a gold wedding band in an emotional bonding ceremony. Students sent devotional letters to Applewhite, praising his wisdom.

The outside world was not so enamored with the strange cult. Ex-members sought out the media and numbers began to drift away. In 1995 the cult took out a lease on a massive palatial mansion in Rancho, Santa Fe. They were quiet and didn't distract their neighbors, although a large internet servicing business was run from the premises.

Applewhite realized that he would not get many more acolytes. With his failing health he felt that the harvesting was complete.

Armageddon

Branch Davidians committed mayhem and slaughter as a result of an ATF raid. Asahara did so to avoid a looming government crackdown. The Heaven's Gate suicide was prompted by a prank call on a crank radio show.

Art Bell's radio show was named *Coast to Coast* and it had a reputation for attracting oddball callers who believed in the paranormal, conspiracy theories and UFOs. Few who listened took the material seriously, but of course there were listeners who took every report as gospel.

On 14 November 1996 an amateur astronomer called Chuck Shramek called and made a claim that would have made even the most jaded listener sit up in rapt attention. After establishing his bona fides as a serious stargazer, Chuck explained that he had taken some photos of an approaching comet. Hale-Bopp, as it is known, was quite clear at this time. It was so clear that Chuck declared that in the comet's tail was the outline of a spaceship. This spaceship was something to behold, with rings just like the planet Saturn. Bell knew a good story when he heard one and got some 'expert' opinions from an organization of psychics. These fellows tapped into the comet and revealed that they had communicated with interstellar travelers who were using the comet's energy to propel their intergalactic craft.

Of course most people dismissed this story as a load of nonsense, especially when professional astronomers examined the photo and found nothing unusual in the makeup of the comet or its tail.

Applewhite seized upon it. He realized that here was the solution to all of his problems. The comet had come just in time. He had become convinced that cancer was soon to end his life. Some state and federal authorities were sniffing around his organization; there was a chance he might have another unpleasant brush with the law. A comet had been passing when he had met Nettles. The law of synchronicity, which had such an effect on his organization, had returned.

Whether there was this much logic to Applewhite's decisions is of course uncertain. Maybe he really did believe the bizarre theology that he promoted. Whatever the reason, Applewhite decided that the arrival of Hale-Bopp would be used to justify the mass suicide of him and his followers.

Applewhite had to convince his followers that this was the time. No expense would be spared. Using cult funds he purchased a large refracting telescope and used it to track the comet. He declared to his followers that there was in fact a large ship with an intergalactic crew of higher-level beings. The best news was, as a delighted Applewhite reported to his disciples, among the crew was none other than the disembodied spirit of Bonnie Nettles. That was why, he explained, his spiritual partner had not been reborn on Earth. She had in fact ascended to the inter-dimensional next level and here she was returning to rescue Applewhite and his acolytes.

But, explained Applewhite, they had to move fast. The comet would not return for many years and by then it would be too late. The environment would be all but destroyed and humanity would be wiped from the face of the Earth. All they had to do was discard their physical containers, their vehicles, and they would all journey to the next, higher phase of immortal existence.

His audience was well primed. There were no dissenters.

There was much to do. It seems that at one stage Applewhite had considered buying firearms and using violence to destroy his followers. This idea was abandoned. He had to make it clear that the complete cohort of his followers went to their deaths willingly. Most were entirely within the thrall of their leader and embraced his unique path with enthusiasm.

It is clear that they enjoyed many hours of harangues from Applewhite, but he gave them the opportunity to give personal testimonies. In what are no doubt the most bizarre recordings of the 20th century, each of the cult members sat in front of a camcorder and recorded why they were taking this step towards suicide. Despite the glowing exteriors and sunny smiles of the members, there is an awareness of the magnitude of their decisions; a nervousness, despite their commitment to carry through the action.

These 'Final Exit Statements' were all taken in the lovely surrounds of Rancho Santa Fe. While a lush lawn and singing birds give a serenity to the scene, their words are chilling. Each talks of how they were miserable before they joined the organization. Isolated and shunned by even their family members. The individuals all describe how Do and Ti gave their life meaning. They can't wait, each explains, to be reunited on the spiritual plane, leaving their primitive vehicles on Earth. There was no way that they would be left behind, bereft of the spiritual support of their leaders and cult companions.

While these videos were being recorded, other preparations were being made. Companies that did business with the cult's IT department received polite emails stating that they would no longer be able to provide programming and tech support.

At the same time, brand new black trousers and shirts were purchased, along with white socks and Nike runners. Embroidered badges with the words 'Heaven's Gate Away Team' were sewn onto the new tops. Intergalactic boarding passes were printed with each member's names and date of birth. Each was assigned a bunk and on small tables next to the mattresses the members placed their IDs, passports and a small amount of cash. There were also duffel bags with a neatly folded change of clothes.

With everything ready to go, Applewhite had one more task. He produced his last video, a call for everybody to follow his lead and carry out suicide. It is possible that this video – remarkable for the staring hypnotic eyes of the guru, set deep in his gaunt features – was taken after the first wave of suicides. There are only 20 or so students in the audience; one or two would be manning the camera and the lights. Maybe the others were already lying dead on their bunks. Applewhite makes one last impassioned plea. God is giving them a chance at eternal life by shedding their vehicles. Ti is swinging by and for a small window Heaven's Gate will be open to those who seek to move to the next level. In seeking to demonstrate his caring nature, Applewhite has the camera pan over the rapt audience. There are only 20 there but, despite his personal bonding with each and every member, he gets some names wrong.

They will attain immortality, but all who remain behind will die. Even though he avoided some of the worst excesses of many of his fellow cult leaders, he proved in that final hour to be an ego driven maniac. His folie á deux had infected his 38 pupils, but Applewhite wished there were more. His final message was: come and join us, anybody can, but don't be too late. You too could get a boarding pass into the Kingdom of Heaven.

The killings went off with textbook precision. The last of the cult's assets had been sold. Clothes had been purchased for all members and the mansion had been scrupulously cleaned from top to bottom.

The members were to die in three waves. The first 15 committed suicide on 22 March 1997. Each was given a serving of applesauce or pudding laced with the powerful drug phenobarbital. This drug's clinical use includes the suppression of fits in epileptics. It slows the central nervous system and can lead to brain death if a dose exceeding 100 micrograms per milliliter is administered. Autopsies revealed that many of the suicides had consumed much more than this amount.

They were all drunk. Many had twice the legal limit of alcohol for driving. Empty bottles of vodka were found neatly arranged around the mansion. After consuming this cocktail of drugs and drink each member had a plastic bag placed around their head and tied around the neck. The stoned students shed their vehicles through a combination of drugs, alcohol and asphyxiation.

One thing attests to the hold that Applewhite had over his flock: none of the deceased had defense wounds. There were no broken fingernails from fighting off their killers, no bruises suffered as they were pinned down to die. It seems that they were so convinced of the rightness of their actions that no one changed their mind at the last minute and tried to fight for survival.

The next day another 15 transitioned to the next level. Applewhite was probably with this group. On the 24th the final nine died. All were covered with a purple shawl and lay peacefully on their bunk. They had five dollars in their pocket and a peaceful look on their face. The final two still had the plastic bags over their faces and did not have a shawl covering their torsos.

The last two sent a message to an ex-member. Rio D'Angelo received a package and an invitation to attend the ranch. He did, on the 26th. As an ex-member he still believed Applewhite's message, but could not adapt to the monastic lifestyle. He appeared with a camcorder and, after recording his grisly find, called the police. Those who had died on the 22nd were already beginning to putrefy. In the months that followed, three other cultists followed Do's instruction to commit suicide.

Applewhite had fooled himself. There was no need for the hasty suicides. His autopsy revealed that he was in fact free of the cancer that had so haunted his thoughts and precipitated the slaughter.

CHAPTER TEN

Deprogramming

Revelation Book 9

20 The rest of mankind who were not killed by these plagues still did not repent of
the work of their hands; they did not stop worshiping demons, and idols of gold,
silver, bronze, stone and wood—idols that cannot see or hear or walk.
21 Nor did they repent of their murders, their magic arts, their sexual immorality
or their thefts.

Once a cult has gained control of a subject, it is almost impossible to leave. The deadly organization to which they belong will break any law to keep them within their spiritual clutches. The very nature of doomsday cults makes it extremely hard for acolytes to leave them. Not only do they have to leave friends and allies, they also have to leave a highly structured lifestyle and a pervasive belief system.

Those who go through an internal process that enables them to see the hollowness of the cult's theology and its destructive impacts are able to move on without external intervention. They may need emotional and financial support, but once these individuals decide to leave, only force can make them stay.

Some of the most tragic stories come from individuals who have seen a doomsday cult for what it is and have left, but have been forced to leave their children behind as their partner refuses to join them. In many cases this had fatal consequences for the children.

The narcissistic personality disorder that most cult leaders exhibit makes them extremely sensitive to perceived slights. Those who seek to leave cults throw down a gauntlet to these leaders; the leader will do anything to bring the fleeing member back into the fold. Years of harassment and legal threats can follow. Many ex-cultists find that to truly escape they must leave the country or assume a new identity.

For anyone witnessing a loved one being damaged by their life within a cult, their aim will be to try and entice them to leave. This is a difficult road fraught with legal and moral implications.

Deprogramming

Deprogramming is a dirty word. During the heyday of cult activities, the 1970s to the 1990s, 'deprogrammers' earned a bad reputation for kidnapping cult members, locking them in isolated locations and using force to get the cultist to renounce their beliefs. Some activists were arrested, tried and jailed for this heavy-handed approach.

Deprogramming is a very expensive and drastic approach as it requires a well-trained (and perhaps well-armed) team to forcibly remove the cult member from their chosen environment. Once the target is in a secure lockup, the individual is subject to hour after hour of intense debriefing. Here the deprogrammers try to use 'ethical' psychological techniques in an attempt to counter the unethical methods of thought control used by the cult.

During the process attention can be drawn to the thought reform techniques used by the cult, revealing that these were used on hundreds or thousands of members. This method seeks to convince the subject that he or she was not really 'special'.

A deprogrammer would reward the cult member for thinking outside of the cult's orthodoxy and try to produce an emotional connection with the subject's former life. This may be in the form of something as simple as eating a hamburger or as complex as having family members sharing their memories of pre-cult life with photos, objects and video recordings.

Maybe one third of these attempts at deprogramming were unsuccessful. But even successful cases left the individuals responsible for the program open to lawsuits or criminal charges.

Intervention

Today a more acceptable response is to call in a cult expert, who can engage the individual in an intervention through a process of exit counseling.

A cult expert is someone who is familiar with the teachings and practices of groups and movements that can be considered to be cults. They are well versed in the methods that cults use to recruit, indoctrinate and keep members. They are trained to encourage cult members to re-evaluate their involvement with the organization and examine its real aims and background.

Interventions usually begin with a request from a family member who feels their loved one is being sucked into a dangerous situation. The next step is to lure the cult member away from the organization's clutches so that intensive counseling can begin.

Many interventions do not progress past this stage. This may be because the cult has located into another country or they defend their personnel within a well-guarded compound. Hyper vigilant monitoring of members is characteristic of the most dangerous cults and members can be forcibly restrained from meeting with their loved one. Aum Supreme and the Children of God were experts in this regard. With their numerous compounds and missions scattered around Japan and the world it was nearly impossible to actually determine where individuals were at any one time.

If the subject is successfully lured away, they will find themselves in a room packed with concerned friends and family members. Often a cultist's first reaction is to run, disgusted that their loved ones are not allowing them to 'make their own decisions' or 'lead their own life.' Once they are convinced to stay by the earnest entreaties of their family, the cult expert swings into action.

In the first part of the intervention, which can go for as long as four or five days, the expert lays out the features of a destructive cult. Groups other than the one that the subject belongs to are usually examined first, before parallels with the subject's own circumstances are pointed out.

During the entire process it is important that no one acts in a judgmental manner and that they deal with the subject sympathetically. The participants will have been coached beforehand.

After analyzing the features of destructive cults and the effect they have had on those involved in the intervention, the principles of manipulative thought reform are examined. Examples from past and present cults are provided and the subject is invited to examine what techniques have been used in their case.

Some interventions last all of two minutes. Some perceive that they have been ambushed. The sign of a successful intervention is when the subject returns on the second and subsequent days voluntarily. It is important to empower the victim; they can leave anytime they want, something true of both the counseling and the cult.

A detailed examination of the history of the cult and its leadership then follows. Lawsuits, criminal convictions, assets – all are put under the microscope. Information is power and a cult member who had been shamed into adhering to a set of beliefs can be empowered by knowledge of the crimes committed by the organizations to which they belong. The testimonies of other ex-members can be useful in this stage.

Pricking the information bubble that a cult has erected around the member is one thing, but it is also important to re-establish an emotional connection. The effect that the subject's actions have had on children, family and friends are dealt with in a non-accusatory way.

Another emotional aspect is showing how much they have been missing out on. Fun things such as overseas holidays and different media are highlighted. These show the limiting nature of cult propaganda.

It is important not to attack the cult with loaded language, but to explore its limitations. Contradictions in the leader's thinking are explored and the entire belief system is deconstructed. Flaws are highlighted. Quoting misleading and disingenuous utterances from the leader highlights the extent of the manipulation.

The advantage of having a cult expert during this phase is critical. As the subject begins to see beyond the intensive programming they have suffered, it is a relief to see an expert there to help and guide them towards a new beginning. The subject has to be treated with respect; their motivations for the initial attraction to the cult are examined to see if these original needs are still being met.

Ideally after an exit counseling program the cult member will decide to move on ... if the cult will let them.

Long-Term Effects

People who leave doomsday cults often have a long laundry list of problems. Many are harassed around the clock by their former cult comrades. Members who fled Jim Jones' People's Temple found cars loaded with aggressive Temple members parked outside their houses, or following them as they went about their business. Rubbish was interfered with and abusive phone calls were also among the tactics used by Jones' disciples. This was not as bad as the experience of those who chose to leave Manson's Family – a bullet in the head, dismemberment and a lonely grave in the California desert.

Provided that they do manage to escape their cult's clutches, there can be a whole bevy of psychological problems. Many feel shame and anger when they realize how badly they have been manipulated and how their assets are now gone. Depression, paranoia, guilt and an all-pervading fear are commonly reported. Cognitive functions may be reduced. They may have difficulty thinking clearly, making decisions, performing everyday activities and analyzing situations.

Moving from a situation where every waking moment and every waking thought was dominated by the cult, ex-members can spend months floating in an otherworldly fog until they get a new focus to motivate them.

They can count at least one blessing. They have left the cult and are free from the pervasive fear of an inevitable Armageddon.

A final word: it appears that the Book of Revelation may have been the last book accepted into the Christian canon and that many early churchmen could have been reluctant to include it in the New Testament. How many lives may have been saved had it been excluded?

Bibliography

Books

Anderson, Scott, *The Four O'Clock Murders: The True Story of a Mormon Family's Vengeance, Dell*, New York, 1993.

Begg, Paul & Fido, Martin, *Great Crimes and Trials of the Twentieth Century*, Carlton, 1997.

Brackett, D. W., *Holy Terror: Armageddon in Tokyo*, Weatherhill, 1996.

Bwire, Robert, *Ashes of Faith*, Frontier Publishing, Amsterdam, 2007.

Clarke, Phil Robin, Hardy, Liz & Williams, Anne, *Executioners*, Futura, 2008.

Goldwag, Arthur, *Cults Conspiracies and Secret Societies*, Vintage Books, 2017.

Gardiner, Philip, *Secret Societies*, New Page Books, 2007.

Hieronimus, Robert, *Founding Fathers, Secret Societies*, Destiny Books, 1989.

Howells, Robert, *The Illuminati*, Watkins, 2016.

Kaihla, Paul & Laver, Ross, *Savage Messiah* Doubleday Canada, 1993.

Kaplan, David E. & Marshall, Andrew, *The Cult at the End of the World*, Crown, 1996.

Lattin, Don, *Jesus Freaks*, Harper One, 2007.

Newport, Kenneth C., *The Branch Davidians of Waco: The History and Beliefs of an Apocalyptic Sect*, Oxford University Press, London, 2006.

Reston, James, *Dogs of God*, Doubleday, 2005.

Stork, Jane, *Breaking the Spell*, Macmillan, Sydney, 2009.

Tormey, Natacha, *Born into the Children of God*, Harper/Element, London, 2014.

Wasserman, James, *An Illustrated History of The Knights Templar*, Destiny Books, 2006.

Scheeres, Julia, *A Thousand Lives*, Free Press, 2011.

Bugliosi, Vincent, *Helter Skelter*, Arrow, 1992.

Bromley, David G. & Melton, J. Gordon (Eds), *Cults, Religion & Violence*, University of Cambridge, 2002.

Documentaries

Order of the Solar Temple, directed by David Cohen and David Carr-Brown.

Wild Wild Country, Netflix documentary, 2018.

Witness to Waco, MSNBC Documentary by Rick Ross, 2009.

Index

Acts, Book of *23*
anthrax *67, 80, 81*
Applewhite, Marshall Herff *187–200*
Asahara, Shoko *8, 14, 15, 68–95,*
ATF (Federal Bureau of Alcohol, Tobacco and Firearms) *57–59, 196*
Aum Supreme Truth 8, *15, 18, 67–95*

Beast, the *8, 10, 24*
Berg, David *8, 19–40*
Berg, Virginia *20–22*
blood atonement *136, 138, 141, 143, 146, 149, 153, 156, 161, 165*
Boilard, Solange *182–185*
botulism *79*
Branch Davidians *18, 41–66, 196*
Brunner, Mary *98, 99, 105, 113*
Buddhism *71, 103*
Bugliosi, Vincent *111–112*

Campbellites, the *20*
Children of God *19–40, 203*
Church of the Lamb *136–165*
Church of Latter-day Saints *136, 137, 139, 143, 146, 152, 153*
Cielo Drive *106–111*

Davidito *24, 39 (also see Rodriguez, Ricky)*
deprogramming *202*

Earth exit statements *194*

FBI (Federal Bureau of Investigation) *59–64, 159*
Fifth Monarchists *9–10*
flirty fishing *36–37*

Hale-Bopp comet *196, 197*
Heaven's Gate *186–200*
Helter Skelter *99, 103, 104, 105, 106, 108, 109, 110, 112*
Hinman, Gary *105, 111*
Howell, Vernon *42–44, 49, 51 (see Koresh, David)*

intervention *203–205*

Jesus-freaks *23, 27*

Kasabian, Linda *106*
Kataribabo, Dominic *115–117, 119, 121, 122, 125, 129–134*
Kibwetere, Joseph *115–117, 119, 120, 127, 130, 131, 135*
Koresh, David *8, 10, 14, 41–66*
LaBianca, Leno and Rosemary *109–110*
Lavallée, Gabrielle *172, 184–185*
LeBaron, Ervil *8, 14, 136–165*
LeBaron, Joel *140–146, 149, 150*
Los Molinos *150, 151*
love bombing *28*

MacDonald, Matthew *185*
Manson, Charles *8, 14, 15, 17, 23, 96–113*
Matsumoto, Chizuo (see Asahara, Shoko)
McVeigh, Timothy *65–66*
Miller, William *10–11*

Millerites 46, 49, 169
Mo Letters *25, 26, 35, 36, 37, 38*
Movement for the Restoration of the Ten Commandments *8, 18, 114–135*
Mwerinde, Credonia *115, 117–121, 123, 125, 127, 129, 130, 131, 134, 135*

Narcissistic Personality Disorder *13–14, 202*
Nettles, Bonnie Lu *189, 191, 197*

Oklahoma City bombing *65–66*
Open Heart Reports *29, 36*

pedophilia *19, 22, 43, 55*

Rancho Santé Fe1 *86–87, 196, 198*
Revelation, Book of *7, 10, 14, 45, 54, 104, 149, 170, 187, 205*
Roden, Lois *46, 47, 53*
Roden, George *47–49*
Rodriguez, Ricky *24, 39*

Sakamoto, Tsutsumi *77–78, 84*
satian *75–76*
Sarin *67–68, 73, 79, 81, 82, 83–93*
Seventh Day Adventists *12, 43, 44, 45, 46, 47, 166, 169, 170, 171, 173, 182*
Shiva *70, 72, 81*
Smith, Joseph 137, 138, 139, 140, 143, *144, 145, 164*
Spahn Ranch *100, 101, 103, 109, 111*
Summer of Love *22–23*

Tate, Sharon *100, 106–108, 111*
Thériault, Roch *166–185*
Tokyo subway attacks *14, 86, 88, 90, 91–93*

Unit, The *19, 31, 36, 38*

Vest, Dean *149, 153–155, 159*
Victor camps *34, 35, 39*

Waco *7, 41, 46–54, 56–57, 60, 64, 66*
Watson, Charles 'Tex' *104, 106, 111*
Wilson, Dennis *100*

Young, Brigham *138–39, 144*

UK £12.99
US $19.99